PRAISE FOR STEVE LACY AND

Steve Lacy: Conversations

"There's no way simply to make clear how particular Steve Lacy was to poets or how much he can now teach them by fact of his own practice and example. No one was ever more generous or perceptive. . . . Steve opened a lot for me in the most quiet way. Music was only the beginning."—**Robert Creeley,** *Poetry Project Newsletter*

"As far back as I can remember, Steve Lacy has represented the sound of the soprano saxophone. Influenced by Sidney Bechet, he has in turn influenced every player of the soprano. His music has always been very personal, and always in search of new paths."
—**Lee Konitz,** *Jazz Magazine* (Paris)

"Steve Lacy's soul-rending sounds emerge out of the chaos of our times like the announcement of the beautiful nonviolent anarchist revolution. In the passionate intelligence of his compositions, every note is the sound of freedom."—**Judith Malina,** actress, writer, and co-founder of the Living Theatre

"Steve Lacy was a universalist whose unending curiosity took him to myriad nooks and crannies of the artistic and intellectual life of his own mind and that of the planet. . . . Throughout his life, Steve collaborated with writers, poets, philosophers, painters, and musicians from everywhere. Along the way, he stimulated and encouraged many of the people with whom he worked to create in ways they never had before. . . . There was also the quality of his mind. Steve possessed an intelligence that was at once poetic, yet clear, precise, penetrating, elegant, often ironic and humorous—much like his own music. . . . Narrow ideological restrictions and categories were not his bag. He was open to everything—seeking, appreciating, and expressing all manner of experience."
—**Richard Teitelbaum,** composer, performer, and professor of music at Bard College, from program notes for a 2005 tribute concert

"Steve Lacy is a superb interviewee, extremely articulate in terms of his music, of the history of jazz, and of the cultural situation in Europe and the United States. Lacy's witnessing to his age is an essential document in the history of post-bop jazz, and in the wider sense—as Lacy's work is profoundly boundary-breaking—of music in the second part of the twentieth century. Jason Weiss has done a superb job gathering these interviews. The range is breathtaking and the chronological arrangement allows the reader to experience the evolution of Lacy as a musician and a thinker. All subsequent theoretical/critical thinking about Lacy and his music will need to refer to this book."
—**Pierre Joris,** poet, translator, and professor of English at the University of Albany

"Steve Lacy was an artist of great importance and influence, not only in music, but in literature as well. This is the first book to emerge in the United States that chronicles Lacy's career, largely through his own voice. Moreover, it is also one of the few U.S. books of any kind on jazz that extensively references non-U.S. sources. Since much of Lacy's career played out in Europe, the European interviews constitute perhaps the best chronicle of Lacy's early evolution as an artist."
—**George E. Lewis,** composer, performer, and Edwin H. Case Professor of American Music at Columbia University

STEVE LACY

STEVE LACY

conversations

edited by Jason Weiss

Duke University Press Durham and London 2006

STEVE LACY

conversations

edited by Jason Weiss

Duke University Press Durham and London 2006

Printed in the United States of America
on acid-free paper ♾
Designed by C. H. Westmoreland
Typeset in Garamond
by Tseng Information Systems, Inc.
Downcome display font by Eduardo Recife
(www.misprintedtype.com)
Library of Congress Cataloging-
in-Publication Data appear on the last
printed page of this book.

Contents

Acknowledgments

I would like to thank and acknowledge the support of Irene Aebi, without whose interest this book could not have been done. Also, I sincerely thank all the many writers and photographers who were so generous in allowing me to use their work and in answering questions; their names will be found alongside their contributions.

In addition, I am grateful to numerous other people who offered their support, provided countless bits of information, and generally encouraged me: Wolfram Knauer, of the Jazz-Institut Darmstadt; Tad Hershorn and Dan Morgenstern, of the Institute of Jazz Studies at Rutgers, Newark; my editors at Duke, Ken Wissoker and Courtney Berger, as well as the managing editor, Fred Kameny; Pierre Joris and George Lewis, who read an early version of this book; Marshall Reese, Mark Weiss, and Vincent Lainé, for technical and tactical advice as well as new clues; Judith Cramer, Steve's niece, and Blossom Cramer, his sister, for details on early family life; Nat Hentoff, Frank Alkyer, Philippe Carles, Chantal Pontbriand, Stuart Broomer, Tony Herrington, Pawel Brodowski, Ishmael Reed, Holly Carver, Robert Rusch, David Gibson, Nathaniel Mackey, Benjamin Barouh, Pete Gershon, and Nathalie Krafft, editors who allowed me to reproduce work they first published; Halley K. Harrisburg and the Michael Rosenfeld Gallery for their permission to use the cover image by Bob Thompson; Patrice Roussel and William Kenz, whose complete on-line discography I consulted often; as well as Irene Devlin-Weiss, Sergine Laloux, Jean-Jacques Birgé, Paul Robicheau, Dalia Azim, Ellen Christi, Steve Goldstein, Rita De Vuyst, Ritchard Rodriguez, Douglas Dunn, Margot Preteceille, Alvin Curran, Joëlle Léandre, Karen Brookman, Terri Hinte, Roger Parry, Bruno Guermonprez, Lisa Hansen, Leo Feigin, and Bruce Ricker for numerous details and assistance. I salute you all.

PART 1

interviews with steve lacy

Introduction

Steve Lacy gave a lot of interviews. For well over four decades people sought him out, and he was always generous with his time and had much to say. He was thoughtful and wise, humble and amused, and constantly aware of the living traditions that he was part of as an artist in his time. He was also a perceptive listener, to questions posed as well as questions implied. Just as he could appreciate a vast range of music and the play of individual musicians in a given moment, so he recognized the quality of searching in all its guises.

If the dialogic imagination has served as a model for literary criticism of recent decades, the very concept would seem to apply first to what musicians actually do: they create by means of a collective dialogue. Theirs is an art of mutual engagement. Moreover, when playing repertory from the past, musicians engage with previous performances through memory in an act of homage, commentary, even provocation. This was where Lacy initially came in during his first decade as a jazz musician. And inasmuch as he was one of a small number of musicians who took up the special challenge of performing solo concerts sometimes, the musical dialogue gained an added dimension: when he played his own compositions, most of these were pieces normally heard in a group context. Thus, the solo work could respond to what had been done or what might yet be done by his group.

The interview, of course, is not a musical performance. And yet it does bear certain dynamic similarities: part reflection, part thinking out loud, depending on the question or where the train of discourse may be heading. The interviewer must come equipped with some kind of plan, while being ready to improvise, to jettison what doesn't fit or may be superfluous in favor of what bears fruit. Lacy, for his part, tried to bring something new to every interview, to further elaborate on a particular project or experience and not take recourse in mere repetition. Not inclined to long speeches, he remained alert to the exchange, the give and take, the sharing of ideas.

Born Steven Norman Lackritz in New York City on 23 July 1934, he had a singular trajectory as a musician, although it began conventionally enough. His parents had immigrated from Russia as small children and met when they were working in the garment industry. He was the youngest of three children from a comfortable family that lived on the Upper West Side of Manhattan. His was not an especially musical household; however, his brother played accordion, his sister played piano, and he himself began taking piano lessons when he was around eight years old, if without great enthusiasm.

Though raised Jewish, he refused to be bound by ethnic, racial, or cultural preconceptions, setting forth on his life of adventure at an early age. As he remarked in his notes to *Sands* (1998), a solo record for John Zorn's Tzadik label, regarding his piece "Jewgitive": "I have been one (a Jewgitive) most of my life, since becoming very disillusioned in Hebrew school (in the '40s), the whole trip seeming not to fit me at all. But, as they say: 'You can run, but you can't hide,' and so, this piece is an illustration of a condition, still being played with." That condition, of belonging and not belonging, animated by a studious transcendence of attendant material circumstances, was to prove auspicious for Lacy.

He discovered jazz when barely in his teens. As he recounted on several occasions, he traced that discovery to when he was twelve or thirteen and had birthday money to spend. He wanted to buy some records and became curious about a set of 78s on the Brunswick label by "Duke Ellington and His Famous Orchestra." Why was the orchestra "famous," he wondered, so he bought the records with no idea about the music they contained. When he listened to them at home, he was hooked. Eventually he switched from the piano to the clarinet and then at sixteen, inspired by Sidney Bechet, took up the soprano saxophone, which practically no one else was playing. For the next five decades he devoted himself exclusively to the soprano, enlarging its capabilities and making its sound indisputably his own. His first enthusiasm was Dixieland and, precociously making his way into clubs while still underage, he was soon playing on stage with many of the legendary figures active in New York.

When he was nineteen he met the pianist Cecil Taylor, who turned him around toward the avant-garde and an entire realm of modernist expression. Lacy continued to work in Taylor's groups (when there was work) until the end of the decade, by which time he was launched into his lifelong investigation of Thelonious Monk's music and had begun his intermittent, though also lifelong, association with the bandleader and arranger Gil Evans. In the summer of 1960 Monk, prompted by Lacy's devotion to his music, invited him to join his group for a while, making it a quintet, as they played sixteen weeks at the Jazz Gallery, with

Family, New York City, ca. 1945. Steven Lackritz, back row center. Clockwise from upper right Martin "Buddy" Lackritz (brother), Sophia Lackritz (mother), Judith Cramer (niece), Blossom Cramer (sister), Harry Lackritz (father). Photographer unknown.

concerts also at the Apollo Theater, the Philadelphia Festival, and the Rikers Island Festival. Curiously, looking back from the vantage of his later work, one can already recognize Lacy's clear, inquisitive, full-toned soprano even in his earliest recordings: the progressive Dixieland sessions of the mid-1950s, Taylor's first date (*Jazz Advance*, 1956), Evans's first (*Gil Evans & Ten*, 1957), and his own début as a leader for Prestige Records (*Soprano Sax*, 1957), which included pieces by Ellington, Monk, and Cole Porter.

Through the first half of the 1960s, Lacy worked with various avant-garde musicians in New York and made a record with the trumpeter Don Cherry. He was also co-leader of a quartet with the trombonist Roswell Rudd, featuring an all-Monk repertory (heard on *School Days*, informally recorded in concert in 1963 but not released until over a decade later). Already in 1958, his second record (*Reflections*) was made up entirely of Monk tunes, something which no musician had done before, and there would be many more Monk projects in Lacy's abundant catalogue. Though Monk is now considered a classic, playing his music was a radical concept for a band in the early 1960s: the quartet never had much work except for gigs that the members produced themselves. Indeed, Lacy was forced to work too many day jobs in those years, and by 1965 he decided to try his luck in Europe.

There were several important developments brewing for Lacy as a musician during the latter half of the decade. Like many of his associates from New York, he sought to explore the realm beyond that was free improvisation. To this end, he made many fruitful alliances with like-minded musicians in Europe. At the same time, he was starting to compose his own pieces, but he was searching for a personal style that could incorporate what he had learned from the modern masters and more besides. So while he wanted to see just how free that free could be, he was also examining the possibilities of structure: how to contain that freedom, how to shape it, what kinds of frame provided the greatest openings. And then, in Rome in 1966, he met the Swiss-born musician and singer Irene Aebi, who was to become his wife and his closest musical collaborator.

His first European sojourn, mostly spent in Italy, took an unintentionally prolonged detour to Argentina in the spring of 1966, which lasted till the end of that year. Lacy had assembled a quartet made up of the Italian trumpeter Enrico Rava along with the bassist Johnny Dyani and the drummer Louis Moholo, both South Africans who had embarked on a European exile only a few years earlier with the interracial band the Blue Notes. Rava's wife was Argentine and had arranged for some gigs in Buenos Aires, so off they went. That band was the culmination of Lacy's free improvisation period, which did not generally find much welcome in Argentina at the time, so the musicians languished there until they eventually scraped up enough money to depart (*The Forest and the Zoo* was recorded in concert near the end of their stay). Lacy returned to New York, where he remained for barely a year, recording with Carla Bley, Michael Mantler, and the Jazz Composer's Orchestra. But finally, concluding that Europe offered more sustenance, he went back to Rome in 1968, leading his own groups and also working with Musica Elettronica Viva, the improvisational collective made up of American experimental composers mostly from the classical realm (Frederic Rzewski, Alvin Curran, Richard Teitelbaum). Indeed, for a while he and Aebi lived in a room of the MEV studio there. By 1970, however, they moved to Paris, where they remained for the next three decades.

Already in the late 1960s Lacy had begun to make use of Aebi's voice by having her declaim texts as part of certain pieces in performance. But he also ventured to think of her in terms of songs: as material for lyrics, he turned increasingly to a wide range of poets and other texts. He had always been a voracious reader, and even before reaching Paris he had written his first song cycle, later known as *The Way*, based on six poems from the Tao Te Ching, the ancient Chinese classic by Lao Tzu; these pieces became staples of his group and solo repertory for many years, though it wasn't until 1979 that the full sung versions were recorded. The 1970s were a period of consolidation for Lacy as a composer, player, and bandleader, as he continued his investigations into what was sometimes called post-free music. Soon he was recording at least several albums a year, for a variety of mostly European labels, and the music played was almost exclusively his own. While never gaining a lot of financial security, he toured often and worked with some of the most risk-taking improvisers in western Europe and beyond: notably the pianist Alexander von Schlippenbach's Globe Unity Orchestra in Germany, the pianist Misha Mengelberg and the drummer Han Bennink in Holland, the guitarist Derek Bailey and the saxophonist Evan Parker in England, and the drummer Masahiko Togashi in Japan. Moreover, he was also performing in many nontraditional contexts, made possible by generous support for the arts in France and elsewhere in Europe—playing at art openings, with dancers and painters, even in workshops with amateur musicians. Most importantly perhaps, by 1972 the alto and soprano saxophonist Steve Potts had arrived in Paris and joined his group, providing an ideal complement to Lacy's own sensibilities. Thus a regular quintet began to take shape, along with Aebi and the bassist Kent Carter, with whom Lacy had worked off and on since the mid-1960s. This foundation of a working group, with a few changes, was to last through most of his time in Paris and helped propel his music to new heights.

In the setting of texts to music, which became the driving force behind much of his composing, Lacy found his most inspired collaborator in Brion Gysin (1916–86), the painter, poet, and inventor whom he first met in Paris in the early 1970s as well. By the time it recorded the Gysin songbook (*Songs*, 1981), Lacy's group had crystallized into its definitive lineup, a sextet with the pianist Bobby Few (and the bassist Jean-Jacques Avenel, who replaced Carter; the drummer Oliver Johnson joined the band in 1977, replaced in 1989 by John Betsch). The partnership with Gysin was the only one at all resembling a songwriting team for Lacy, although it was clearly more far-reaching for them both: for some fifteen years, they exchanged texts, sounds, recordings, ideas, images, and advice, influencing their other work along the way. They also performed their songs occasionally as a duo at poetry festivals in Europe, with Gysin's delivery more spoken than sung.

Clearly, Lacy's music—challenging, exhilarating, and very hip, in the unique balance of structure and freedom that he achieved—was coming fully into its own. From the late 1970s on, the Swiss label Hat Hut and the Italian label Soul Note became his most frequent record producers (enlightened individuals at big labels eventually caught on to him as well). He began to conceive larger projects, especially with dancers and based on sequences of songs. *Sands*, from three French love poems by Samuel Beckett, and *Stuff*, using Gysin's lyrics adapted from William S. Burroughs's novel *Naked Lunch*, were two ballets performed on the same program in Italy and France, though never recorded in their full versions. In November 1984 Lacy gave the première of a spellbinding, evening-long spectacle drawn from twenty poems by Robert Creeley, *Futurities*, an exploration of love and marriage featuring two dancers (Douglas Dunn, Elsa Wolliaston), his group augmented to a nonet, and a luminous, altar-like chevron by his old friend the painter Kenneth Noland that served as a set, changing colors according to the lighting. Later song projects, without dance, included *Clangs* (1992), for double sextet, based on painters' texts and originally composed twenty years earlier; *Vespers* (1993), for octet, based on texts by the Bulgarian poet Blaga Dimitrova; *The Cry* (1999), for septet, a sort of jazz opera based on works by the Bengali poet Taslima Nasrin; and another work long in the making that became his final record, *The Beat Suite* (2003), for quintet, based on ten Beat poets. As Lacy noted in *Clangs*: "The unity between *all* the arts, as well as the infinite possibilities of collaboration between artists in different disciplines, and of different persuasions, has long been apparent to many of us. However, the actual work in common, and the combining of the elements involved, remains a very delicate affair."

If material survival and maintaining a sextet remained always somewhat of a struggle, still there was recognition and assistance in the form of prestigious awards: a Guggenheim in 1983, a five-year MacArthur "genius" award in 1992, a one-year DAAD residency in Berlin in 1996; the French ministry of culture named him a Chevalier of the Order of Arts and Letters in 1989 and a Commander in 2002. Lacy wrote over two hundred songs, but his emphasis on the textual element was difficult for some listeners, as well as players, to digest. In addition, purists were befuddled by Aebi's singing style, which owed less to a jazz lineage than to classical training and the European art song. Eventually Lacy had built up such a backlog of his own compositions that only a small portion could be developed by the full group. It was necessary to get back to the essentials, to a pared-down approach, in order to give wings to more of the songs. As a parallel to working with his group, he took to performing as a duo with Aebi, and sometimes in a trio: *Rushes* (1990), based on poems by the Russian poets Marina Tsvetayeva, Osip Mandelstam, and Anna Akhmatova, and *Packet* (1995), based on poems by his old friends Judith Malina and Julian Beck of the Living Theatre, both featured Frederic Rzewski on piano along with Lacy and Aebi. This activity reflected a more open-ended use of Lacy's regular group, which finally disbanded in the mid-1990s even as he continued to perform in a trio with his rhythm section of Avenel and Betsch.

Remarkably, despite the accolades Lacy could not secure enough work for his sextet to enable it to survive. When he and Aebi went to Berlin for their residency they thought that they might stay, or at any rate thought that it was at last time to move on from Paris, which no longer felt as hospitable an environment as it once had been. But they returned for another five years, aided largely by a change of neighborhood: for over twenty years they had lived in a loft in the heart of the Marais district, a block from the Centre Pompidou and two blocks from Gysin's apartment; in

1997 they moved to a small house with a lush garden near the outskirts of Paris, an easy cab ride out to the airport. By the time Lacy was offered a position at the New England Conservatory of Music in 2002, they were ready to go. For a year, living in Brookline near Boston, he enjoyed a busy teaching schedule with many eager and promising students, which still allowed him time to travel and give some concerts. But in the summer of 2003, soon after turning sixty-nine, the age at which his own father had died, Lacy was diagnosed with liver cancer. For a while the experimental medical treatments seemed promising, and he continued to teach and perform. However, the following spring, his condition worsened. He died on 4 June 2004, honoring his commitments, even performing with his students, almost to the end.

This book seeks to convey some sense of Lacy's spoken voice, if not as sound then at least as text. More than that, it offers a measure of his thinking as articulated on a number of occasions over the course of more than forty years. Through these texts, edited to minimize repetition, the artist may be glimpsed at various moments of his career, and so the person, whose life was made up of much movement and many challenges. The interviews—taken from American, French, British, and Canadian journals, as well as a few books—are arranged chronologically, rather than chopped up and pieced together according to theme, because in this way the reader can better appreciate the lived experience. Where a subject inevitably recurs, such as Thelonious Monk's music or the circumstances of being an expatriate in Europe, Lacy's comments offer a layering or accumulation of reflections as seen from the shifting perspective of time and growing older. Given that much of his career took place in Europe, it should come as no surprise that half the interviews included here are from French sources, most of which were conducted directly in French; I have done all the translations.

Anyone who has spent a significant amount of time living abroad, especially in a culture different from one's own and where the spoken language is also different, knows that one is forever changed by the experience. Attempts to characterize those changes are never quite adequate, for a mysterious and irreproducible chemistry has taken place inside. The particular difficulties and opportunities in being a foreigner, depending on how one meets them, are an education unlike any other: sooner or later one has no choice but to ditch the shell of national pride and embrace the world. Soon after returning to the United States to begin teaching,

Lacy reflected on such matters: "As for being an 'American composer,' one's origins are certainly interesting and perhaps significant, but destiny and fulfillment, and the path and order taken by each artist is, to me, much more so. We all have our nature, and its fullest possible realization must be the real goal" (letter to Molly Sheridan of the American Music Center, 14 September 2002).

Steve Lacy flourished precisely because he went off to the open terrain of Europe and made those musical friendships, which helped carry his art beyond the early influences. If his work remained mostly unrecognized in his native land for many years, it was only because American listeners had to catch up to where he had gone. Certainly he could not have created the music he did had he stayed behind in New York; he had to go outside to find it. In that respect, this book may also serve as a chronicle of the voyage.

Finally, a personal note is in order. I have been listening to Lacy's music since the mid-1970s, so when I moved to Paris early in 1980 for what turned out to be an entire decade, I hoped to find some excuse to meet him. That summer I went to Brion Gysin's home to do an interview for a newspaper article, and there were Lacy and Aebi. Over the years I interviewed Lacy three times, and wrote about his music on a number of occasions. But soon I also became a frequent visitor to his and Aebi's home on the rue du Temple, where he and I talked of books more than any other subject. There I first heard of Robert Musil, Elias Canetti, Ryszard Kapuscinski, and other writers, including various Russians, in whom Lacy had a keen interest. Often we lent each other books, though I was much younger and it seemed that he had read everything. In that way I learned of certain sensitive areas: when I broached the topic of Latin American writers, I saw him shy away somewhat, evidently still smarting from his Argentine experience of long ago, about which I had known nothing until then (and yet, over the years, he would speak of writers as diverse as Jorge Luis Borges, Miguel Angel Asturias, and José María Arguedas); after I brought him Edmond Jabès's *The Book of Questions*, a new discovery for me at the time, I realized that it was probably too Jewish for his tastes. Once, somehow, we got on the subject of the distinctive shakuhachi master Watazumi Doso, whom Lacy had met on his first visit to Japan in 1975: to my delight, he lent me six records of him, released only in Japan, which of course I duly copied onto cassettes.

Perhaps I knew subconsciously that I was already working on this book over twenty years ago. Having contributed a number of pieces to the French journal *Jazz Magazine*, I took advantage of my access: on one or another visit to the journal's offices on the Champs-Élysées, I spent a long hour photocopying pieces that interested me from back issues. Foremost among these were a half-dozen interviews and articles about Lacy (as well as an excellent interview with Steve Potts). The day after I learned of his illness late in the summer of 2003, the idea for this book popped into my head. Considering how extensive was his catalogue, including over 150 records, a book of conversations with the composer seemed long overdue.

1

Introducing Steve Lacy

By the time of his first interview, less than a decade after he picked up the soprano saxophone, Lacy had been playing all over New York and traversed the full range of jazz history. He had already recorded several Dixieland sessions as well as first dates with Cecil Taylor's and Gil Evans's ensembles, and he had also recorded his own first two albums, *Soprano Sax* and *Reflections*, the latter devoted to Thelonious Monk's music (and the first of many recordings with the pianist Mal Waldron).

Soon after the Monk album came out, this interview appeared in the *Jazz Review* (September 1959), edited in New York by Nat Hentoff and Martin Williams. Presented as an extended monologue of Lacy talking, it had an unattributed introduction that laid out his itinerary up till then:

> Steve Lacy, 25, is a native New Yorker. He has a wife, two children, two cats, and lives in a loft just off the Bowery, over a cellophane bag factory. Being in a manufacturing district enables him to play his soprano saxophone any hour of the day or night. Steve began playing jazz about eight years ago. His first gig was at the Stuyvesant Casino (not far from his present neighborhood), and he was billed as the "Bechet of Today." His work in Dixieland continued for the next couple of years with men like Rex Stewart, Max Kaminsky, Buck Clayton, Pee Wee Russell and Lips Page. He spent six months in Boston at the Schillinger School of Music (described by him as a fiasco during school hours, but at least making possible sessions at the Savoy that proved enlightening). At the school he was a curiosity as the only Dixieland musician and the only soprano saxophonist. It was during this period, through records, that he started to absorb Lester Young and more modern jazz. . . .

Lacy began by speaking about Monk's music:

When I heard Monk's record of "Skippy," I was determined to learn it if it took me a year. It took me a week to learn and six months to be able to play it. I had such a ball learning it that I started to look into his other tunes. I had previously recorded "Work." Each song of Monk's that I learned left me with something invaluable and permanent, and the more I learned, the more I began to get with his system. Soon I realized I had enough material for ten albums.

Monk's tunes are the ones that I most enjoy playing. I like his use of melody, harmony, and especially his rhythm. Monk's music has profound humanity, disciplined economy, balanced virility, dramatic nobility, and innocently exuberant wit. Monk, by the way, like Louis Armstrong, is a master of rhyme. For me, other masters of rhyme are Bird, Duke, Miles, Art Blakey, and Cecil Taylor.

I feel that music can be comprehended from many different levels. It can be regarded as excited speech, imitation of the sounds of nature, an abstract set of symbols, a baring of emotions, an illustration of interpersonal relationships, an intellectual game, a device for inducing reverie, a mating call, a series of dramatic events, an articulation of time and/or space, an athletic contest, or all of these things at once. A jazz musician is a combination orator, dialectician, mathematician, athlete, entertainer, poet, singer, dancer, diplomat, educator, student, comedian, artist, seducer, public masturbator, and general all-around good fellow. As this diversity indicates, no matter what you do, some people are going to like it, and other people not. Therefore, all you can do is to try to satisfy yourself, by trusting the man inside. Braque said, "With age, art and life become one." I am only twenty-five, and I trust that I will one day really be able to satisfy myself and at the same time express my love for the world by putting so much of myself into my playing that others will be able to see themselves too. Jazz is a very young art and not too much is known about it as yet. You have to trust yourself and go your own way.

Since there are no soprano saxophone players, I take my inspiration from soprano singers, as well as other jazz instrumentalists, painters, authors, entertainers, and that thing that grows wildly in New York, people. I like to observe people on the subways, what they express just by sitting there. I had a ball during the newspaper strike this past year, because people couldn't hide as they usually do. I would like to be able to portray what I feel for my fellow creatures. My horn has a texture, range, and flexibility which is ideal for myself and my purposes. I have been grappling with the difficulties of it for some time now and can very well understand why no one else has attempted to play anything on it more complex than the stylings of the '30s. The instrument is treacherous on several levels: intonation, dynamics, and you can't get gigs on it. At this point, I am beyond the point of no return and my wife and children have agreed to go with me all the way.

The most gratifying and enlightening musical experience for me in the past few months was playing with Gil Evans's fourteen-piece band for two weeks at Birdland opposite Miles Davis and his marvelous group. It was the first time that I had ever played with such a large ensemble and it was the start of my investigations into the possibilities of blending my sound with others. I was the only saxophone in the band and sometimes played lead, sometimes harmony parts or contrapuntal lines, other times obbligato, and quite often I was given a chance to blow with the whole band behind me—perhaps the greatest thrill of my life thus far. Gil is a splendid orchestrator, a brilliant musician, and a wonderful friend. Sometimes when things jelled, I felt true moments of ecstasy; and recently, when a friend of mine who worked with the Claude Thornhill Band in the '40s, when Gil was the principal writer, said that some nights the sound of the band around him moved him to tears, I knew exactly what he meant. So does anybody else who has ever played Gil's arrangements.

The contemporary saxophonists whose work most interests me are John Coltrane, Sonny Rollins, Ben Webster, Ornette Coleman, Jackie MacLean, and Johnny Hodges. Being a saxophone player, when I listen to these men I not only can feel what they are doing artistically but also follow their playing as a series of decisions. While working at Birdland those two weeks with Gil, I naturally had a chance to dig Coltrane and appreciate his, at times, almost maniacal creativity. He has a fantastic knowledge of harmony and, like the other members of Miles's group, including, of course, Miles himself, seems to be really searching out the vast resources of scales.

Sonny Rollins, on the other hand, rather than concentrating on scales, has devoted a large portion of his mind to plastic values and the effects of various shapes on each other. Sonny's playing, it can be clearly seen, derives largely from extremely intensive research into all facets of saxophone playing per se. Ben Webster is the master of sound. His use of dynamics indicates the great dramatic sensitivity of this most mature of all saxophone players. His masculinity and authority can only be matched in jazz by that of Thelonious Monk.

Ornette Coleman is the only young saxophone player who seems to be trying for a conversational style of playing and is the only one I have heard who is exploring the potentialities of real human expression, something which has a tremendous impact on me. I have yet to hear him in person but his playing (not his writing) on the album I did hear moved me. Jackie MacLean has the most rhythmic vitality and so far, the least discipline of all these saxophonists. He expresses his own personality with his sound and has tremendous swing and energy. Hearing his blues sounds has always been for me a haunting and, at the same time, exhilarating, experience. I have always loved Johnny Hodges. He is a true aristocrat.

The difference in the personalities of all of these men, who manage to indelibly express their uniqueness in their music, is to me the most profound demonstration of the validity of jazz, because I feel that the communication of human values is the main purpose of any art.

Besides jazz, I enjoy the works of Stravinsky and Webern and certain works of Schoenberg, Berg, Bartók and Prokofiev; also African and Indian music. When I get dragged with everything, I try Bach. I find they all help my ear enormously. As far as the way these musics influence my own playing, all I can say is that *everything* is an influence. When I say everything, I mean just that, from the rhythm of children's speech to the patterns of the stars. I believe that the only way for me to develop myself is the way thoroughly proven by the men who have made jazz what it is—that is, to play as often and as publicly as possible, with as good musicians as will tolerate me.

My Favorite Thing

Lacy's discourse on the soprano saxophone appeared in the longtime jazz journal *Metronome* (December 1961), edited by Dan Morgenstern. The music of Thelonious Monk continued to dominate in Lacy's development, as the source of more than half the material on his next two albums. In 1960 his unusual quartet (with Charles Davis on baritone saxophone) recorded *The Straight Horn of Steve Lacy*, two months after his summer-long stint playing in Monk's quintet. That same year, after hearing Lacy play, the tenor saxophonist John Coltrane began to take up the soprano and recorded his first album on the instrument, *My Favorite Things*. A year later, just before the following article was published, Lacy recorded *Evidence* in a quartet with the trumpeter Don Cherry.

The straight B♭ soprano saxophone is one of the least familiar of all the saxophones. The jazz audience today is largely unused to the sound or even the sight of the straight soprano, which is not to be confused with the curved, toy-like soprano saxophone that is considerably easier to play and sounds much like a higher, thinner version of the alto. On sight many people think it is a gold metal clarinet.

Back in the '20s, however, the soprano was considered a standard double for the average reed player, but as techniques and section difficulties increased, the intonation problems, which are considerable with this instrument, outweighed the desirability of its use. Only a few players continued to employ it.

As far as its being the sole instrument played by an individual, Sidney Bechet stood almost alone throughout the '30s and '40s. And even he also played clarinet until the last few years of his life. In 1932 Bechet had organized a violent little band with Tommy Ladnier on trumpet. They made half a dozen sides for Victor, which are fiery examples of his remarkable drive. To me these sides remain among the most exciting jazz records ever made: "Shag," "Maple Leaf Rag," "I Found a New Baby," etc. In the early '40s he recorded, again for Victor, an excellent series of sides with Kenny Clarke, Sidney de Paris, Charlie Shavers, Teddy Bunn, Sid Catlett, and others. Throughout his European career he was a featured soloist, sometimes accompanied by a large orchestra. Bechet would sometimes play the trumpet part, the soprano having the normal trumpet range. More often, though, he would fill the traditional embellishing role of the clarinet, sometimes switching to the clarinet itself. As everyone knows, Bechet was one of the pioneers of New Orleans jazz. He and others of that time were largely responsible for the perpetration of the idea of jazz being "hot" music. The heat in Bechet's playing was a result of the intense swing and the passionate involvement of himself with his music. Bechet was no architect. He was harmonically naïve and rhythmically unsubtle. However, he had a natural plastic sense and could capture the imagination of his audiences with sweeping melodramatics. He had a very personal sound that will be remembered by all those who heard him play. Many did not care for this sound owing to his excessive use of a very wide vibrato. My own feeling is that this was a means, perhaps, of covering the natural inaccuracy of any given note on the horn itself.

Certain portions of the soprano's range are intrinsically out of tune with the rest of the horn. All instruments have "bad" notes here and there, but the soprano has whole segments of such notes. Several solutions to this problem are available to the serious player. Bechet had one, the above-mentioned wide vibrato. This is stylistically distasteful to many musicians who might rather prefer to use a small chambered mouthpiece and play at a low volume level, thereby minimizing the difficulties. If one wants the power of, say, a Bechet without the vibrato, one must humor each note, bending it to the desired pitch. This requires long and assiduous practice with much frustration, or else a high natural sensitivity, coupled with extreme lip flexibility. The amount of time necessary for complete memorization of all the necessary adjustments discourages doubling the instrument.

Johnny Hodges was an early student of Bechet and is a brilliant alto player. He was also, to my mind, the finest soprano saxophonist until the mid-'40s, when he gave it up for reasons of his own. Most of Hodges's recordings are unavailable on LP, but on the original 78s there are numerous examples of his warm, suave, lyrical improvisations. Outstanding among these are "Indigo Echoes" and "Tough Truckin'," using for that, or any other time, the very unusual instrumentation of cornet, soprano, baritone, piano, and two basses. Other good discs, both with small groups and the full Ellington band, are "Blue Reverie," "Blue Goose," "Tired Socks," "That's the Blues, Old Man," and "Harmony in Harlem." Hodges's great coloristic flexibility and marvelous control, combined with his delicate ear, enabled him to handle the soprano in the same relaxed manner as his own alto, without having to resort to Bechet's vibrato.

Now, largely through my own efforts and those of John Coltrane, Lucky Thompson, Budd Johnson, Barney Wilen, and a few others, the instrument seems headed for a resurgence of popularity.

Coltrane was looking for a relief and contrast to his tenor and also an extension of the higher register, and found it quite naturally in the soprano, which is both in the same key and exactly one octave higher than the tenor. His playing combines great harmonic complexity, a dry, almost Eastern sound, and unflagging propulsion, which when used in his present format (sometimes with two basses droning hypnotically) produces quite an exotic mood.

I heard Bechet on records about twelve years ago and bought my first horn. As my ear was not very good in those days, I was unaware of the pitch problems inherent in the horn. By the time my ear had improved, I was too far gone to dream of switching to another horn. Instead, I gave up the idea of doubling altogether and really started to get down to work. I certainly was not primarily concerned, however, with the promotion of the soprano per se, even though it was and still is a challenge to master this devilish instrument.

This instrument can fulfill an extremely valuable function in today's jazz. Like all saxophones, its range, with practice, can be increased beyond the normal limits to four full octaves. It is the only treble instrument able to be played percussively enough and with enough power and brilliance to fit into the stylistic demands of contemporary jazz. The lowest part of the soprano's range, which is right in the heart of the tenor saxophone range and quite similar to it in sound, can be played with extreme intensity. If the range of the horn is extended upwards to the extreme limit, the top notes are remarkably like those that Cat Anderson can produce. Between these two extremes a great diversity of colors are available, thereby making this instrument potentially one of extreme expressive power.

As Charlie Parker increased the technical and expressive possibilities of the alto, Milt Jackson the vibraharp, Kenny Clarke the drums, and Jimmy Blanton the bass, one of my personal aims is to do the same for the soprano.

The Land of Monk

Throughout the early 1960s the most regular formation that Lacy played in was a quartet he co-led with the trombonist Roswell Rudd. Intended as a repertory band, they soon decided to concentrate on a single composer, Thelonious Monk. The band did record some sessions for Columbia and Verve, but these were never released. The only album to be made available of that group, recorded in a performance at a New York coffee house in March 1963, did not come out until over a decade later (*School Days*). This unattributed interview was published in *Down Beat* (10 October 1963), two months before Lacy performed with Monk's big band at the Philharmonic. The following year, he began to break out of Monk's orbit.

"I think of it," Steve Lacy said, "as an analogy to *Alice through the Looking Glass*. If we can get through the mirror, there's another country on the other side."

The twenty-nine-year-old soprano saxophonist was speaking of the curious and fascinating discipline his quartet has been undergoing: limitation of its repertoire, for the present, to the music of Thelonious Monk. The experiment is nearly two years old. But, Lacy said, "it's no longer just an experiment. It works."

It is hard to say with certainty that there is no precedent for what the group is doing. But none comes readily to mind. Rarely, if ever, has a jazz musician or group of musicians limited the repertoire to the music of one composer—not even when that composer is himself. Duke Ellington plays music by other composers, and so, for that matter, does Monk.

But Lacy even has more Monk material active in his group's repertoire than Monk does. Monk usually has about twenty of his own pieces in performing shape with his group at any given time. Lacy has fifty-three—"the complete recorded body of work of Monk," as he puts it.

He added, "We don't do Monk's arrangements of other people's tunes, and we don't do some of his improvised piano blues. Otherwise we're doing all his things.

"The Monk material has given us a sound, a direction, a point of view, a technique as well as an excellent library of material, material we don't get tired of and that inspires us every night.

"The immense variety and joyous profusion of rhythms and shapes and lengths and tempos and moods is such that we never get tired, and we can go three or four days without repeating a tune. And each night will be just as interesting as the others."

The saxophonist said that what they're after is a group in which everyone speaks the same language—or at least speaks compatible languages.

"When you get through to the other side of the mirror," Lacy said, "there's a new language, derived from the vocabulary of the material we've been playing.

"We could have done the same thing with Bird tunes, or Duke's material, but Monk's was the most fetching, the most challenging—the most seductive. No other body of jazz compositions that I've found has been as real, as pure. It never encroaches on pop music, though I believe that in time it will become as popular as pop music."

Lacy's group consists of himself; Roswell Rudd, the young Connecticut-born trombonist who this year was chosen a talent deserving of wider recognition in *Down Beat*'s International Jazz Critics Poll; Dennis Charles, drums; and Lewis Worrell, bass.

Finding a bassist who could accommodate himself to the group and to the Monk material was a serious problem.

"We've had 17 bass players," Lacy said with quiet humor. "It's given me an education in bass playing and caused me to rewrite the bass book several times. I found that the regular method of naming chords was inadequate, arbitrary, and elusive. We've had four or five versions of the bass book in the attempt to make it clear."

Of those players who have worked with the quartet, Lacy said, four—including Worrell—fit well the group's approach and musical vocabulary.

How did this in-depth exploration of Monk begin?

"I was at the point," he said, "where I realized nobody was going to hire me to play the material I wanted to play—the Monk material. And so I got a band with my pals who also wanted to play Monk. That sounds like a bunch of amateurs, doesn't it? But that's the way it happened."

The problem was to get the sound of the music right for these four instruments—no mean task, Lacy is quick to assure, because all the tunes have not only a melody and a bass line, but two or three inner voices as well.

"And if you're going to reduce something," he elaborated, "you'd better get the essence of it or not bother."

At the time he made his decision, nearly two years ago, Lacy also had some Kurt Weill, some Ellington, and some Cecil Taylor material in the book. The group played a few gigs, and it didn't work. It was too eclectic and scattered, he said, so they decided to concentrate on the Monk tunes—but *all* of them.

"We felt the answer lay somewhere in the act of doing that," he said. "And we were right.

"What we wanted to do was to eliminate the compromises Monk had had to make recording them, due to the lack of sufficient preparation of his sidemen. It seemed there wasn't a strong enough relationship between the improvisations and the piece itself. This was true not only in the Monk records but in most of the jazz that we'd heard.

"Roswell and I listened to the Monk records many, many times, trying to find out what the pieces meant and what would be practical for us in them.

"At first, we were quite stiff about performing the tunes, and we'd do them in a rather Wagnerian manner. After about half a year we got a little looser, and after a year the approach began to crystallize.

"Now we're at a point where our flexibility is at least equal to that of any of the so-called free players. However, our freedom has been won through a long—and, some people would say, arbitrary—discipline. It's also been an extremely enjoyable one.

"We're after a more active participation not only by the players but by the listener, so they can follow the events more clearly than in most of the jazz around."

Lacy's study of the Monk material began about seven years ago. Three years ago he worked in Monk's group for several months, an experience that increased his insight into the material. He and Monk have remained on warm and personal terms.

It can be assumed that no one, aside from Monk himself, knows the contents of Monk's works any better than Lacy does. And he has some surprising observations to make on them.

He says that the body of Monk's work is a portrait of New York City in its various aspects, somewhat as Utrillo's paintings were a compound portrait of Montmartre.

"Or rather," he amended, "taken all in all, the music is a self-portrait of Monk with a background of the city and all the people Monk knows.

"Some of the things are about stickball, tugboats, the railroad yards, parts of Central Park, Broadway, and even some of the neighboring areas of New Jersey. They're all in the music somewhere. Monk's neighbors, past and present, and even some of his relatives are there. He's been living on the same block for years, you know."

The strict limitation of the quartet's work to Monk material may be drawing to an end. Lacy intends eventually to expand the repertoire—once he feels that the discipline has worked its magic. He plans to start doing material by Ellington and Parker. And both he and Rudd have written material for the group, though they have not performed any of it publicly.

"The approach, the vocabulary, can be applied to other music," Lacy said. "It's really we who can be applied to it. We're already better players because of it."

As one might anticipate, Lacy's uncompromising dedication to the music of Monk and to his discipline has created problems, both for himself and for his group. First of all, no one has recorded the quartet as yet. And bookings were hard to come by.

The coffee houses of Greenwich Village offered a hospitable refuge when the standard jazz clubs weren't interested. Of late the group has been working at a club called the Phase 2. Its owner, Paul Blau, has proved sympathetic to the group's approach and encouraged them to continue with it.

Monk, too, is sympathetic to the experiment.

"He has given us full encouragement," Lacy said.

"He hasn't heard it yet. He told me, 'I'll hear it when I'm supposed to.' It fits right into his system of life.

"It makes sense to me too."

Goodbye, New York

interview by Garth W. Caylor, Jr.

In this unpublished interview, recorded at Lacy's home on 12 April 1965, he takes stock of his itinerary as a musician thus far and reflects on his growing discontent with New York. Just prior to his departure for Europe, it marks a moment of fertile uncertainty in his life.

The text itself has an unusual provenance. Caylor came to New York City to do his architectural internship after graduating from the University of Oklahoma in 1963. An avid jazz fan, he recognized the unique time that the music was going through in the city and proceeded to interview musicians for a possible book, starting from a similar set of questions on how they viewed their own involvement in all that was going on. Nor was he sectarian, for his subjects included, besides Lacy, Roger Kellaway, Herbie Hancock, Zoot Sims and Al Cohn together, Freddie Hubbard, Jim Hall, Art Farmer, Jaki Byard, Paul and Carla Bley together, Steve Swallow, Lee Konitz, Sunny Murray, John Tchicai, and Archie Shepp. The reel-to-reel tapes were transcribed and typewritten, but the book never found a home. In recent years Caylor began to look through all his materials again, and when he read about Lacy's death he sent a copy of this interview to Jean Morrow at Spaulding Library of the New England Conservatory of Music in case anyone would be interested, where it was duly forwarded to Allan Chase, the dean of faculty.

How did you happen to read Selden Rodman's *Conversations with Artists*?

I didn't read it. I read *at it* in bookstores. Because I hang around bookstores and I like paintings.

I notice Dennis Charles's name on the door downstairs.

Yeah, we've been friends for a long time. He stays with us sometimes. He's uptown right now.

He was on your early records, the Transition one and the Verve one with Cecil Taylor. I like those very much, and the New Jazz one, *Evidence*, too.

Oh! Well, you've heard just about the whole recorded history of me. The start and finish of it anyway. So far. Even *Evidence* is four years old. Nothing's happened for me on records since then, except a couple of sides with Gil Evans. The concert at the Jazz Composers' Guild was taped last night.

How did that go?

It was all right, I was glad I was there. It was tough sometimes, but I liked it. It's uncomfortable music to play, a lot of it, because I'm not conditioned that way. I recognize a different provocation than they provide. So I have to invent my own, and it requires quite a lot of effort. It doesn't come naturally, but it's very good for me and all in all, it serves me right, the whole thing. I wouldn't miss it.

What do you mean by provocation?

Well, I've played with Cecil, with Gil Evans, with Monk, with Giuffre, all different kinds of carpets to stand on, you know, different kinds of prongs in the ass, but this is something else again, what's going on now, these Seventh Avenue people. I like that. I like what it did *to* me, and once in a while I liked what I could do *for* it. I really feel like almost a half-generation before those people. I don't know if they come in halves, but the music seems younger than I am.

How old are you?

Thirty. A nice round number it just happens to be. Yeah. And I can't find my music yet, except, you know, I have come across it in the last few years, now and then. But at the moment I can't find it, and that's why I'm going to Europe, because I want to play *nightly* for a while. I'm tired of waiting. I have at least a month's work over there, probably more after that, with different rhythm sections.

But this is with your own band?

No, my band is dead. . . . That was a good little band. It was alive for about three years, until last fall. We couldn't keep it going any longer. Roswell Rudd, Dennis Charles, and twenty-eight bass players!

[The telephone rang, and he discussed air fares to Copenhagen and smallpox shots, and mentioned his day job. After he hung up, I asked what kind of a day job he had.]

I work for a market research firm. I'm called a coder. I translate housewives' answers to surveys into numbers, then my endeavors are fed to an IBM machine and tabulated. I've been doing it for about six months; hating every minute of it, too.

Has a day job been necessary to sustain you all along?

No, that was the first steady day job I'd had in about five years. But it had gotten to be nearly a full-time occupation *avoiding* a day job, and I couldn't make it anymore. Playing jobs were just nonexistent. So I'm looking forward to getting away for a while. I've been here too long.

You taking all your troops? [He has a wife, two step-children, and several animals.]

No, they're coming later when school's out. Goodbye, New York. I'm confused by it now, and I don't dig that. I don't understand it anymore, this island. I've been a musician all along, but I've been other things at the same time that distracted me. I've gotta be *just* a musician now. Especially when I'm getting paid for it.

What did the Composers' Guild Band play last night?

The works of Carla Bley, Mike Mantler, and Bill Dixon.

Does that band rehearse?

Sure, we had two private and two public rehearsals before the concert. There are about fifteen pieces in the band. I don't know if it will stay extant, now. There are several reasons, one of which is my departure, that it may fold now, for a while, anyway. I think Carla wants to rest from her Herculean labors for a while, too.

What's the band doing, musically?

Whatever she asks it to! [Laughs.] Which is a good situation—that's where it's at now, it'll do anything. Anybody's willing to try anything you ask them to if they trust you to a reasonable degree—even if they don't trust you—because the experimental days are with us. Cats are willing to freak off in public, and own up to it afterwards. That's just the way it is. You know, it's both healthy and unhealthy, like it always is. I can't tell which is more or less, because like I say, I've been embroiled in it too long.

Have your viewpoints changed in the last couple of years?

Sure. Of course. But you know certain things are constant, like in everything else. Your values shift, and your proportions maybe remain the same.

Are your old Verve sides valuable to you now?

I don't even have a phonograph, and I haven't for a long time, so I don't know. It has just happened to work out that way, so I've had a period of listening to a little music live and my own playing. I don't think I'd like them now, though. When I think of them, I think of the flaws rather than any kind of strength that might be there. That's the way I feel about nearly everything I've recorded—it seems not to be what it should be. Or not what it is now. That's what drags me, because I don't have anything even nearly recent out that somebody could hear. I was talking to a German promoter, and the work of mine that he is familiar with is eight years old. He liked it, and that's fine, but it's disconcerting to be accepted on that kind of basis. But I'm glad people still like that stuff, I really am. Listening to older things for me is like time-traveling: it takes you back to things that were happening at that time, and it's more of a "human" experience than a musical one. I don't listen to those old things any more.

Do you think that has anything to do with the fact that people don't play standards anymore, since these extramusical associations come into play?

Well, not everybody *doesn't* play standards—some people play standards. I still play them sometimes. When cats get together like last night they don't play standards, but I wonder what they do when they're by their lonesome, you know. The scene really isn't very communicative now; people are willing, as I said, to get up and play off the top of their head, and be responsible for it, but they're not willing to talk to each other about what they're doing. It's very dangerous right now, musically: the music is *precarious*. It seems that way to me, like the music I took part in this last weekend—I dug it, but it made me feel a sense of danger. Maybe that's one of the things it's about. Some of the things that people did that didn't interest me would get a response from someone else. Somebody would get up and say, "Yeah! Crazy. Wonderful!" I don't know what they heard, but it wasn't what I heard. There's a lot of daring involved in the music now. Anything goes, but your own integrity tells you that everything doesn't "go." So it's a very delicate situation. It's the play of one set of values against another: your own, and the collective sensibility of where it's at now. What to expect. That kind of a musical chance situation makes you play a different way; you have to get up there and *play*. It's all quite new. Quite raw. Quite dangerous. Really, though, there wasn't much goin' on last night that Cecil Taylor wasn't into almost fifteen years ago. He was where it's at now. He's really been the secret leader of the whole New York jazz scene for fifteen years, the unacknowledged shaper of where it goes and what it does. Long before Coleman hit town. Powerful as Ornette was, Cecil was already making earthquakes and tornadoes and cyclones, but there were only a few people who listened to it, much less dared to play that adventurously. There were a very few who, like myself, were innocent enough to play that way without being self-conscious about it. But it's interesting that people are willing to go through that. Old things come out and they throw you, you know, it's hard to keep the thread.

What specifically was Cecil Taylor doing that far back that is happening collectively now?

He was doing more than is happening now, to my taste. He did it as an entity, and the elements are hard to discuss apart from the whole thing.

He was way ahead, his music was more of everything than I find now. It was more dolorous and more frantic, and more beautiful and more ugly, and it was more alive. That's what it was, really, more alive. That music was really supercharged. Of course, what he's playing now is wonderful too. He's just, you know, a "champ." That record he did with Gil Evans is something special, *Into the Hot.* The three pieces by Cecil—"Pots," "Bulbs," and "Mixed"—are the best examples of his writing on record. He's a great composer, like Monk and some others. His composition really sticks out. My wife and I went to his Town Hall concert, and we were very moved by that, too; it was beautiful. Everybody knows there is a Cecil Taylor now, but they don't know what that is, and most of them shy away from the reality of the music. His Fantasy record with Sunny Murray is more difficult for me. I don't understand Sunny Murray's drums. I heard Cecil play at the Five Spot with Tony Williams and it was wild. They really had it together. It melted me. Everything succeeded, everything worked, nothing was arbitrary—where I find Sunny Murray's drumming arbitrary, pointless. But there's probably some *other* point to it. He lives twenty-four hours a day, too.

You've used that word "arbitrary" before, in describing Thelonious Monk's music.

I've been running from it for a long time. I shun it. I mean, a lot of my endeavors have been a flight from what I consider to be the "arbitrary" at any given moment. A search for something more meaningful, something that makes sense right then and there—that's the only criterion. When you play, you just try and make sense to yourself at the time, that's all you can do. It's an active process. I've thought a lot about Monk's music, in the past anyway, it's a part of me. The band I had was involved with the complete music of him, and for years before that I had been thinking about it and trying to play it.

[We came back to the Jazz Composers' Guild of the night before, and he told me that they played Carla Bley's "Radio," among other things. I asked him if he had a solo on "Radio," and he nodded, and I asked him how it related to the composition.]

I don't know—ha! The composition had a lot of melodies. It had a collective melody, a displaced melody with several aspects of itself at one time, like a cubist painting. And chance was involved in it all. The rhythm wasn't pre-set. The length of time wasn't really suggested for the different elements, the different events that took place. That had a lot to do with the success or failure of it, the proportions that happened. Very interesting!

What do you mean by proportions?

Relative sizes, volumes, lengths. In time. Three seconds for this and five minutes for this, and the whole in three quarters of an hour. Certain amounts of high and low, and dynamics, fasts and slows. Relative sizes of things from the whole range of possibilities. A lot of the proportions of last night were chance, and a lot of it was motivated by what was written. It was a very beguiling mixture of these two provocations: what was caused first by what was written, and what was caused by who was there and how they were feeling at the moment.

Material and response.

Yeah. Subject and situation.

[He spoke to his wife on the phone, and she said she'd be home in a while. He had mentioned earlier that he was trying to rent his apartment and I asked him if it was safe for his wife and children on the Bowery.]

Sure. These people down here are the coolest. They have an unwritten code among themselves of "no trouble." There are strong relationships between them and the place they live. They're not just anonymous and they can't remain in isolation. Not many of them even get drunk alone. I've lived here and just around the corner for eight years, and there's never been any trouble. But that's enough, and I'm ready for a change of scene.

Were you attracted by it?

No, it was just the only place we could afford, and at the time I had the band and wanted a place to rehearse. So much of life is arbitrary, too. The hardest thing in the world is to make decisions, the ones that you actually make. I try and avoid not having a determinant except when a lack of them is called for. There is a place for such things. In practicing, for example, you seize things for no apparent reason except that it's Tuesday, and you need a place to start, and you work with it and see what happens. It may get somewhere not arbitrary; it becomes useful for further exploration. It's what Stravinsky calls the principle of "speculative volition." That's a good term—he's a master of language. That's why he gets so mad at the critics all the time, he believes that this principle is inviolate. The fishing mind, going places that it hasn't been before. Like "he who thinks of something first, that's the way the universe goes." I don't know who said that. Mallarmé? People go about thinking new stuff all the time. You can't be aware of everything at any one time, just a few things. While you're thinking about those few things, you're missing ten zillion other things! So who's to say? It's very mysterious business. There's a lot of mystery in the world.

Mystery.

I'm a big one for words. I've read a lot, especially by and about artists. So I have a headful of notions, and that isn't always good, you know. The instinctive silent life is beautiful too. It has advantages that the other doesn't.

Is this Monk's life?

It's funny that you should say that, because I was thinking about Monk, although he's more aware and articulate to himself than most people realize. He doesn't feel it's necessary to verbalize, and he's right. If you got him at the right time, you'd get a lot of meaningful words with a lot of silence around them. You'd have to leave the silence around them, or you would spoil the proportions.

I'll remember that. [We were back around to music, to the little dichotomous relationships he had touched upon before his wife had called.]

There are all kinds of things you can base improvisation on. What motivates you shouldn't stick out when you hear the music, although you can get intellectual pleasure from the relation of form and content and what-not. If the music is good enough, you're not thinking. You're just hearing it, taking part in it. It's real plastic phenomena. If it's real and good enough for a particular time-space situation, you're not thinking how it came to be. It's better than any thought about it, when it's like it's supposed to be. *Thought* about it is retrospective. You sit back and say "wow" if it's good and tangible and palpable. It fills the room, it fills peoples' heads and hearts and stomachs and feet. Everything, you know. It envelops people. It sweeps everything away. You try not to lose the thread of it when you're playing it, and the listener is going through the same thing. That's when it's really happening, and it's a beautiful process. [Pauses.] I wandered off there, I was thinking about other things too. I can't remember who said it—whether it was Kline or Pollock, they probably both said it, and de Kooning too—about when you lose contact with it, it's a mess. It's as simple as that, you just try and stay with it, that's all. When you're not playing you think of all kinds of stuff, but at the time, you just try to keep contact. That's why you hear guys talk about *receiving* their music, as if you were not there, as if it were almost involuntary. I don't know, it gets mysterious again. I heard today that the Russians achieved contact with outer space, did you hear that? Radio beams from other beings, that's contact of another sort!

Those analogies are interesting. Another reason I've read a lot about painters and what-not is because a lot of the writing about jazz is not good enough. It just doesn't seem hip enough. There's certainly nothing about jazz as enlightening as Klee's notebooks. And there are no monographs about jazz musicians like there are about Gauguin or Goya.

But those people are older, and you can print their paintings.

Yeah, jazz is young. But you can't see it all at once. You have to see the man's whole output, and that's several museums full, in the case of a very prolific cat. Somebody like Dubuffet, you couldn't get all his things in one museum. So it would take as much time to dig that as it would Stravinsky's music. You have to come back to it again and again, in the same way. How many of these things do you really have time to do? I've done more than my share, because of the lack of work I've had. I've really investigated a lot of life's works, artists' total outputs.

What have you found lacking in the writing about jazz?

The other hours of the day, and the other days of the life. Even a pickpocket lives twenty-four hours a day—he does other things besides pick pockets, he had a mother and a father and a childhood too. The things I've read have been thin, limited. The biographical things and the critical things too. There are some exceptions, but it hasn't had its [Bernard] Berenson yet. I read writing about jazz, but it isn't as rich and rewarding as other stuff—or, as Berenson would say, as *life-enhancing* as the other stuff.

Do you think that the music itself is worthy of that kind of attention?

It's pretty damn good. The really great music since at least Louis Armstrong and the '20s and Duke and everybody, it's been good enough to spend a life on. It's that weighty, same as classical music. Jazz is an alloy, but it weighs just as much. It's worth a life, and that's as much weight as there is. You can fulfill yourself completely in it, either from the inside or I assume from the outside.

That sounds like the measure of it to me!

That gets us back to proportions again, whether all the things it has and all the things you have coincide to enough of a degree to permit complete personal fulfillment by spending your life in it: to where you can get out of it everything you have to give to it.

Cecil was the first person I met who was really articulate about jazz, and I used to listen enraptured while he spoke about it, years ago. And then I began to think and talk, and he didn't dig what I had to say, and he was right—I was very naïve about it. And we kind of drifted apart for a while, but we've always had our relationship. We've spent a lot of time in music together and there's a lot of love involved. Do you believe in cycles? I don't know if events fit patterns and all.

Are you superstitious?

I try to be, but I can't quite bring it off. [Laughs.] I love what can't be explained, though. I like that.

Mystery!

Right, but that word doesn't taste right right now.

Does that word characterize the works you like best?

Consider Jean Dubuffet. He's had all my time for a few years now. One of his little pithy sayings is, "The world is not what you think it is." I like that, and I also like the opposite, which he didn't say: The world *is* what you think it is. So in answer to your question, "The most valuable part of things is the part that can't be explained." Braque said that, and it's good. He too seemed to understand things and was articulate about it.

Do you think he was more articulate than painterly?

No, he had nice proportions of both. I like his total body of work, including what he said. He had a nice estimate of himself, as an artist, and he knew what to do. And he did it. Like a number of them. Miró, too. Painting is nice, because I don't have to do it. I can see it more clearly than music, because I'm not so involved in it. I can't *savor* music at this point, that's what I want to say. I can't get far enough away from it to be able to see it, so I'm leaving New York for a while.

Faithful Lacy

interview by Philippe Carles

In the spring of 1965, Lacy went abroad for the first time, to Copenhagen for a month's engagement at the famed Montmartre Club, where he was joined by the trumpeter Don Cherry and the pianist Kenny Drew, who was already living there. Although he had lately recorded with Gil Evans (alongside Eric Dolphy) and with the Jazz Composer's Orchestra, he still struggled to find enough gigs in New York. "I'm tired of being in the underground. I want to play for people—lots of people—every night," he told *Down Beat* (17 June 1965) before leaving. "If at all possible, I want to move my family and settle in Denmark. They are tired of underground living too. I'm tired of seeing jazz fed upon by all of American music and not being fed in return." All the same, his wife and stepchildren did not go with him: the trip was open-ended, and Denmark proved to be only the starting point. He was seeking new possibilities for his music, and though an avant-garde revolution in jazz was on the move in New York, he had to go abroad to partake of it on his own terms.

Indeed, he was optimistic about his departure: "I'm not running away from something; I'm going toward something." By the end of that year, he recorded a trio date in Rome (*Disposability*) with the bassist Kent Carter and the drummer Aldo Romano, which was the first appearance of Lacy's own compositions, among other pieces; less than two months after, the trumpeter Enrico Rava made the trio a quartet on another recording (*Sortie*) made up entirely of Lacy pieces. In between these sessions, he also made a record in Holland (*Jazz Realities*), as part of the quintet he was working in as well, which included the trumpeter Michael Mantler and the pianist Carla Bley, in addition to Carter and Romano.

The following interview from *Jazz Magazine* (August 1965), and a shorter one in *Jazz Hot* at the same time, were the first with Lacy to appear in Paris. *Jazz Magazine*, and its longtime editor Philippe Carles, were among his most faithful supporters in the French press throughout the subsequent decades.

Is your real name Lacy?

No, that's not my real name. I changed my name ten years ago. In fact, it was Rex Stewart who changed it for me: he couldn't pronounce my name, Steven Lackritz. "I'll call you Lacy," he told me. I replied, "All right, that's fine with me."

Besides Rex Stewart, you've played with Max Kaminsky, Jimmy McPartland,

Buck Clayton, Charlie Shavers, Zutty Singleton, Hot Lips Page, all of them more or less representatives of the "old style" . . .

Yes, years ago. That's where I started. I started with New Orleans and Chicago, I mean the Chicago style. Only for a few years, at the beginning.

Why did you choose the soprano?

I fell in love with it . . . Because of its sound, above all.

Who were your favorite players?

Sidney Bechet, of course, and then Johnny Hodges too. At the time, they were my favorites. But not anymore. These days, my favorite soprano saxophonist is me . . . I am my favorite.

John Coltrane plays soprano . . .

I like it, but not from a musical point of view. It's . . . *très amusant.* I prefer Coltrane on tenor. He doesn't have a serious knowledge of the soprano. He lacks training. He could have more technique. For him, the soprano is a toy. He's better on tenor. It's not a toy for me.

How do you explain that very few people use the soprano?

It's a very difficult instrument to manipulate, to master in terms of accuracy. That accuracy is a big problem. It's very difficult to control the accuracy on soprano.

You've always lived in New York. Have you ever been tempted by California?

No . . . Or rather, I wanted to go there, but was never able to. I can't go every place that attracts me. I have to work first.

Is music like a job for you or something more important?

Music is everything for me. Music, only music.

Was there an interest in music in your family?

No, not at all. Neither in jazz, nor classical music. It was as if music didn't exist.

Why did you become a jazz musician?

L'amour . . . l'amour de la jazz. I fell in love with jazz.

Do you like other kinds of music?

Yes, I like Stravinsky, Webern, Berg, Prokofiev, Nielsen, Bach, Bartók . . . Schoenberg, Harry Partch . . . an American composer. I don't think he's known in France. He's excellent.

Does folk music interest you?

No . . . Although, some. That depends on the folk culture. Indian music, for example. I especially like listening to it when the weather's hot out. It's a summer music, a music for hot temperatures.

Can it bring you something in particular?

Yes, inspiration. But not in technical terms. It's very different music. The rhythmic concepts are fantastic in Indian music, very sophisticated.

And among the composers you've just mentioned, has their work helped you?

Webern, for example. I transcribed a number of Webern's pieces written for soprano voice. I transposed them so I could play them on soprano sax. It's very difficult, the rhythmic changes, rhythmic nuances are extraordinary. As training, it's excellent. It's not a question of playing that in public, of course. For me, that would hold no interest.

Do you prefer that people understand your music or that they like it, even without understanding anything?

I prefer that they like it, that's better. I only ask them to give me a little of their time. It's not essential for them to understand. It's enough for them to come, to be there.

Do you think of your audience when you play?

No, not while I play. But in between times, yes.

When you play, are you thinking of something in particular? A memory, a landscape, a woman, or simply a matter of chords . . .

No, I never think of chords, nor of chord changes. Never that sort of thing. In fact, I don't think of anything. I only try to follow the music, to stay with it, to not lose sight of it. If you lose it, you're in trouble, you make a mess of it, but if you don't lose it, that's perfect.

Do you believe in God?

I believe in what's good and right. I really think it's the same thing, God and good. I'm very religious, but I have my own religion. I read Lao Tzu. The *Tao Te Ching,* only that book. For me, that's enough. Everything is there. The *Tao Te Ching,* in English "The Way of Life," I read that. It's my bible.

You don't read anything else?

Oh, yes! I like Proust and Robert Musil. By him, I prefer *The Man without Qualities.* I always find time to read. But I also love painting. To look, not to paint! I like all the painters, from Giotto to Dubuffet. I enjoy more looking at painting than listening to music, I get more out of it. I'm not as caught up in it as in music. So I have more freedom to appreciate it. I don't have to worry about judging it or analyzing it. I can simply look and enjoy.

And film?

I especially like Antonioni's films. *La Notte,* in particular. *The Red Desert* is the only one I haven't seen yet. Monica Vitti is my favorite actress in film.

Are you proud or satisfied to be an American?

No, not of being just an American. I'm happy to be an American jazz musician.

When you listen to a jazz record, can you tell if the musician is white or black?

Usually, yes. Often, for the most part . . . Mainly because of a certain virility . . . But it's not important.

Do you like listening to your own recordings?

No . . . A few, though, sometimes. The one with Don Cherry, for example. But not the one with Cecil Taylor, it's not good enough. I'd like to do it over. With Gil Evans, I do like certain things. I enjoyed playing with Cecil Taylor and I enjoyed it also with Gil Evans. I hope to play with him in the fall.

Do you prefer playing in a small group or a big band?

I like both. If the big band is good, I'm happy to play there. If the small group is good as well, that's good too.

How many records have you made as a leader?

Four have come out under my own name. The first was bad, the second a bit less so, the third better, and the fourth was the best. If I make a fifth, the sixth one will be better yet . . . In addition, there are two that were never released.

What does "free" or "freedom" mean for you?

For me, it can only mean one thing . . . to be free, to play freely, all of that involves knowing, knowing perfectly what you want to do. The more you know what you should do, the more you are free. It's not a matter of knowing nothing, but rather of knowing everything. I'll give you an example . . . you're playing a piece. If you know it really well, then and only then are you free. Freedom has never been about playing just anything.

Can you imagine jazz without swing?

No. Absolutely not.

Have you heard Jimmy Giuffre's latest works?

No, I haven't had the chance yet. But I played with Jimmy Giuffre when I was in New York. I like him a lot, he was a good friend, but musically we're not at all on the same track, our kinds of music are incompatible. For me, friendship is very important. Most often, if the friendship is really good, the music is very likely to be good as well. When I meet someone I like, I know I'll like his music. A few days ago, I met a singer. I haven't heard her yet, but I know I'll like her style.

Do you like to accompany singers?

Oh, yes, a lot. Unfortunately, I was never able to accompany the best, those whom I'd have liked to play with. I've accompanied two or three singers in my career, but they weren't famous.

Do you have close friends in the jazz world?

Not at the moment, no. But I have had some, at the time when I was playing with Cecil Taylor, for example. I was very connected with him, then with Roswell Rudd, the trombonist. With Roswell I formed a band. In New York, we've played together off and on for three years. It's a good group. We play all of Thelonious Monk's tunes.

Who are the other members of the group?

The drummer is Dennis Charles. As for the bassist, about thirty bass players have passed through this quartet. Twenty-seven, exactly. John Ore, Steve Swallow, Henry Grimes, Wilbur Ware were among the best.

How do you explain so many changes?

Well, when a musician finds a better-paying job, it's normal for him to go. And that often happened.

But why was your drummer always the same?

Dennis Charles, you see, is an excellent musician, but he's not very enterprising about finding work. It's not that he's lazy, but rather he's not aggressive enough. It's not that he's shy either. He's just not combative. In New York, you always have to fight for work. Especially if you don't have a manager.

Are good managers easy to find?

No, there are very few. But a manager is absolutely necessary. I don't have one and I hope to find one, unless he finds me first.

How important is money for you?

Money is necessary, like the air you need to breathe. When I have some, it's not important; when I don't, it's crucial.

What did you do when you couldn't find gigs?

In New York I've done a lot of very different things. I sold records and books. I was also a business representative. A lot of ridiculous things, it's not even worth talking about.

How old are you?

Thirty-one.

Are you married?

Not anymore: I'm separated from my wife. I have two children, but they live with their mother. That's a mess now, you see, a big mess . . . In New York, for example, I no longer have a fixed address. Sometimes, I end up staying at Gil Evans's place. In any case, I'll be staying in Europe for the whole summer. I'll be moving around, of course, according to the engagements I'm offered. When I return to New York, I don't even know where I'll live.

Have you found what you hoped to find in Paris?

No, I found much more. I mean that the city is even more magnificent than I imagined. The jazz here is not very good, because it's something rare. It's one of the rarities of Paris. Paris is chock full of rarities. The city itself is a rarity, in every domain. I won't be staying long this time, but I'll be back, because I love Paris. I'm in love with this city. A very beautiful city.

Does the place where you play matter much to you?

I always like to play and the place matters little. Every place where you have the chance to play is interesting. Some can stimulate you more than others, of course. There are some that I prefer, but in fact I can play anywhere. I played at the festival in Bologna, at La Bohème (*chez* Buttercup), at the Chat Qui Pêche, and I've enjoyed playing in all of them.

Are you an optimist?

Optimist? Yes, I am. No doubt because *je suis fou.* If I wasn't an optimist, I would have dropped everything a long time ago. Discouragement keeps you from playing jazz. Still, I have gotten depressed sometimes . . .

What role does the blues play in your music?

A very big role. The blues is everywhere in jazz, it permeates any piece you play. You don't have to play the blues for it to appear in your music. All of jazz is saturated with the blues. I have on occasion played blues, but one can play anything in the spirit of the blues. Even "The Marseillaise."

Django already did that . . .

Oh, I've never heard it! That must be fantastic!

Do you have any specific projects?

No, on the contrary, my projects are very vague. After Paris, I don't know where I'll go. But I know that I'll be back . . . When? As soon as I have work. The only thing I'm sure of is that I want to play every night, six nights a week. I want to play with the best so that the music is best. That's all I want to do. However, one day I'm going to write an opera. But for the moment, playing is enough. It will be a jazz opera. I'm really stuck on this idea, but I don't know when I'll do it. Maybe I'll achieve it in nine months, maybe in nine years. I don't dwell on it, it will come by itself. Even as I'm playing, it's getting ready. It's not a matter of choice for me, but of something that will impose itself. Right now, I'm still quite far from that . . . Composition interests me so much that I'm sure one day to put this project into practice. It will happen almost inadvertently.

How important is Monk in regard to your work?

Monk represents for me the defense of a supreme equilibrium by the importance he gives to rhythmic values, to harmonic proportions. If I chose to play his compositions with my quartet, it's in order to understand the work that I absolutely had to know. So it was not an arbitrary choice. Monk was the only one I could choose, for a number of reasons. First, no one else but him was playing his music. He was there and his music was neglected. When I started playing it, no one else was. That was nine years ago. Nine years later, no one plays it and I'm still playing it. Another reason, of course, is the quality of his music. It's very fine music, better than most. I mean that for me, to play it, it's what I've found best. That doesn't mean I don't like other kinds of music besides Monk.

What musician currently seems the most important to you?

These days, there's only me. I mean that for me, the only musician who counts, who interests me, is me. I have to be concerned with following my own path. But if you mean "what musician has brought the most to others," I'd answer Duke Ellington, always Duke Ellington. He's been the king of the music, and he still is. If he's influenced me, it's in every way possible.

Would you like to play with him?

Oh, yes, of course!

Do you think interviews are useful?

I don't know, but sometimes they're interesting. In any case, I read them. As for me, I'm not sure if I like it, I don't think about it. All I know is that I like the coffee (he says indicating his *crème*). Only in Paris do they make it like that. The *café crème*, that's another thing I've only found here!

What do you think of the association founded by Bill Dixon?

It's a very good idea. I know all the members of that association. In effect, musicians have to defend their interests. Among the founding members is one of my students, John Tchicai. But I don't really like teaching.

Why do you do it?

Because people ask me to.

What are you going to do now?

Go up to the top of the Eiffel Tower, to see the whole city. Maybe visit the Jeu de Paume museum where there are terrific paintings, by Cézanne, etc. And then try to meet the friend of a friend of a friend of a friend who knows someone who can get me a seat at the Opéra so I can hear Stravinsky's work . . .

Twenty-six New Jazzmen Put to the Question

Toward the end of that same year, still on his first trip to Europe, Lacy was among a varied group of young musicians who replied to a questionnaire submitted by *Jazz Magazine* (December 1965).

What do you call the music you play? Why?

I call my music jazz: that's what it is. I don't see any other name for it.

Does your music follow a general understanding of the fate of the world and of man? Politics, religion, philosophy, do they play an important part in your art?

Music is part of life. All life is in correlation because politics, religion, etc. are only angles of vision brought into focus. (Braque: with age, art and life become one.)

Do you think before or while you improvise? If so, of what?

The question's too personal.

Are you concerned about swing when you play?

Naturally!

Do you take pleasure from playing? And do you try to give pleasure to those who listen to you?

Playing is too difficult for "taking pleasure," but it's my reason for being and I play with pleasure.

When you create, is beauty your objective?

Beauty is not my concern. Music is the result of the musicians' encounter with the spirit, in space and time.

What is freedom in music? What relationship does it have with mastering the instrument?

Freedom is an irresistible mirage. The greatest musicians are *relatively* free. Some of the *least* interesting musicians have the greatest technique on their instrument. In jazz, the nature of technique is generally misinterpreted.

Can you make a living from your music?

Yes.

What is your most cherished project? Do you hope to achieve it in the near future, and with whom?

To become myself. I hope it will take me my entire life. I hope to realize this project with the cooperation of everyone who's willing.

How do you see the future of jazz?

It will get better, it will get worse, it will stay as it is. There will be a handful of giants (different, I hope) who will change the course of the music and many, many to propagate it; certainly, some will do it better than others but everyone will influence the progress of the music, in partnership, let's not forget, with the public.

Steve Lacy Speaks

interview by Paul Gros-Claude

The latter half of the 1960s was an important time for Lacy, full of movement and creative ferment. Early in 1966 he met the Swiss musician and singer Irene Aebi in Rome, and by the spring they went off to Buenos Aires with his quartet for what turned out to be a difficult eight months. That band—with Enrico Rava, trumpet; Johnny Dyani, bass; Louis Moholo, drums—was the culmination of Lacy's free jazz period, at a moment that was hardly propitious for such music in Argentina. Toward the end of the band's stay there, it recorded *The Forest and the Zoo*. Lacy returned to New York from Buenos Aires and proceeded to work intermittently, recording on projects written by Carla Bley (Gary Burton's *Genuine Tong Funeral*) and Michael Mantler (the Jazz Composer's Orchestra's "Communication No. 8," featuring Cecil Taylor). But there was not enough to keep Lacy active or interested, so he and Aebi went back to Rome early in 1968. There he worked with Giorgio Gaslini, Enrico Rava, and many others, especially with the composers' collective Musica Elettronica Viva. In '68 he also wrote "The Sun," a bright, illuminated piece based on a text by Buckminster Fuller; performed for German television, it marked the first time that Aebi sang in his group, which included Rava, the vibraphonist Karl Berger, the drummer Paul Motian, and the bassist Kent Carter. The following year Lacy recorded two sextet dates, with Aebi on cello and mostly Italian musicians: *Roba*, the first of his records for the French label Saravah, and *Moon*, for BYG, also in Paris, which included the first appearance of a piece from his Tao cycle ("The Breath"). Though the music was mostly improvised, these dates began to move beyond free jazz to see what was next in terms of structural or thematic elements. In 1970 Lacy and Aebi moved to Paris, encouraged by all the expatriate musicians living there. At the beginning of '71 his quintet recorded the first full version of the Tao cycle, *Wordless*, without the text. The following interview, in *Jazz Magazine* (February 1971), was published there soon after.

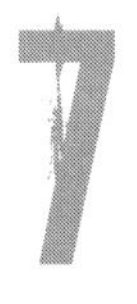

At what point were you attracted to music?

In 1950 I began to think about it seriously. I entered the Schillinger School, where I lasted six months, dissatisfied with the academic music teaching there. As for the Manhattan School of Music that I attended, I decided it was even more classical, just as tiresome, and thus dissatisfying, besides being absolutely useless with regard to jazz. I prefer the life of clubs, where one really learns something. Attracted by Dixieland music, I would take photos of musicians, and it was in bringing some negatives to tenor saxophonist Cecil Scott that I had my first contact with a jazz musician; so, I asked to study music with him. For two years, I studied clarinet and soprano with him. He used to sit at the piano, playing all sorts of chords and, on my end, I would try to improvise without knowing what he was really doing. It was very good for training my ear, although in a certain way it gave me the bad habit of thinking in terms of chords, which doesn't suit me personally. Everything I learned was useful to me, but one must approach music from every direction, this way, that way, from above, from below, inside out. What's bad is to close yourself off in a single path. The apprentice musician must invent his own method.

What was your first contact with modern jazz?

Until 1952, I didn't know about bebop—Parker, Monk, Dizzy, etc. The first record of modern jazz that I heard was a recording by Miles Davis. I was fascinated by that music: it was so mysterious! Between 1952 and 1956, I was still playing with the veterans of vintage jazz: Charlie Shavers, Zutty Singleton, Pee Wee Russell, Rex Stewart. Those encounters were decisive for me, to the extent that I felt more and more integrated into jazz: those musicians impressed me by their conviction, the purity, the finesse, and the depth of their playing. It was also at that time that I met Cecil Taylor. I was playing in a Dixieland club where he came one night. He approached me and said, "You're young! Why are you playing that music from the past? Music is a language and you have to invent your own language." I didn't understand what he meant until later. Cecil was my teacher for the next six years and I learned a huge amount from him, particularly on the political level, which he linked closely to the music—that was new for me. He showed me how there is no separation between life and music. Nonetheless, those beneficial encounters one after the other were not decisive with regard to the choice of a personal style. Besides, I don't think that we ourselves decide on the elements that shape our personality as a musician. Everything is fixed, everything is there, programmed in advance: all that's left is to find, to find oneself. One can be helped, influenced, interested in others (and when we are interested, it's proof that we're alive, that we're capable of emotions), but all that's left is to bring oneself to completion. While working in Cecil Taylor's quartet, with Buell Neidlinger on bass and the drummer Dennis Charles, I had contacts with other pianists, Gil Evans in particular, which had a huge importance for me. It was a fantastic experience working in Gil's orchestras starting in 1956 and studying composition and arrangement with him. Besides, that's my main concern at the moment: composing.

Taking part in Gil Evans's projects opened my eyes to many problems that the composer faces. At the time, I was trying to compose my own music but it was very bad. So when I first recorded with my own quartet, I used tunes written by others. In that period, until 1965 in fact, I used to play what seemed the most perfect to me, Thelonious Monk's tunes; I've only been playing my own compositions for the past few years. Monk is a terrific person! He's a consistent musician and, contrary to what one might think, easygoing. He understands people, he knows them, and he can get along with them. Knowing Monk's music so closely, I can understand the man that much better. I heard him recently in Italy: he is as marvelous as ever. Each time I hear him, he plays new music with a new quartet, new shoes, a new hat, a new suit.

How do you see yourself in relation to jazz today?

I think that the period of free jazz ended around 1967. We are now in the post-free, although some musicians continue to play what you call free jazz. I don't listen to a lot of other musicians; speaking only of myself, I can say that my group in 1967 was free. Nothing was preconceived: no limitations, structures, chords, harmonies, tempo, nothing. Just complete improvisation. Then I was asked in New York to do music for the film *Free Fall*. I realized that total improvisation was impossible in that case: the imprecision of the musical language would not have fit with the exactitude required for the scenes unfolding on the screen. Therefore, I devised certain limitations of time, timbre, tempo; certain instruments had to play a given part, others had to stop at a given place. When you make use of that kind of limitation, you cannot say that you're expressing yourself in the free idiom, as I do in my album on ESP, *The Forest and the Zoo*, recorded in Buenos Aires in 1966. Although it's approximative, one could characterize this "free" with reference to the painting of Fautrier, where the substance of things is disclosed, the nature of a free improvisation revealing itself in the informal, but all that is relative because, in resorting to an example taken from another artistic discipline, we remain in imprecision. So after that film, I had apparently arrived in the post-free period. Certain works started to carry structures, texts, notes, which is very important for me now because you cannot go back to the language of free when you've already passed that stage. Free jazz, necessary in its time, was not varied enough; that's the reason why it ended: it gave rise to monotony. It's up to the musician to bring about the changes, to arrange for something to happen; what you get by limiting yourself is the real freedom.

How do you choose your musicians and the texts that appear in your compositions?

To achieve a certain unity in my productions, several criteria determine the choice of my current musicians: friendship, their possibilities, their temperament, and, in addition, something indefinable. I've known most of them for at least five years: the bassist Kent Carter, the drummer Jerome Cooper, and my wife Irene Aebi, who speaks, sings, and plays cello. I met the trumpeter Ambrose Jackson in Paris. Regarding the texts, sometimes I use my own words but most of the time I prefer ancient Chinese texts, those from the *Tao Te Ching* in particular, which I've been working on for almost ten years.

Do you think you'll stay in Europe a long time?

I'm going to stay in France this year. Life is easier for me here than in Italy, for example. The arrival in Paris of Sunny Murray, Frank Wright, the Art Ensemble encouraged me to come here because I knew that good music was being played and that a public formed by these musicians was attentive to all kinds of new musical expressions. I think I'll return to the U.S. next year and I'm preparing compositions for my group in order to present them there; that music will be much like our current performances. We can define it as post-free jazz (although I don't like the expression) or as "program music," a little in the spirit of the Art Ensemble, which interprets "stories" on specific themes. It's closer to the music on Ellington's first records than to the "athletic music" of bebop. Perhaps it will take a long time for me but look at the example of Cecil Taylor: he had to wait twenty years to be able to live decently. During those twenty years, he was in advance of everybody: best composer, best pianist, best leader. In New York, it was very difficult for him to find employment: the critics wrote detestable things about his music, the musicians refused to play with him. After twenty years, George Wein took him on a tour and then he was officially accepted. For Monk, it was the same thing. He waited until 1956 to be recognized. On average, it takes twenty-five years for one's ideas to be accepted, if one is really original. My music has been evolving for almost twenty years: when everything's in order, it will all work, business will take care of itself and the clubs will contact us. There are exceptions to the rule, of course. Miles Davis is one, although we're not talking about him as a composer; he doesn't write like Monk, Ellington, Taylor. At any rate, I believe in Miles because he is always very receptive emotionally. Whatever routes he takes I have confidence in him, and I've been following his development for a long time. I was in New

York when Coltrane began in his quintet. No one knew Coltrane, who played awkwardly and expressed himself with extreme difficulty. Then, night after night, Coltrane progressed until the detractors at the beginning recognized their error, whereas Miles was convinced from the first second of Coltrane's worth.

Improvisation

interview by Derek Bailey

Since the 1960s, the guitarist Derek Bailey has been a pioneer of free improvised music in his native England and beyond. In 1974 he did a series of radio interviews with musicians, including the following piece with Lacy, for what eventually became his wide-ranging book *Improvisation* (1980), a study of its nature and practice in music.

Lacy's own music was developing by leaps and bounds in the early part of the decade, and his increased activity as a composer matched new opportunities for playing. On the one hand he launched a solo career, starting with the overdubbed studio recording *Lapis* in 1971, and his first live performances a year later in Avignon (*Solo*, reissued on *Weal & Woe*). In 1972 his quintet took shape with the arrival of the alto and soprano saxophonist Steve Potts, who became a close collaborator at the core of his band for the next two decades. Already the quintet made three records that year: *Estilhaços*, recorded in concert in Lisbon; and *The Gap* and *Mal Waldron with the Steve Lacy Quintet*, both for the short-lived French label America, which managed to record the most innovative American musicians then in Paris. The following year, Lacy diversified further with guest appearances in Vienna and Milan; his modified quintet, performing in London (*The Crust*) with Derek Bailey on guitar, marked the first of his many collaborations with Bailey (on several Lacy projects, but also as a duo and in the improvisers' collective Company). For a while in 1974 his band grew to a sextet, with the pianist Michael Smith (*Scraps*; *Flakes*); late that year he worked with Bailey again, in his augmented saxophone quartet for a concert in London (*Saxophone Special*).

The American soprano saxophonist Steve Lacy, like many jazzmen in recent years, has chosen Europe as the base for his activities (firstly living in Italy and then for the past few years, Paris). During the 1950s and early '60s he lived in New York and at that time took part in many of the developments and changes then taking place. Events which led to what was later called "free jazz."

I suggested to Steve Lacy that the extreme changes that came about in the late '50s and early '60s were possibly due to an increase in self-consciousness on the part of jazz musicians, an increase in artistic self-awareness.

"Of course, the thing comes more to the surface. The longer you do something, the more aware you become of it. That's inevitable, and you lose your innocence, collectively and individually. And you lose your youth and the music loses its youth."

We discussed how jazz in earlier times didn't seem too concerned with its past—its "roots." It seemed more of a totally contemporary activity.

"For me that's where the music always has to be—on the edge—in between the known and the unknown and you have to keep pushing it toward the unknown, otherwise it and you die. The changes which began in the late '50s and were probably completed by the middle '60s came about because in the '50s jazz was no longer on the edge. When you reach what was called 'hard bop' there was no mystery any more. It was like—mechanical—some kind of gymnastics. The patterns are well known and everybody is playing them. When I was coming up in New York in the '50s I was always into the radical players but at the same time I was contemporary with some of the younger accepted players. And sometimes I would go up and play with them. People like Donald Byrd and Herbie Hancock. They were the newer accepted people. I was also working with Cecil Taylor, Mal Waldron, and other people who were the radicals. I was really mainly concerned to work with the radical people but at the same time I couldn't ignore the nonradical elements. But for me playing with the accepted people never worked out. Simply because they knew all the patterns and I didn't. And I knew what it took to learn them, but I just didn't have the stomach for it. I didn't have the appetite. Why should I want to learn all those trite patterns? You know, when Bud Powell made them, fifteen years earlier, they weren't patterns. But when somebody analyzed them and put them into a system, it became a school and many players joined it. But by the time I came to it, I saw through it—the thrill was gone. Jazz got so that it wasn't improvised any more. A lot of the music that was going on was really not improvised. It got so that everybody knew what was going to happen and, sure enough, that's what happened. Maybe the order of the phrases and tunes would be a little different every night, but for me that wasn't enough. It reached a point where I, and many other people, got sick and tired of the 'beat' and the 'changes' and the '16 bars' and the '8 bars' and the '4 bars'—everybody got tired of the systematic playing, and we just said, 'Fuck it.'

"But I think the question of appetite is very important. Some people are of a progressive bent and some are not. And you can't ask either of them to change. Some people are interested in carrying on an old tradition and they can find their kicks in shifting round patterns and they are not in any rush to find new stuff. They can rummage around the old stuff all their lives. People become obsessed with not just maintaining a tradition but with perfecting it. Some people search for the perfect arrangement of the old patterns and that is progress for them. Other people want to beat down the walls and find some new territory.

"What Cecil Taylor was doing started in the early '50s. And the results were as free as anything you could hear. But it was not done in a free way. It was built up very, very systematically, but with a new ear and new values. But there was complete opposition to what he was doing in the '50s. To me in New York he was the most important figure in the earlier '50s. Then when Ornette hit town, that was the blow.

"On the one hand there were all the academic players, the hard-boppers, the 'Blue-Note' people, the 'Prestige' people, and they were doing stuff which had slight progressive tendencies in it. But when Ornette hit the scene, that was the end of the theories. He destroyed the theories. I remember at that time he said, very carefully, 'Well, you just have a certain amount of space and you put what you want in it.' And that was a revelation. And we used to listen to him and Don Cherry every night and that really spread a thirst for more freedom.

"But I think the key figure just then was Don Cherry. Cherry was freer, in a way. He didn't worry about all the stuff that Ornette was worrying about and his playing was really free. He used to come over to my house in '59 and '60, around that time, and he used to tell me, 'Well, let's play.' So I said, 'O.K. What shall we play?' And there it was. The dilemma. The problem. It was a terrible moment. I didn't know what to do. And it took me about five years to work myself out of that. To break through that wall. It took a few years to get to the point where I could just play.

"It was a process that was partly playing tunes and playing tunes and finally getting to the point where it didn't seem to be important and it didn't do anything for you, to play the tunes. So you just drop the tunes. And you just played. It happened in gradual stages. There would be a moment here, fifteen minutes there, a half-hour there, an afternoon, an evening, and then all the time. And then it stayed that way for a couple of years. No tunes, nothing. Just get up and play. But it all had a lot to do with the musical environment. You have to get some kindred spirits. And at the time, that was in the air. It was happening everywhere. But I think that jazz, from the time it first began, was always concerned with degrees of freedom. The way Louis Armstrong played was 'more free' than earlier players. Roy Eldridge was 'more free' than his predecessors, Dizzy Gillespie was another stage and Cherry was another. And you have to keep it going, otherwise you lose that freedom. And then the music is finished. It's a matter of life and death. The only criterion is: Is this stuff alive or is it dead?"

For Steve Lacy, a musician who has always valued independence and freedom, the commitment to jazz through improvisation remains unchanged:

"I'm attracted to improvisation because of something I value. That is a freshness, a certain quality, which can only be obtained by improvisation, something you cannot possibly get from writing. It is something to do with the 'edge.' Always being on the brink of the unknown and being prepared for the leap. And when you go on out there, you have all your years of preparation and all your sensibilities and your prepared means, but it is a leap into the unknown. If through that leap you find something, then it has a value which I don't think can be found in any other way. I place a higher value on that than on what you can prepare. But I am also hooked into what you can prepare, especially in the way that it can take you to the edge. What I write is to take you to the edge safely, so that you can go on out there and find this other stuff. But really it is this other stuff that interests me and I think it forms the basic stuff of jazz."

Evidence and Reflections

interview by Alain-René Hardy and Philippe Quinsac

9

The spring of 1975 was a busy time for Lacy: as a guest with Alex von Schlippenbach's Globe Unity Orchestra in Berlin, the first of many song collaborations with the artist and writer Brion Gysin (*Dreams*), and also his first trip to Japan, where he made four records in different configurations (including two with the percussionist Masahiko Togashi). While in Japan he met the shakuhachi master Watazumi Doso, from whom he had a lesson. As he told Richard Scott many years later about this encounter (in *The Wire*, June 1992): "[Watazumi Doso] is perhaps the greatest improviser I ever heard in my life. The sound is more modern than anybody in jazz, the concept [he has] of sound as material is timeless, ancient and super-modern. He's playing with the components of sound, the vibrations. This man rises every morning and goes into the forest near his house and practices until dawn with the birds and the wind. And he is a master of wind himself, he has a complete mastery of sound. His diaphragm is astonishing, uncanny. His playing is extremely dramatic, daring, full of invention."

In the spring of the following year, Lacy returned to New York after several years' absence, where he reunited with the trombonist Roswell Rudd for a quartet date (*Trickles*), and performed his first solo concerts in North America. At the beginning of that year, 1976, he gave the following interview to *Jazz Magazine* (April 1976), joined by Irene Aebi; it was the first such occasion when he spoke directly in French. Of his facility in the adopted tongue, the writers commented that he "uses a French that is, if not fluent, then fluid, and only a few times did he have to struggle to express himself in a foreign language. We did not want to translate into an academic written language, with its discursive and intellectual nature, an interview that unfolded with much simplicity, cordiality, and spontaneity. On the contrary, our constant objective was to preserve in Steve Lacy's speech its oral specificity and particularly its rhythm, his musical construction—in a word, his authenticity."

Hardy: How do you assess, Steve Lacy, your recent three-week engagement at the Cour des Miracles?

Lacy: It was good because we played every night. Playing sixteen times in a row like that is magnificent because it multiplies the favorable occasions. When you play one night and you know that you'll be playing the next night too, that changes what you do. You can take more risks . . . There's nothing better for the music than to play regularly. It's like a plant that's given the possibilities to develop . . . and for the audience as well.

The audience and us, that forms a unit, and the more it was unified, the better it was. The music was always more or less good, and if it was less good, it was on the way to getting better again. Like a child . . . In the end, it's always good because it's alive. There was never a dead day, that's what was positive about the engagement. It was three lively weeks, three weeks that gave us the possibility to live, because a musician who doesn't play is dead. If we play, we are alive.

H: And in material terms?

L: It's painful . . . We don't earn anything. It's a disaster. We can't earn money like that; it's an economic sacrifice. If we don't play every night, we can find an engagement for a concert where we'll earn four or five hundred, but when we play every day, we earn very little and we spend it at the bar, there's nothing left at the end . . . It's not for the money that we play, that's for sure. We try to play well, to do something original, a bit new, but it's not easy to sell, it's not commercial. Maybe it will be some day, I don't doubt it. If the music is good, it turns into gold, it's alchemical. But that takes time.

H: Although you've lived in Paris for a number of years, the specialized journals seem to have kept silent about your work. Likewise, your absence from most of the French festivals has struck me . . .

L: Maybe the jazz magazines have been silent, but there is no silence around me. We're playing, and not only in France. We travel a lot, we play in Japan, in Italy, in Germany, in Holland. I play solo, I play with my group, I play with other groups too. That's how we manage to survive. Otherwise, we cannot. If we counted only on Paris, we could starve. We're ignored because we're too available. At the Cour des Miracles it was the first time I've worked in Paris since September, and how much did I earn? Nothing. In September, I did a few solo concerts and I earned very little. But between September and December—that's long—nothing, and in order to survive you have to earn a certain amount each month. If we play once every three or four months, people come to hear it and think, "Ah, he plays all the time." But that's not true, that's not true at all . . . And while we wait, we could starve.

H: What do you do during those slow periods?

L: I practice, I study, I compose. We rehearse, we wait, we study other things, but without an audience it becomes very abstract, we need to play before an audience.

H: Would the word "love" be out of place to qualify the feelings you bring to the audience?

L: I prefer a word like "sharing." If there's love, that's OK. That's a beautiful word. But it is a sharing. Love is a degree of sharing. In an experience like a concert, there is a sharing between the audience and us and the music and the instruments. It's an experience in common. What I do doesn't exist without listeners, without takers. If I do it in the void, that's crazy. If the public isn't there, it makes no sense. It's only a thing in common. I do one part of that, the audience does another, but it's really the same thing. When the music is good, there is no division, no separation, there isn't even the word "sharing," there's nothing. It's only that. It's a fact, an event, a thing that exists. There is no question . . . We can't say anything . . . There really is nothing to say, not for the public, not for the musicians. It's only when the music is less good that there are questions.

H: That would produce a sort of communication?

L: "Communication?" I don't know, that's not an effective word for me, it's a term that never occurs to me. Because that implies something I refuse a little, it implies that there is something else. For me, in the music, there is nothing else, it signifies nothing else but itself. It's a substance, and it contains whatever you like, it contains a life, and all the values therein, but it communicates nothing else but itself. It's a substance: we eat it, we taste it, we share it, we ignore it, we make it, but communicate, about what? Time? What does that mean, communicate? That's outside, communicate, and for me, in the music, there is nothing outside. I am making that substance, I try to put whatever I like inside, I want it to be good for you, for me, for everybody, but communicate, what does that mean?

Quinsac: What do you have in mind by "substance?"

L: Substance is . . . stuff . . . it's a material, an object, a real thing one can touch, it's a fluid, like a sound, it's a material, a story, it's whatever you like. We share the same substance. It's like cooking. We eat the same dish, and it's good. When it's good, there is no question. I want to make music like a substance that comes from me. It's not even music, it's very rare for it to become something that I call music. It's a substance, stuff, shit, the thing I do. It's too intimate, too personal . . .

H: The fact that your music is so personal, does that complicate the contact, the sharing with the public?

L: If the music is good, the divisions instantly disappear, it conquers all. Music is a medicine. It has a therapeutic effect, it erases divisions, it *silences* the cries, it soothes. Music is for responding to a call. We need music.

H: That concept of music approaches its practice in traditional societies, African especially . . .

L: I don't know. There are a lot of musicians now. Long ago, there was a certain number of musicians for a certain quantity of people. They played their music before people, their music was the same as the people. There was the right quantity of musicians for the right quantity of people. Now . . . You have all these records, each one is a different kind of music, and there are lots of musicians as well. That produces a multiplication, which is maybe a form of pollution. That is, we're no longer in Eden now, it's not paradise anymore, it's a mess. If you go to a record store, there are a thousand records, most of them are bad. There's no sense anymore in these things. So you have to find what you need for yourself, as a public or as a musician. There is no more innocence, that's all finished. The music of the East travels to the West, the music of the West travels to the East, it's a mess, there is no more sense. There are only messes now. Me, I struggle for purity, for an authenticity of means, of music. I want to eliminate the questions around the music, I want to make music without questions.

H: Do you regret the lost Paradise?

L: Of course I do. Now, I have to compete with Beethoven, reggae, with all that. Me, I'm there, reggae is there, Beethoven and all the others, Bach, Coltrane, Verdi, Bill Haley, all that, I exist with all that. Sometimes I get the feeling that I'm supposed to compete . . . it's a pain . . . I can't ignore all that. I worked at a record store for a few years, and I heard twenty-five versions of Beethoven's Seventh Symphony, every possible version. Beethoven doesn't interest me at all, nor the Seventh Symphony, but I know every interpretation, each one a little different. I was obliged to hear all that, I can't ignore it, it's a part of me, even if it didn't interest me at first. My desire is to play a certain way, but it comes from the Beethoven that I heard also, I can't ignore Beethoven, nor the amount one listens to Beethoven, and my music is a reaction against that somewhat. The pollution is everywhere. There's too much music. It's ridiculous.

H: Would it be justified to connect what you've just said to the fact that your music is often a discordant music?

L: But discordance becomes accordance. That's very, very ephemeral. Those categories don't last. Beethoven was also considered very discordant. People have less and less difficulty following me, I should go faster, because they're coming too fast. That's too easy now. One could say that five years ago—not anymore.

H: Since we're talking about your music, can you explain your preference for pieces organized along the pattern of collective statement of the theme/breaking out and individual improvisation/coming back together on the theme?

L: Because there is the space to go into the new. It's the new that interests me, I have a progressive ear. I like new things, new music, and a new public, new situations. It's a question of taste, appetite, tendency.

H: In those conditions, why not forms that are open from the start, deliberately open, like in the music of Frank Wright, for example?

L: I did a lot of that years ago, playing without structure or theme. But it always grew tiring after a while . . . Because I like structures. I'm a materialist. I like limits, lines. I'm a composer, I like pieces, precise atmospheres. I like craziness too, within certain limits, with other things around it. It's a question of need, appetite, preference. What I'm searching for is a certain rapport between the piece and the playing. Something that makes a unity between the structures and the playing. I'm seeking a music that unifies these different things. For me, composition and improvisation must be the same thing, it forms a whole. For example, on *School Days*, it was on the way toward that. We were playing pieces by Monk and we improvised upon them, because we were searching for a rapport between the way of playing and the piece that provoked the playing, we sought a homogeneity between the piece and the playing. Now, we're looking for the same thing—it's no longer based on Monk pieces but on pieces I write myself. But there, it was on the way. That's why I called it *School Days*, because it wasn't our music, but Monk's music.

H: Does the release of that record make you want to leave Paris and go back to work in the United States?

L: I want to work all the time, like everyone. I hate vacations. I would like to travel a lot, but instead of that I stay in Paris. I would like to do anything, play anywhere . . . I don't care . . . I love Paris, New York, Tokyo, all the cities where I can play. If I don't play, it doesn't interest me. However, in Paris the public is good. They've heard of a lot of things, they have rather high standards, they really understand. They're demanding. It's not easy to play every night in Paris, because the same people come every night and they are there on the last day, to see what we're going to do that night. So it becomes a bit burdensome. But we don't care, we practice during the day, we prepare new things and we're ready and we go to it . . . But we really like leaving that and traveling in the provinces. Both are necessary, Paris and the provinces. One without the other isn't good. In the provinces as well, it's a good public. They haven't heard anything, they never have anything, so they're very happy if you come to play for them. We did a children's workshop in the Southwest, there was no problem. We played a sound, and they'd react right away to that single sound, whereas in Paris they don't react because they've heard too many things. With the children, we'd do "bof," and right away: "ha, ha, ha!" It was fantastic. That's a demanding public as well, but not by the same criteria. For example, you can't joke with them, they're not informed—if you joke with them, they go right to sleep.

H: And the American public?

L: Vast, and very backward . . . more difficult maybe. But I'm going to see this year, we're going to do a number of concerts there. I think it's going to be a big shock . . . for them, not for me. I played in New York four years ago, *underground* concerts, and it was a shock already. Even this record, *School Days*, which has come out now after twelve years, it's a little shock for everyone. But when we played that twelve years ago, it went completely unnoticed. There were only four or five people who liked it, the business people had no interest at all, and we had no work. Now the record comes out, a lot of people buy it, they like it, no problem. That's the *gap*, the distance between things and their appreciation—it's different for each music. For one kind of music, it takes a year, for another, it's ten years, for another, twenty.

H: If one defines jazz as the music of black Americans, do you consider your music a "black music?"

L: Jazz has always been mixed, it's a mixed music. In New Orleans, there were good creole musicians and good black musicians, and there was a certain quantity of whites. It's always a mixture, and all those strict categories, that's an illusion, it doesn't work at all. LeRoi Jones wrote his book, *Black Music*, but it's ridiculous, because he ignores certain people. To write that book, he has to ignore this fellow and that fellow . . . But the exceptions ruin all those categories, and I'm an exception too. Maybe there are only exceptions. What is a black music? It's absurd, one can't say that . . . Which black? Where? I like things by anyone, whether the person's white or black. I don't like everything. I'm discriminating. I think it's important for musicians to be discriminating. That's an idea I stole from Thelonious Monk, because one night he told me: "Ah, you have to be very discriminating." To choose. But it's dangerous if that becomes like black music/white music. That's ridiculous. It never worked in the music, a racial thing, never. For me, Roswell Rudd is the greatest trombonist I know, I don't know a black musician who plays better than him, but if you ask him, "Hey, Roswell, do you play black music?," he'll punch you in the mouth. Among musicians, it's no secret who plays well and who doesn't play well, it's always clear. And among whites and blacks, it's never a question of that, but rather: "Do you want to play? Let's play." The one who plays well wins, the one who doesn't play well loses, whether they're white, red, black, green, yellow. There's always been a musical battle between musicians, it still exists, especially in New York, not much in Paris. Paris is a dream, it's easy. In New York there are a lot of musicians, and you could always get crushed musically by a fellow who was stronger than you. So you were beaten, you lost the battle. Then you practiced a lot, and after, you ended up winning perhaps. That was the reality. I know all the musicians, I know who plays better than me, worse than me, and they know it too, there's no doubt. And it's never a question of the color of one's skin.

H: Steve Potts plays a bigger and bigger role in your quintet . . .

L: He has always been the hero of the group, the guy who does the solo and everyone applauds. He's always been like that, and he's even more comfortable now in the music we're doing . . . so he relaxes more, he's more confident, he can let himself go more, and he finds things much stronger than before. It's magnificent, and if it wasn't like that, I would change it to become like that. I like that feeling. I want to give him every possible freedom so he'll always do that, and I'd like him to stay with me my whole life . . . always with that feeling.

H: Do you consider him like a disciple?

L: No! Rather I am his disciple. I learn each time he plays. I always learn something. It's been four years and it continues, and I'd like it to continue always. That's very normal for me. I like playing with people who are stronger than me, that way I learn something, and it inspires me a lot. If Potts plays well, everyone in the group is happy. We arrange it so he'll feel good in order to play well. And if I play well, everyone is happy also.

H: What does that mean, "a person who is stronger than you?"

L: He plays more than you, he crushes you. When I played with Cecil Taylor, when I was young, I always had the impression during those six years that he was a lot stronger than me, and it was true. Even practicing eight hours a day, I couldn't catch up with him, he was gone, he was stronger than me . . . It was magnificent and frustrating, but it pushed me to progress. It's magnificent to get beaten by a person who is magnificent—he kills you, but in such a beautiful way that what can you say?

"Thanks!" That's love, it's a sort of love. Now, in my group, there's Steve Potts who plays like a madman, each night more than the night before, and I never manage to catch up with him; I can only encourage him. It's perfect . . . There are nights where I tell myself: "It's crazy, he plays too well, it's not possible." I love that. If you play with people who are not as strong as you, you have no inspiration, it's not stimulating. There are nights when Potts plays so well that I wonder what can I play after that, but all the same I have to play something, so I launch forth, and I find something, and I surpass myself . . .

Q: Do you prefer recordings in concert or those you make in studio?

L: In public, there's a certain warmth, a certain reality. It's harder in a studio perhaps, but sometimes we manage to do things that we cannot do in public, for example the new record on Saravah, *Dreams*. But in studio we generally record what has already been worked out in public, if that's possible. It's during the public engagements that we cook things . . .

Aebi: We don't have a lot of time in studio. We do things preferably once, twice, three times, rarely more. It's not like pop groups, who have the studio for three weeks. For us it's different. We can't play the same thing many times because, otherwise, the musicians get bored.

L: The music we do is too hard technically to repeat many times in succession. On the other hand, in studio we can sometimes reach a certain perfection in our interpretation.

H: What led you to singing?

A: I've always sung. Since I was very young I sang . . .

L: It's very important. The most interesting event in the music we do is the introduction of the voice. When it happens really well, there is a unity between the voice and the instruments, but it's not easy, and it takes time . . .

A: I'm still not comfortable yet. It's a big effort for me to get up and sing before the mike, it's still not very natural, it's hard. Behind the cello, I'm much more comfortable—I float there, I'm well surrounded. But when I sing, I feel really . . . exposed. There's a kind of . . . fear, really! It comes out, but I'm never content.

H: In other words, you're not an exhibitionist?

A: The pieces are really demanding. It's not improvisation, first of all. The texts are very beautiful, texts by Lao Tzu, moral reflections. You can't be an exhibitionist with texts by Lao Tzu.

L: How are you going to be an exhibitionist singing about the morality of not being an exhibitionist?

Q: What development led you to sing, since you seem more comfortable on cello?

L: She was singing before she played the cello.

A: I sang before . . . I played the cello in order not to sing!

H: Do you still like to play the music of other musicians?

L: I've done it a lot. I've played with a thousand musicians. Before I came to Europe, in the 1950s, I played with so many musicians . . . it was fantastic. That's an irreplaceable experience. It happens less now. From time to time, I play with Mal Waldron or with Schlippenbach's Globe Unity Orchestra, but I like to do it only when I can also play one or two pieces of my own. Otherwise, it's a mercenary job, and I have to be really well paid—and so I stop my own work temporarily, I go there, I play their music, I'm well paid, and I come home, and I get back to my music, because I have a lot of things to bring to fruition now, a lot. I can keep busy every day for the rest of my life. I have enough, and I'll write other pieces if it's not enough. So I can only allow myself to drop that for a day or two, or a week, or a month, but not too much, otherwise I wouldn't have the time to create what I have to create. The music is so demanding . . . it gives you the instructions, it tells you what to do. It's the music that tells you—not you—what to do. It's me who follows it, and not the contrary. It's the music that's demanding, it's not me.

[Earlier in the evening, before the interview as such, one of us had asked Steve Lacy if he could explain where the characteristic sound of each great master of the saxophone came from, that sound which after a few measures, even a few notes, allows one to recognize without a doubt Ayler, Shepp, Coltrane, Ornette, or . . . Lacy. Here in substance is what he replied:]

L: One often thinks it has to do with the instrument, or else the mouthpiece, or the reed. Some try lots of different mouthpieces, but the sound doesn't come from there. If Coltrane takes another musician's sax, he'll make it sound like Coltrane. The sound, you have it inside you. All your musical work aims to (re)produce it. It's like a carrot before you, that makes you run. But we can't say *your* sound, *my* sound. It does not belong to you, it's you who belong to it.

H: Where does that music come from that is inside you?

L: It comes from very far away, very deep, and from nowhere, and . . . I don't know . . . For example, I make music that is based on two-thousand-year-old Chinese texts, and the music comes directly from the words. So where does that music come from? I can't explain such a thing. It's so distant, so old, so new, so mysterious. One cannot explain that: you have to do it. There is a realization to do. But it comes from things that are very ancient and I know they'll still play this music in the future, even after my death. It's completely crazy. It's useless to talk about it, because these things I have to realize in music. It's like evoking a thing that doesn't exist, but it does exist, that's all. It's very clear for me. It's useless to speak of it, it's better to realize it and after, we'll talk. If I say, "I have a song, blah blah blah . . . ," useless to talk, I have to sing it. A musician has to realize certain things—I insist on the word "realize," *make real*—but not to discuss, speculate . . . All my questions are musical, and I can respond to them musically. This whole discussion is a diversion for me. It's OK, but it has nothing to do with the thing, and the thing for me is a musical thing, a substance, a musical substance, and all my responses are in that substance, in the music I'm going to leave here. I deal in the musical substance, I'm not a talking kind of guy . . . Like Coltrane . . . he's gone now . . . he has nothing more to say . . . He left that, the traces of his work, the musical substances . . . that's it, his thing.

H: Is it important for you to leave a trace?

L: I love making records. I've made a lot, I want to make others. Not only records, but traces in the memories of other people, and of musicians too . . . Yes, the music leaves traces. For me who makes it, it's a substance. I work a lot every day on that substance, and tomorrow I'll have to keep working still. It's a natural thing. Like a baker makes his bread, I make music. I work all the time. Today it was good, but tomorrow, I'll make something else better with that . . . to stay alive. If I make the same bread tomorrow, that bores me . . . I have to remake it, I have to do better. Today's bread isn't good for tomorrow. I'm always looking for the bread that I had the idea about . . . the ideal bread.

10

On Play and Process, and Musical Instincts

interview by Raymond Gervais and Yves Bouliane

In March 1976 Lacy performed first-time solo concerts to packed houses in New York and Montreal, released on record many years later as *Snips* and *Hooky*. Two lengthy interviews appeared in the fall of that year as a result of these visits: with the poet Ron Welburn in the third issue of his improvised music magazine *The Grackle*, published in Brooklyn; and with the French Canadian artists Raymond Gervais and Yves Bouliane, in the art magazine *Parachute*, published in Montreal (autumn 1976; a hastily translated English version appeared in *Brilliant Corners*, spring 1977). Gervais, a multidisciplinary artist with a special focus on the phonograph record as artifact and experience, is also a jazz producer with a massive record collection; Bouliane is a painter and musician.

You've dedicated a piece to Rothko.

I didn't know Rothko personally. I had seen certain things by him in New York when I lived there and it didn't impress me. But some years later, after he died, there was a big Rothko show in Paris. I saw it several times and was really astonished. I found it magnificent and it inspired me to put my impressions into music a little. For me, those canvases were like flakes, each canvas was like a sort of flake on the wall. It was very beautiful. But "Flakes" [on *The Crust*] is also an ice-skating piece. It's dedicated to Rothko and signifies the flakes, canvases, but also little flakes on the skates . . . A lot of painters interest me: Paul Klee, Miró, Picasso, Braque, Mondrian, Matisse, Rothko . . . I also have a good friend, Kenneth Noland; I love what he does. I know a lot of others too, not very well known . . . Van Gogh was maybe the first painter who interested me when I was very young. His letters too.

Were you interested in painting before music?

Yes, perhaps a little before. I don't know. It's something that has always interested me. I did a tiny bit when I was very young.

And you no longer do painting or photography?

No, but what remains the same for me is the act of seizing something and putting it into music or on the wall. It's always the fact of seizing something that has a path in life.

Have you worked with other painters or artists on multimedia pieces?

I've tried that sometimes, but it hardly ever worked well. It was always a bit artificial as a marriage because the form wasn't right . . . Sometimes I take a part of a piece and exaggerate the gesture that goes with it, or I say a few words. It's a temptation I can't resist, sometimes. But with me, it's always a matter of sound first.

Do you feel close to John Cage and his philosophy of the environment, of natural sounds?

He once told me that I was looking to make popular music more serious whereas he looks to make serious music more popular [laughter]. I liked that, but I don't know if it's true. If it is true, I prefer his role to mine.

Each time you improvise on one of your tunes, do you have some kind of mental scenario for moving around inside the improvisation?

No. There's a space for the improvisation and I leave that "free," I leave it open. I'm looking to establish a certain rapport between the playing and the theme and the idea of the theme is to provoke another sort of playing. Especially for solo concerts, it's important to have a good variety of pieces to maintain interest . . . I think every way of doing it is good. If it works for you, it's good. Each person has their own way. A well-known musician told me one time that when he plays, he really thinks of a scenario: it's like a story he's telling. When you hear this pianist, you have no idea of that scenario; it's improvised music like that, but for him it's very precise. So I think there's always a big difference between the inside and the outside of something. For example, in that piece for Rothko, I'm thinking: ice skating, Rothko, painting, all that. But when I play that piece, I don't say anything, right? People are free . . . each piece is always very precise for me, very specific. It's always about something or someone, yes, always.

Morton Feldman, Christian Wolff: are you influenced by their music?

I adore Feldman, I'm crazy about Feldman, and Wolff too. I like Cage a lot, all of them, yes, Harry Partch, Varèse, Stravinsky, Webern, Bartók, Schoenberg.

Can you speak to us of your work with Giuseppe Chiari? For example, those photos in "Teatrino"?

Those were photos from a duo concert. We did two or three concerts like that, in Rome, Trieste . . . It was a very fragile music, completely improvised. He was doing whatever, and I was also doing whatever. He called that "Strimpellare," which in Italian means: to play in a very relaxed manner, not like a professional but like an amateur. We also worked together with Musica Elettronica Viva (MEV). That's where I met Chiari for the first time. It was at a concert with MEV in an occupied factory or something political like that. He arrived there with a megaphone and I wondered: Who is this guy and what's he going to do in our group with his megaphone? Then he began to play, to improvise with his megaphone, and it was fantastic. I've never forgotten that. It was so funny, so inventive, and it was good. He used it as instrument and as object. The two were inseparable, the comic things and those for the ear, it was a single thing. I've never seen a guy like that, not before, nor since. I loved that. After, we worked together several times.

You made music that was totally improvised each time?

Yes.

Was it like musical theater?

Chiari was completely theatrical and me, maybe I danced a little but not on purpose. I was really looking to play. If I dance, it's an accident, see. I don't dance publicly like that; I move normally and maybe that seems like a dance. But him, he's a great actor, a great player, a great improviser, a great composer too. After that, I studied some pieces he had written and we gave several performances of them. For example, that piece called "La Luce" (The Light), we did five or six performances of it in Milan, in Paris too.

What did you do in that piece?

It's a fantastic piece, only a noise and the light. The piece is a combination of sound/no sound, light/no light, that's all. A piece so classic, so perfect. Everyone can do this piece like that, with the light and a noise. And it works. For example, it begins, darkness/sound; the second line would be, darkness/no sound; the third line, light/no sound; the fourth line, darkness/no sound . . . It's organized like that, very dramatically . . . we used electronic sounds or sounds played by amplified instruments; we did five or six different versions of it, but it's so simple a piece and so classic that everyone can play it.

Have you written pieces like that?

Inspired by that, yes. A lot of my things are inspired by this minimalist idea.

Where a piece can be played by nonmusicians, for example? Does that interest you?

Yes, a lot. For a long time I was preoccupied with things that anyone could do and for situations like those.

How long have you been connecting music and politics?

Since Cecil Taylor, since the 1950s. At the time, I was starting to learn what music is and the politics of survival, playing music that no one wants. For me, politics is a question of social values and music is an act . . . it's also an economic question. You have to struggle for it and that becomes political because you have to survive. You have to be paid for that music no one wants. Cecil Taylor was really prepared to struggle. And Chiari taught me other things; Chiari is very strong politically. One of the phrases he said or wrote, and which impressed me a lot, was: for an artist, the only way to be political is to stop making works of art and to make only political gestures that become works of art.

He also wrote somewhere: "The only value of a work of art is the value it gives to other people."

Yes, of course. Sartre said the same thing. It means that once it's done, it's not yours anymore, it belongs to everyone and it's for them to do something or not notice.

Did your social commitment come into focus with your stay in Europe?

Yes, a lot. It's given me a great sense of the realities. New York is crazy. If you live only in New York, you have no idea of the planet.

In New York you were often not paid; you say, "We invented work." Have you done the same thing in Europe?

Yes, a lot, always, in Rome, in Paris too. It's very aggressive, all that; it's part of the music. For me, the gig comes before the music. There is no music first, without a gig.

You've been interested for a long time in the texts of the Chinese philosopher Lao Tzu. In those texts, as in certain others from Indian sacred literature for example, they often preach a detachment from material things which creates a kind of contradiction with that type of social and political commitment you speak of. How do you reconcile the two?

Yes, but I'm not a hermit on a mountain separated from the world. I live in big cities above all and I'm very much a materialist; so perhaps there is a contradiction. I am a materialist in the sense that I work with a material, music, in a world that is real, the world of people, of the commercial machine, all that, and all the music that exists already. I exist in the context of Beethoven, the Beatles, Stockhausen, Bach, Dylan, all that; I am a part of that whole world, I cannot deny it. So I am one person among others.

Tell us about the relation between the Tao and your compositions that are like a reflection upon it, like a musical version of the Tao.

There are six pieces I play that form a cycle and which are called Tao. I use texts from Lao Tzu for these pieces and they're sung. They are words set to music. Up till now, I've only done it instrumentally; but with the group, we've already begun to realize a version with the texts. Which means they're conventional songs like that but using a two-thousand-year-old text with new music. They're not fully realized yet. I play the tunes but my wife Irene sings them. It's not on record yet, but we've worked on it a lot already in Paris. It's a long process. The text took two thousand years to reach me. So now, it can take several years to become realized vocally like that. But soon, it will all become clear.

They'll be the standards in times to come?

I believe so, yes.

What do you think of Albert Ayler's music?

Ayler's language seemed very shocking in the beginning. But what shocks ceases to shock quickly enough, more and more so each year. There are no more surprises, not in that domain . . . The first time I heard Ayler was in 1964, and I laughed a lot; it made me laugh like a fool. I thought: this guy is crazy and I didn't understand. It really made me laugh. And I said: no, it's not possible, he's not serious. But soon I became aware that it was funny, yes, but it was also serious, and it was true, it was new. It didn't take me long to travel from one point of view to the other. The public as well gets accustomed rather quickly today to what is "no" and very soon becomes "yes."

With Steve Potts in your group, we sometimes see a collage of instrumental languages.

I'm interested in a real marriage, but that takes time. With Steve Potts, we've been playing together for four years now, and it's only this year that I find it really homogeneous, really together. And Kent Carter, I've been playing with him for ten years now. We've made progress together, but it's taken some time.

Is your language accepted by most musicians today?

In Paris there's no problem, nor in the provinces. In France, in Europe, no, there's no problem anymore. I haven't played in America except recently in solo concerts and three years ago in a quartet at Sam Rivers' place, and no, I didn't have a problem there either. For the past few years, it's become clearer and clearer.

Your record *Lapis* counts among the most important recordings of improvised music in the 1970s. One really has to live with it to appreciate its true value. On that record, there is like a Zen attitude, that is to say: don't seduce, don't seek to please.

It's interesting because it is precisely that record that's responsible for my trip to Japan. Because of that record, a fellow came to see me in Paris, to get me to come to Japan. The Japanese like that record a lot. They find it a bit Japanese.

It's close to shakuhachi music, for example.

Listen, I was in Tokyo, I was giving an interview in a coffee house and I was about to leave. I was in the street and they put that record, *Lapis*, on the stereo. I heard that in the street, in Tokyo, and it seemed to me typically Japanese, you see . . . but, up to that point, I would have never thought of it. I've always been interested in the Orient, Japan, China.

Would you agree that your record *Lapis* was like a turning point?

Yes.

It's your first solo album. You overdub several tracks on it.

At first I had to do it like that, then it gave me the confidence necessary to do solo concerts. The record in Avignon was the first solo concert I gave. But that was after *Lapis*. The first was not too difficult but after, it became very difficult, and now it's easy again. But it's always demanding.

You had a rather difficult stay ten years ago in Argentina, I believe.

That's right, yes.

Are you interested in the ethnic music there, the tango for example?

The tango, oh yes, I liked that a lot. When it's authentic, yes, it's fantastic.

Did you meet musicians like Astor Piazzolla?

Yes, we played on the same bill and we had a big fight with him.

He didn't like your music.

Not at all. He said that we played with a knife between our teeth, very aggressive. After he heard us, he took refuge at home and listened to Vivaldi all night. He said that in an article.

You didn't play with Argentine musicians?

No. We were a quartet: Johnny Dyani, Louis Moholo, Enrico Rava, and me. We were really like immigrant workers there, unwanted. We were really blocked there.

There was no improvised music?

No, there was nothing. There wasn't even traditional jazz. I thought before that it was colonized, but that wasn't true; it was virgin territory. And at that moment, it was very bad politically. It was right after the colonels and generals had their coup. There were tanks in the street, all that. And there were posters in the street: "Revolution in Jazz." People didn't want to hear the word "revolution." It was a complete mistake.

So you had some serious problems to solve.

All sorts of problems. But above all, the misery, the lack of money, of lodging, of food, all that. Eventually we turned the situation around and had a bit of success. At the end, there were people who liked us a lot. We developed an audience there, in eight months. But it wasn't easy. I wouldn't want to go through an experience like that again.

Can you tell us about your work with Sonny Clark, to whom you've dedicated a piece?

I knew everyone in New York because I was very active there for fifteen years, from 1950 to 1965. So I knew musicians of every style and I had played with them on occasion, for example people like Kenny Dorham. But with Sonny Clark we worked together in a coffee shop. It was one of those "invented" engagements. We passed the hat and the owner took out most of it before it reached us. Later, someone killed that guy because he was really mean. It wasn't a musician who killed him. Our group consisted of Sonny Clark (piano), Tommy Turrentine (trumpet), Carl Brown (bass), Billy Higgins (drums), and myself. Sometimes there was also a tenor—I don't remember his name. We played together for several weeks, some bop things, pieces by Sonny Clark, simple things, a bit like "La Motte-Picquet" [Lacy piece dedicated to Clark, on *The Gap*], a bit less complex maybe. That was in '58 or '61–'62. I don't remember exactly anymore.

And what is your impression of New York these days?

It's very interesting. Now, there's much more activity than before, more clubs, new musicians who are very interesting, and a bigger public than ever. I feel the music is part of New York's "bloodstream" a lot more than before; it's truly part of the city. And that's a little different. It's no longer as "underground" as it was; it's normal to hear it in taxis, at home, everywhere. There are even radio stations that play jazz twenty-four hours a day.

Do you intend to return to America?

Yes, I don't know when or how exactly. But there's work for me and a public as well to develop.

Your music seems very European to us compared to American improvised music.

I don't know. Maybe it's because I've lived in Europe for ten years, maybe too because my parents were of Russian origin. At any rate, yes, I make music that is a bit European. But in Europe, maybe they find my music very American, I don't know.

How do you manage to live financially in Europe?

Now it's all right. When I play, I'm paid respectably. But sometimes I also accept a gig along the way for less money; for example, last night I played in Toronto for a percentage because I was there. It wasn't a good take, but it covered the expenses. Anyway, that's not the main point. It's a political fact that a worker or anyone, if he works, should be paid correctly. I've played a lot for nothing but I don't do that anymore if it's possible, except for a benefit concert or something of that kind.

In Europe, do you feel like a musician in exile?

Now, no . . . no, but sometimes yes . . . But it's too late for all those sentiments. A musician has to travel a lot. I live where the music is and where the music is, that's where I live. I don't care if it's Paris or New York or wherever. So when I'm doing all right, I don't feel like an exile or an émigré at all.

You've done recordings, for example with Verve [1964, with Roswell Rudd], that never came out. What do they do with those tapes? Do they throw them out, do they lose them?

No, they come out, they all come out. Each day, I hear a new story. Now, they tell me there's a guy who has a tape of me with Monk, and he's selling it. I didn't know it existed. He ought to pay me or at least let me know, but one always knows after.

What writers do you like?

There's no specific one who is close to what I'm doing, but if you take twenty-five of them and put them together, there is something similar overall.

You dedicated a piece to Elias Canetti.

Yes, "The Wool" [on *Solo*]. He wrote one of my favorite novels, *Auto-da-fé*, in 1936, I think. It's a book that was lost during the war; now it's beginning to get known. In this book there is a fabric, a sort of wool . . . a great mastery of the stuff of life . . . it's difficult to explain.

"Wool" refers to a texture. When you write arrangements for the band, do you think in terms of a sound texture, almost tactile?

Ah, yes. What I would like is always music one can see or touch; that is, something precise, particular.

Does electronic music interest you?

Yes, a lot, but I don't have much talent for manipulating electronics. I prefer to work with good musicians who are specialists, like Richard Teitelbaum. We did a lot of things together ten years ago.

You recorded a tape with him, "Connected" [Rome, 1968, with Irene Aebi, cello].

Yes, that was a very good record. I have a copy of that somewhere. It never came out because the company went broke.

Don't you think that most electro-acoustic music proceeds always by collage

rather than fusion, given the nature of the instrumentation and the differences of articulation?

I think, if you're obliged to stay together with a person, you can surely find something after a certain time, and you can end up getting along with anyone in the right circumstances. With Richard, it was always good. There was never a problem of sound, texture, all that. It's a question of friendship, too.

Tell us about your work with amateur musicians and nonmusicians.

I've done a lot of that; each time was a little different. With Musica Elettronica Viva, we did "Zuppa" (Soup). That was for nonmusicians, for the folks who had never touched an instrument but who needed to participate in a collective session like that. Before they came, the people didn't know they were going to play. Right away on entering, they saw the musicians completely letting loose, and lots of instruments available there. Then without saying a word, one guy takes a trumpet, he makes a sound. It's not a proper, conventional sound; it's an utterly unheard of sound. And at the time, that interested us a lot, the unheard of sounds. So for us it was perfect. There was material for us to work with, starting from that sound offered by some guy. So we took that sound and added another sound right after. You had to be really on your toes, in a better than normal state to make music; that is, if a fellow doesn't know how to play an instrument, he can't make a phrase, he can make a sound that might be more interesting than a whole phrase by a musician. But you mustn't lose that sound. You have to seize it immediately, in a way that encourages him to produce another sound. It's a sort of psychological game like that and it was fascinating. Everyone loved that. But it was also a very fragile situation. We discussed lots of notions about musician/nonmusician, public/nonpublic. And we put into question precisely all those categories. It was in the air at that time, not just for us in Rome, but for lots of people in different places, for example the Living Theatre, Fluxus, Merce Cunningham, Cage . . . Lots of people were interested in breaking barriers. We no longer wanted a difference between the public and the musicians. But for us it didn't last, and after six weeks we stopped that and started to do the normal concert again. It was like the myth of Prometheus, really. The public will tear you apart if you expose yourself like that. After a while, they no longer appreciate it and they start to destroy everything. We didn't know it would be like that but it was. Why? I don't know. It was very mysterious, a bit frightening too. But I noticed the same thing in my "workshop" for amateur musicians in Paris. Everyone practiced together once a week. After a year, it was still terrific. Then, the second year, it began to decline like that, the quality, the spirit, the attitude, and people didn't appreciate the opportunity anymore. They began to abuse it. We felt very sluggish, you see; we had lost the freshness of the situation because it was an artificial situation, effective but which didn't last forever.

It was more a social situation than a musical one finally?

Yes. The fact is that the participants were becoming mean. At the beginning, they were very grateful and nice, and after a while they became mean. I don't know why.

Wasn't it because you were destroying your status as a well-known professional musician, on a pedestal?

Yes, something like that. Even so, I don't regret it. It was really good for us and for them too. And it was better for us, because they didn't continue. That's what is really artificial and it's the reason why I don't give many lessons. If I continue for twenty-five or thirty years, the others are only passing through.

More and more people are playing soprano saxophone.

It's crazy, huh? In New York this time, I saw millions of sopranos [laughter]. I was at the same shop where I bought my first instrument twenty-five years ago and then it was the only one in the whole shop. Now in the window, there were a thousand, a thousand in the window and another thousand in back, of all sorts. It's like flowers, no? I found that funny. It used to be overlooked, no one would touch it. I began . . . but it's really Coltrane who took hold of people's imagination, who took hold of their ear with that sound.

Are there musicians playing soprano in an original way that you particularly appreciate?

Steve Potts, he's terrific. He plays a lot of soprano on the last record that's coming out now (*Dreams*). Oliver Lake plays soprano very well, and Wayne Shorter, Evan Parker, Trevor Watts also. On the new record for Emanem (*Saxophone Special*), there's a piece for four sopranos.

And how does that sound?

Like chickens [laughter]. Animals are a very important factor in my music. That's why I mentioned the writer Elias Canetti. He's one of the only people who understood the rapport between animals and music . . . and men too.

Animals love and make music.

Yes they do, and they only like certain music, they don't like other music.

Do they like your music?

Dogs like my music a lot. Cats take refuge immediately. The sounds are too sharp, it disturbs them a lot. In Paris, I have a cat who doesn't like it when I practice. But I have a good rapport with dogs.

Do you often go to zoos?

Yes, often, always. In a city, that's where certain animals live. Some zoos are sadder than others and some aren't sad at all.

How do you translate an animal into music, ducks for example?

Well . . . Quack! That's already a sound, and if one does "Quack! Quack!" that's already a rhythm [laughter]. But in that piece, it's rather a question of personality, of the movement of animals and their relation to certain people. That piece, "The New Duck," is dedicated to Ben Webster. Initially it was called "The Duck," and then it was rewritten, "The New Duck." Ben Webster had a way of playing that was very expressionistic; he had an aggressive side too. When he was young, they used to call him "The Brute."

What does *Roba* mean?

"Roba" in Italian means material, thing. At the time [of that piece], we were living in Rome. We had a group with amateurs and professionals mixed. And we played every day without a theme, without anything, without a word. It was a sort of material, *roba*, thing; there was no name for it and we called it *roba*. In Italy, especially in Rome, they use that word for no matter what. They say, Ah, what *roba*! It means a thousand different things, a situation, an object, a material, a music, a drug, anything. And that word interested me, that word above all. I like it a lot.

Do you sometimes use quotations in your improvisations?

In certain cases, the quotation becomes part of a piece and there are other moments where it occurs to me to quote something. I'm surely capable of quoting a lot more than I do presently. So that means I sooner avoid it, it's too easy, dangerous, and it stops the music. When the quotation happens, the music stops for a moment. But if it's done in another way, it doesn't stop. I don't like when the music stops for something else. For example, in Holland they love comedy and often the Dutch musicians stop the music to play around; me, that leaves me cold, but for them it's the contrary, they love that. So we don't agree. It's in the blood, it's a temperament, it's a preference. The music has to be alive, it's the only thing that counts, either alive or dead: that's a universal standard . . . It's the idea of *roba*. Often I use free improvisation as a source of material and later we organize structures around that to provoke another sort of *roba*. But it's the *roba* that comes first and the structure that is applied after the research.

These days, a lot of music gets composed without knowing who is going to play it.

I prefer "the old Duke Ellington" where the pieces were composed specifically for certain people. When I write, it's always for someone precise. And now I'm writing a lot. We can't play all that I'm writing. We don't have the time and not enough gigs. But even so I'm in the habit of writing for my group or for myself, and I'll continue. I never write things abstractly but always for someone specific. I write because we need material to play. So it's for us, for me, for the group.

In contemporary music, a lot of composers who are not instrumentalists compose music that doesn't correspond to a need because it doesn't correspond to individuals, to a tangible reality.

Yes, it's very forced, very bad sometimes, things that are truly unnatural. In Paris, it's crazy what they present as contemporary music, things that are hardly natural.

Your music, on the contrary, is very organic, like the ambient surroundings, nature, air, water . . .

I would like to be that way, yes, something that goes, that moves along . . . It has to work, it has to be playable, listenable, consumable, it has to be good, without question, without explanation, without anything.

So your music must have a function in the environment, a healthy social function?

Yes. There is a certain morality, there are values in any piece of music, a whole world of values: durations, proportions, certain repetitions . . . And each musician uses these values in his way. And sometimes it's long after he's dead that we can appreciate them. But the true value of a piece of music is the use one makes of it. If it remains in a drawer, it doesn't serve a thing. After a short time, it turns into dust, nothing at all. If you look at old issues of avant-garde music magazines, *Source* for example, they're already dust. It's very amusing, very interesting at the time, but weeks later it's no longer anything. Music has to be alive, it has to last, like a tree; if it dies, it no longer does anything. But maybe it has provoked something else to become alive; that was its function. So you have to be careful, because something that doesn't interest you at all can be very valuable for someone else.

Your pieces are almost all dedicated to someone. Is that fairly recent for you?

No, but I don't always say it because otherwise it becomes a double title, it's too cumbersome. And then, it's a personal thing. All my pieces are dedicated, but I don't say it. That blocks the listening if you have too many things in mind. In general, I don't announce the titles of pieces in concert because that keeps people from relaxing, really.

In "Paris Rip Off" [on *Lapis*] you clap your hands . . . What does that piece mean?

There was a rhythm [clapping hands]: "Paris is a rip-off / Paris is a rip-off / Paris is a rip-off." The piece is a bit mean. I had had a scuffle in a Paris café, a window broken, an argument with a customer, a whole mess . . . and I put that in this piece, that anger.

Your tunes are very easy to hum, without much effort. They flow all on their own.

It's *strimpellare,* that manner of singing like that, yes, that interests me a lot. It's like when you sing in the bathtub. But you know, Chiari caused scandals with pieces like that in the Italian churches. There was this concert in a church where he sang: "Ta ra ta ta ta ta ta, ta ta ra ta da da," and people went crazy: Who is this guy, this composer, and why is he singing like that? . . . Yes, I really like things that are imperfect, instead of perfect; all my things are a bit askew.

On the record *Lapis*, where you use sounds recorded out in the environment, are you provoking an encounter between your music and the environment, the better to inscribe it into that environment?

Yes, to be part of nature, like the rain, like the noise . . . everything. Eventually it becomes like that, certainly. After I'm gone, if the music remains, it will be part of the environment like that. At any rate, on that record, I used a lot of natural noises: there are keys, the telephone, traffic, there's a record, all sorts of noises. There's even some silence that I recorded in the park at Vincennes, with a cassette recorder. I taped a lot of silence, about twenty minutes of nothing, to have a bit of space, a bit of air, and I mixed that silence in the studio with the sound in "Precipitation Suite." You don't notice it, but it changes the sound, it gives a lot more air in the sound. So there's the noise and there's also the silence mixed in; that record is full of tricks like that.

That silence is not artificial like the silence of a studio?

No, it was in order to compensate for the sound of the studio, to put in a bit of air, to change the air.

The air on the cassette.

That's right, yes, and that record was a bit influenced by Duchamp. I was really impressed by Duchamp when he did his *Large Glass*. He said that one could put absolutely anything into a painting, any idea, and I agreed: I thought one could put anything into music too. And when I was making that record, I was thinking about that.

You only play soprano saxophone. A lot of musicians these days play several instruments.

I went through a period in Rome, when I was playing with Musica Elettronica Viva, where I touched on everything: I played the soprano and I played the wall, the floor, the objects, the sounds, all sorts of things. That was the period of *roba*. But it didn't last long. I still experiment with other things, but I find that I can do everything with the horn, everything, and that's enough for me. There are always other things to discover, but each musician has his temperament and maybe some need to change instruments in order to change style. It's a question of preference, of taste, of temperament . . . but for me, it's a question of laziness too. I like to carry around only one saxophone and I don't feel limited by one instrument.

Have you ever played with musicians from other musical traditions?

Not a lot. It happens sometimes, but it's rare and it's really something else. In a situation like that, I can adapt more easily than they can; so it's not fair, because they don't have the experience of abandoning their music, while I'm used to abandoning my music and playing with them, to find their style, the surface . . . and it's a bit artificial, a bit forced. It's good for one time like that, to have fun, but if we really want to make music together, we have to play together a lot. And I've never spent a lot of time with someone from another tradition.

When you were a child, was music important to you? For example, did you hear Russian music at home?

Tchaikovsky, yes, I liked him a lot when I was little, some of the classics, Gershwin, Ravel's *Bolero*, things like that.

Does one find a bit of that music in your music now?

Yes, it comes back, it comes back, it's funny. All the things come back. With that experience of *zuppa* that we had, the most extraordinary for me was when we were obliged to improvise in that crazy way, things from far, far away would come back, by necessity; that is, a fellow would make a sound that was so unexpected, for example, that my response was something from far, far away which I had completely forgotten: a quotation from old music that I hadn't heard in thirty years or so. It came back like a flash . . . we were in a very strange state then, it was like a sort of therapy. It's always surprising to see something come back from far away.

Do you like the music of Debussy, Ravel, and Satie?

Yes, a lot, all three. I have pieces dedicated to each one. For me, the dedications are a way to pay back a debt. I have a debt toward all my influences, all the people I took something from, and I repay the debt with the music. That's why I don't say it; it's a personal debt between me and the person.

Is the fact that you are of Russian origin important for you?

Yes.

Do you like that Russian music which is very melancholy and emotional, like gypsy music?

Yes, when it's good I like it a lot. I like all music when it has a real feeling.

Do you personally feel a part of Russian tradition?

Strongly enough, yes. It's in the blood, that's for sure . . . My parents had forgotten Russian; they came to America when they were very, very young, and they didn't relate to anything about it. But there's something inside that comes out again when I read Russian writers or listen to Russian music. I think one can't ever lose what's really in the blood, one can be unaware of it, one can forget it, but it's always there. It comes out in certain phrases, certain sounds, certain values, certain harmonies, certain preferences, certain tendencies . . . But it's not for me to analyze that, I don't have the necessary detachment.

Before we end, is there anything you would like to add?

What's important for me is the history of the music, what's already been done, the classics, the whole history of jazz and of improvised music. I know it fairly well and it has always interested me a lot. I hope that what I do, and will do, will contain all that's happened before; that is, I'd like to do something that's a part of the whole thing, part of the history. I began with Louis Armstrong, Duke Ellington, Sidney Bechet, Jelly Roll Morton—all that—and for me, what I do is part of that. I'm trying to see all that more objectively because I've been living inside it for a number of years. I approach it in a virgin manner, meaning that with any music, even music I know well, I'm always trying to get back to the first time, as if it were the first time.

It's important for you to travel, to see other countries, other people.

It's music that is the other country for me, really. The place where I am interests me a lot, but I go there for the music. And along the way, I find all sorts of things. It used to be there were a few musicians who made music for people at home and that was enough. There were no records, nor voyages, whereas now it's a casino. So today, you have to travel a lot. People consume one music after another, and you have one kind of music, not every kind. I must go to another city, therefore, and after me they'll consume another kind of music.

The shock of all kinds of music creates a tension. Doesn't that complicate things, i.e. doesn't it make authentic creativity more difficult?

It's everything at the same time. It's sad, it's interesting . . . that's how it is. It's useless to speculate. Paradise was lost a long time ago. Lao Tzu speaks about lost paradise. He's speaking about something much older than himself.

In the Spirit

interview by Roberto Terlizzi

In the early summer of 1976, Lacy's quintet was among the featured groups scheduled to play at the first Pisa jazz festival in Italy, whose artistic directors were Roberto Terlizzi and his fellow critic Stefano Arcangeli (Lacy' s sextet would later perform, the same night as Sun Ra, at the festival's grand finale in 1982). The opening of the festival that year was marred by riots and ideological conflicts, and some concerts had to be canceled. Lacy agreed, however, to perform at a smaller venue instead, Balalaika, a *casa del popolo* (bar and meeting place) owned by the Italian Communist Party, which could fit about sixty people. The following interview, published in *Coda* (January–February 1977), took place the morning after.

In August of the following summer, 1977, Lacy had another unique experience worth mentioning: he was invited to the large festival at Châteauvallon, near Toulon on the French Riviera. There he held a number of workshops, rehearsing and performing his music for a week with not only his quintet but many other musicians as well, both professional and amateur, culminating in a forty-nine-piece big band.

How far do you go back to the roots of jazz? Do you go as far back as African origins?

Well, I go much further back than that: to me it's a long, long story, goes way back, to me it's thousands of years, there were many strains; I can feel them, but only some of them I know about consciously; but I can feel the old ones, thousands of years old, that I really can't name: it's just in the blood, in the memory, in the spirit.

When did your music begin to take shape?

It began to form around 1965; I started to become a little bit clearer about the way of improvising. But it was only in 1967 that I wrote my first piece that I still play now. Before 1967, everything I wrote I just threw away. We played that first piece last night. At that point things started to unfold, to become clear.

Your music is very open: last night I heard a calypso . . .

All kinds of things are happening; I just play.

How did you venture into solo saxophone concerts?

From practicing, really. If you practice an instrument alone many, many hours, you are playing alone, and it's just a small step from there to doing that in public, though it's a big step too. The one who helped me get over there is [Anthony] Braxton; when I heard Braxton successfully, that gave me the idea I could do it too. It's a different story to group music because it's one voice. You have to control very carefully your material, you can't bore people, you must hold their interest, you must keep the whole space alive yourself; you have no drums, no help, you must keep the thing alive by a change of material; and that was a challenge for me to organize my material so that I could keep the interest alive with a single voice. I try to concentrate on the rhythm, which is the most important element in a solo concert. In other words, rhythm for me is when you do something and what you do afterwards and the distance between and the proportions. Rhythm is the most difficult thing in solo concerts and also the sound because it's based on sound and no sound; that's all you have in solo performances.

Do you let yourself go, or is it structured from the beginning?

Most of it is a let-go. If a concert is two hours long I may have a minute here and a minute there where everything I do is very precise; but most of the time it's improvisation, free.

To what degree does an audience affect your music?

At the highest level possible. That's beyond everything, that's what it is for, what it is about. I'm just like a workman, I'm trying to get the evening to a certain point, where we are all together, where I disappear and they disappear, and it's just one thing, that's it.

Is it very difficult to be always creative?

Yes, like a permanent revolution. Coltrane used to start from zero every day. It's a matter of life and death. If you don't do it, you're dead.

Are you afraid of wearing out your energy in this process?

I used to be, but not anymore because I know better than that now. Before I knew how it worked I thought it would go away, but now I know it doesn't go away. *You* can go away, but it doesn't go away. It goes on and on, it's always there. If you go after it, it's there.

What is the relationship between the words and the music?

What you heard last night are old Chinese texts from Lao Tzu, that's two thousand years old and came to me mysteriously many years ago. I can't explain that because it's too old. How can I know what happened thousands of years ago? And why is my job to be in music? I can't answer that, it's too mysterious for me really. Those pieces are moralistic pieces; we do other pieces which are more amusing, poetry and politics and architecture, and Buddhism. We have about thirty-five pieces with words.

How about the titles?

The reason you give a name to a piece is to call it, so when you need it you can call it, you say: hey, come here!

You love animals . . .

Yes, they're very important to me as a source of life and music too. I study animals a lot. And every time it rains I have the chance of studying the rain for its musical qualities; that adds to my information, so I can perform the music better. I think that one of the most important things in music is the reappearance of the voice in jazz. I think it's rare but it's coming back, the mixture of the human voice with instrumental music. The importance of the words is that the singer who sings them must be believable. Irene, my wife, is a certain type of a person, so she could only sing certain things that sound believable; if she sang the things that Billie Holiday sang, she's not that kind of a person—it wouldn't be believable, it would be imitation, it would be artificial. When I look for texts I try to find things that fit her, that she would feel like singing.

You are also interested in religion . . .

I'm interested in many religions, spiritual matters. To me Lao Tzu was not a religion, it was a fragment of a way of life, an ethical system, ethical nonsystem, really. But I am also interested in Buddhism, in Catholicism from a certain distance. We have Buddhist pieces and another piece which is a Spanish Catholic song; we do that at Christmas time only. So, if you put all these pieces together, you would see what it's all about. But it's too soon, after I'm gone one can do that.

Do you still go and hear other musicians?

Sure. Tonight I'll go see Dizzy Gillespie. But I also listen to younger musicians twenty years old, seventeen years old, and I learn much from that. I follow Braxton's records and Cecil's records and Gil Evans's.

Do you know the new generation of musicians like Leo Smith, Oliver Lake?

Sure, I know all these people: it's very important to me that those people exist because they reassure me in the continuity of the life in the music. It keeps me alive knowing that they're alive.

Is it the same also with European musicians?

I've got a good relationship with many of them. People like Alex Schlippenbach, he doesn't know a lot like me in the tradition, but it doesn't matter, he follows with open ears, in a very good way.

Even a Peter Brötzmann or an Evan Parker are in the tradition?

Sure, because it's an expanding universe. Jazz has always been a music that defies restrictions. So if you have a rule that says "it's always like this," someone will come along and break that. Music is about freedom, a freedom fought for.

Do you feel like playing every day?

I always feel like playing, and if I have a job I have to play, even if I don't feel like playing, the music is there waiting. So, when I go to play, the music comes and I feel better.

Do you think your music is presented in the wrong way?

Less and less. When the music was not clear, the people were not clear either; but as the music gets clearer, it becomes easier and easier to understand. Sometimes the music is hard to understand, but with time it becomes easy. It is not promoted as it should be, anyway.

What is your reason for that—fear, or what?

Ignorance, apathy, and also it is dangerous music for the other musics. Most music is uncreative, it is just like soup and what we do is against that, it threatens that. I think the soup will melt if they let us play in front of the public as much as we wanted to; well, we would take the place of the soup. Probably they would make money anyway, but it hasn't to do with money.

Do you think creative musicians would still starve, whether they were black or white?

If you look at the history of jazz you see that everybody knew everybody else, there were no race problems. Louis Armstrong knew Bix Beiderbecke, Frank Teschmaker knew Barney Bigard, and they used to play together all the time. Good musicians know the other good musicians always. Some people have a pathetic story, there are many tragedies in jazz, people who died before they got their recognition. I know some musicians who are starving even today, fantastic musicians, in New York for example; most of them are obscure, but to me they are fantastic. I wouldn't want to say names, there are many really. Art Williams, the trumpet player, he never works. There are musicians who hardly ever play, once in six months; other people play every day, there are very difficult stories. That's why I left New York. New York is hard because there are many musics going on at the same time, many musicians; competition is very intense, competition is on music and the right to work. It has to do with space, with how many jobs there are, how many places to play, how many promoters, how many record companies. In Chicago they were clever, they had a good organization [the AACM, the Association for the Advancement of Creative Musicians, founded in 1965] and they had solidarity, they had Richard Abrams and they had space, the idea and the spirit, and they knew how to survive and they learned from the errors of other people; so, Chicago was a very special case. Now all the people are inspired by that and they also organize. I think musicians have to organize to survive, but in New York there's no organization, it is just like a war.

Getting back to your music, do you think your music has influenced other musicians?

Yes, sometimes I hear the echoes come back, quite surprising sometimes.

What's your relationship now to musicians of older styles, people like Rex Stewart or Cootie Williams, who limited their creativity to one style?

People like that are always interested in creating. Cootie Williams is still playing, still sounds fantastic; Rex Stewart, I heard him at the end of his life, he was beautiful.

What about the drugs?

Music like that is hard to do, it puts you beyond the normal life, in a way. I understand why musicians are attracted to drink and drugs, because the way they live they're sort of outside society and so it's like a tool or a crutch. You may call it bad, but it's understandable to me that musicians were attracted to them. But there are some people who never touched them, other people who died of them, and each one has a different story.

Do you think your music has something to do with the social situation?

Yes, quite a lot. While the Vietnamese war was going on, the last year and a half of it, we were playing a war piece [*The Woe*] which was terrifying, just terrifying; we didn't want to do it, but it had to be in the music; that was the only thing we played for a year and a half, a half-hour piece, like a war melodrama with all kinds of tapes of war noise. It was a terrible piece, we don't do it anymore; when the war was over, we stopped playing it. That's just an example of how life gets in the music. You can't keep life out of the music. Whatever is going on in life is also going on in the music. But I know other musicians who try to keep life out of the music. I don't believe that; I believe that everything can be viewed critically, can be viewed politically, musically. Everything contains everything.

What of the opposite? To what degree can a work like Max Roach's *Freedom Now Suite* influence people?

At the deepest level; what about *Guernica*? At a point beyond life, because it lasts a long time, beyond one person's life, it goes on and on for hundreds of years. Like what Goya did, the *Disasters of War*, the echoes of that go on and on and people who see that are moved by that, but they're only moved in a way that they're going to go anyway, so one person will ignore that, another person will see it. But I think they're powerful because they are like tools to help people move. One more thing. You said, "your music, your music." The music that I do, it's not my music, I don't think of it that way. It's just something I do, it's a music I'm involved in; sometimes I do it alone but I have a lot of help too, it comes to me, it's my job to do it, but it's not mine: I belong more to it than it belongs to me.

The Spark, The Gap, The Leap

interview by Brian Case

By the late 1970s Lacy's music had come fully into its own. He was busy on multiple fronts, performing solo, in duos, in other groups, and above all with his quintet, which recorded five albums in those years. He was also a guest artist in groups led by his old friend and collaborator Mal Waldron, as well as with Company in London and the Globe Unity Orchestra in Germany, and he was reunited with Musica Elettronica Viva and Gil Evans on projects in Rome. In a reflection of his varied activities, he was the featured artist for the last ten nights of 1978 at the Théâtre Campagne Première in Paris, which hosted "Steve Lacy's Free Encounters," a series that included members of his regular group as well as the pianist Frederic Rzewski, the trombonist Albert Mangelsdorff, the flutist Robert Dick, the violinist Takehisa Kosugi, and the reeds player Michel Portal.

The following interview originally appeared in the British journal *Melody Maker* (7 April 1979) and was reprinted in the première issue of *The Wire* (summer 1982), which took its name from a Lacy composition.

"Music has a mind of its own, and at the time you have to just watch the road . . .

"The spark . . . the gap . . . the leap. Robert Musil talks about that for three big books (*The Man without Qualities*). Zen literature, too. What we're talking about is magic. That's what's interesting in any kind of art—or athletes, or cooks.

"When I used to work with Monk, he used to say, 'Let's lift the bandstand.' That's magic, man, when the bandstand levitates, I didn't know how to do it—but I knew what he was talking about. Old dreams but they're still valid."

Any artist sharing Steve Lacy's above-stated belief in the near priestly function of art is in for a thin time in our society. Touring England with Company, Steve has been occasionally depressed by sparse audiences.

"In the kind of music we do together, the whole thing is: Is it interesting? Is it alive? There's nothing else to say. All the other criteria fall by the wayside.

"England is rough because of the quantity of rock 'n' roll going on, the proportions. It's hard to cope with all that. I used to love Hendrix, Stevie

Wonder, the Beatles, Otis Redding, but the ordinary bulk just makes me sick. I can't stomach it at all.

"Last night, I was walking by the university here, and I heard some ordinary rock they had coming out of a party there—just some typical stuff—and *loud*, you could hear it for three blocks!

"Me, personally, I got sick to my stomach. I couldn't stand it. It's just like everything I do is against what this is. And that was current normal stuff with loads of people having a good time to it, no problem—except I was walking down the street and I was suffering, and I was the only one who was.

"It's hard to deal with a phenomenon like that. You have to consider that you're a specialist, you're a freak—and you have to live with it.

"The only thing important in music, as in anything else, is life and death. Any kind of style, any kind of way is valid, if it's alive. Life and interest are two things I equate. Once a thing is sufficiently interesting, it becomes alive. I don't care whether it's Dixieland, Flixieland, Pixieland, or a private or public joke or no joke at all—if it's alive, I'm for it.

"In my own case, I don't want to be put to sleep, so I don't want to put others to sleep."

You can sometimes judge a man by the company he keeps. In the case of Steve Lacy, it is possible to infer a high seriousness and heft from his title dedications. A man of vast cultural grasp, tributes to writers like Elias Canetti, Kafka, and Dostoyevsky and painters like Paul Klee appear alongside the more expected jazz masters in his personal pantheon.

Canetti's *Auto-da-fé*, a novel of nightmarish intensity which foresaw the rise of Nazi Germany, started our trace.

"He was beyond even what he knew himself," said Steve. "The power of observation, the burning inspiration, the prophecy. I've read everything I can get my hands on in English, which is not much. My wife reads German, so she was able to tell me about the journals and other stuff.

"To me, writing has to get to a certain level, a certain heat, before it interests me really. The greatest writers and the greatest players are the ones who write or play beyond themselves—above and beyond the rational. For example, Gombrowicz said that after he'd read something he'd written, he became that—but before writing it, he didn't know what that was."

And Klee?

"I studied his lecture notes and works like *The Thinking Eye* and I think I learned as much from him as I did from many musicians. He's all about rhythm and proportion and structure, thicknesses and thinnesses of lines, the effect of one thing on another, visually.

"I've translated this into my own musical terms. Klee is trying to seize something and fix it and put it down. His work covers a vast area of human dealings and endeavors, and he's found ways of dealing with all these phenomena in plastic terms. That's what a musician does too, so it's very close."

Continual practice and periods of totally free playing armor him for his role as a vehicle for the music.

"It's good to have something in the bank, as it were, before you make that leap. It's good to be steeped in the technical aspects, because otherwise you're going to break your neck. Free playing is a kind of research for me, a kind of pushing. You extend the language and you come up with a few things, but I find it hard.

"The danger is dryness, the drying up, a tendency toward aridity. For me, these are a way of ensuring variety, wetness, a kind of fertility. I can do it in addition to what I normally do, but I can't only do that. The thing is to change up—play on a theme, off a theme. I like a variety of approaches in conjunction with each other."

Few musicians have Steve Lacy's iron determination. He worked with Thelonious Monk for four months, and spent the next twelve years working out the possibilities of Monk's compositions. He and Roswell Rudd, an ex-Dixielander trombonist, concentrated exclusively on the Monk repertoire from 1962–65, and Lacy has recently returned to it again.

"It became like a kind of Dixieland, yeah. Part of learning that stuff is to fool with it, and to arbitrarily change certain aspects of it so as to see what will happen. It's a way of orientation, and I do that with my own material too. I try and play it in different tempos and see why it won't work.

"I don't worry about the Monk stuff like I used to. I try and get the theme right, but once that's over, I don't have to take it too seriously. I used to try to get each measure correct, but now it's sort of behind me, and I can relax with it more. I think I do a better job now."

Two major influences in the emancipation of Steve Lacy were Cecil Taylor and Don Cherry. The period with Taylor was seminal but both men have since developed apart.

"That influence isn't apparent now in what I'm doing—if it was, there'd be something wrong—but it is chemically related. Some of the stuff that he was writing back in the '50s that we used to rehearse has disappeared, and he never went back to it. On the contrary, for me it formed an integral part of what I did, and was the basis of some of my own writing.

"Those pieces on a record like *Into the Hot*, they gave me a key. That was kind of a gift to me. I really got into that kind of composition, whereas he got out of it, and went beyond that. Even the titles, 'Bulbs,' 'Mixed,' they're kind of like my titles, too."

Cherry's arrival in New York with Ornette in 1959 bowled him over.

"To me, he was the vanguard of the vanguard—the freest edge of the free thing they had going then. We got to be fast friends and sort of brothers, and we spent a lot of time playing together in my house in New York.

"He'd say, 'Well, let's play,' and I'd say, 'OK, what do you want to play?' And he'd say, 'No, let's just play.' This was revolutionary to me at the time because I was into Monk tunes, and thought you had to have a tune, a structure, and chord changes, the whole thing. He didn't have any problem that way. He'd just play, and when he played it was really alive.

"This started me thinking a lot, and it took me over five years before I reached that point myself, and a lot of hard work and struggle to break the shackles. His way of going into the beyond and just taking off—to not worry about where you were coming from, but just to go—I wanted to be able to do that myself. It had something to do with my concepts of life and death and music."

The steadiness of his musical advance and the single-mindedness of his compositional output indicates a methodical mind.

Example: why do you use an off-station radio on "Stations"?

Answer. "It had several aspects to it. One was a desire to get into the now, to keep the music absolutely now, and have nothing to do with then. When you turn the radio on, it's really now. Whatever you catch, you have to deal with. Next, the element of inspiration from John Cage. Thirdly, it was dedicated to Monk, and the structure, harmony, and rhythm that I superimposed upon the radio is very Monkish. So that's what that was all about."

That species of QED makes it difficult to relate to Lacy's leap beyond logic.

"It's a progressive appetite for wanting to take the leap, because unless you do, you're not really alive. If you're not secure enough to take the plunge, then you're really in trouble, and you'd better go back and practice until you are secure enough to drop the security. It isn't random at all."

But the concept of the leap conjures up associations of a bracing of the muscles, of strain. Don't most musicians report that during the creative act, their minds are a blank?

"Not exactly a blank—more like a blink. You try and stay out of the way. You try and not lose touch with the music, and let the thing happen. It's not you that does it—it's *IT* that wants to be done. You get yourself in good shape and be in tune and on your toes, have good chops—and not mess it up. It can only go one way, and it's not you who decides, it's *IT*."

Stuyvesant Casino, New York City, 1952. Left to right George Wettling (d), Lou McGarrity (tb), Herb Fleming (tb), Jimmy Archey (tb), Steve Lacy (ss), Henry "Red" Allen (tp), Cecil Scott (ts), Pee Wee Russell (cl). Photographer unknown.

Lacy's first record under his own name, *Soprano Sax* (1957). Cover photo: Esmond Edwards (courtesy of Prestige Records).

New York City, 1961.
Photo: Larry Fink.

Steve Lacy and Roswell Rudd,
New York City, July 1964.
Photo: Larry Fink.

Steve Lacy and Roswell Rudd, New York City, July 1964. Photo: Larry Fink.

Museum of Modern Art, New York City, 1967. Left to right Enrico Rava (tp), Aldo Romano (d), Steve Lacy (ss), Kent Carter (b). Photo: Raymond Ross.

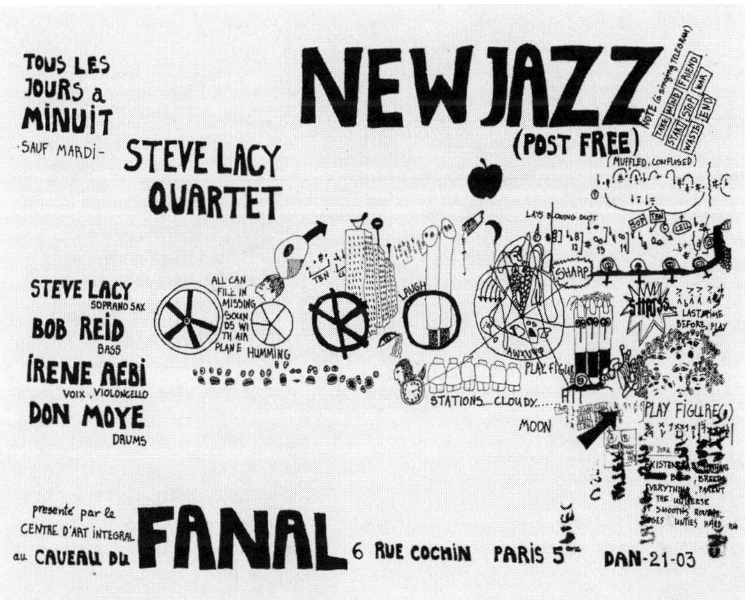

Homemade flyer for concert, Paris, 1970.

(opposite) At a junkyard outside Paris, September 1969.

Photo: Guy Le Querrec.

Irene Aebi and Steve Lacy at home in Paris, 1974.
Photo: Roberto Masotti.

Musica Elettronica Viva, at Alvin Curran's studio, Rome, 1975. Left to right Richard Teitelbaum, Steve Lacy, Frederic Rzewski, Garrett List, Alvin Curran. Photo: Roberto Masotti.

Workshop at Châteauvallon festival, France, August 1977. Left to right Jean-Jacques Avenel (b), Kent Carter (b), Steve Lacy (ss), Oliver Johnson (d). Photo: R. Eyraud.

At a café in Paris, 1976. Photo: Roberto Masotti.

Quintet, at the Workshop Freie Musik, Akademie der Künste, Berlin, 1977. Left to right Oliver Johnson (d), Irene Aebi (c), Kent Carter (b), Steve Potts (as), Steve Lacy (ss). Photo: Roberto Masotti.

13

In Search of the Way

interview by Jason Weiss

Starting with the release in 1980 of *The Way*, featuring the full sung version of his song cycle based on Lao Tzu, the new decade saw a number of Lacy's big projects brought to fruition. That same year, his quintet grew into a sextet with the addition of the pianist Bobby Few (also, Jean-Jacques Avenel replaced Kent Carter on bass), a transformation that added more texture and a fuller sound to the band. Meanwhile, as Lacy returned to performing Thelonious Monk's music on the side occasionally, back in New York Monk had been ailing for some time (he died early in 1982). The following interview—which appeared in the international edition of *Jazz Forum* (February 1981), a journal published in Warsaw—took place in September 1980, shortly before Lacy was to tour North America for the first time with his group.

On your recent solo album *Eronel*, you play only Thelonious Monk tunes. Hadn't you stopped performing Monk's music for some years?

Well, I first heard it around '55 or '56, and became more and more involved with it for about twelve years. Then I put it away for about ten years, and now I'm back into it again. There's the solo Monk record that just came out, but usually I do it as part of a solo concert. This season I'm also supposed to do some all-Monk things—with Muhal Richard Abrams in Italy, with a Swiss band in Hamburg, and something else in New York maybe in June.

Why have you gone back to doing Monk tunes?

Well, first of all, because the stuff is so great, and it just seemed like it got more interesting with time. And second of all, it was an idea of having Monk get well. I can't go and nurse him or anything like that, but I did go back to his music. I thought maybe he would hear about it and it would cheer him up. In fact, the record was meant as a get-well card.

What did working with him teach you that you couldn't learn from the tunes themselves?

Working with him was like about five schools rolled up into one. In a way, the materialistic part was the least of it, and the spiritual part was the most important. The ideological, philosophical, and political thing—all that stuff was much more interesting even than the material, which I could learn myself just copying records.

It was how to play and what to do, and mostly what not to do. Monk showed me what not to do and that was invaluable. He gave me a lot of tips that were fantastic. In other words, don't play so much bullshit, stick with the melody, don't lose the beat, make the rhythm section sound . . . I mean, the only way you can do is to fuck up and have somebody stronger than you say, "Hey, you're fucking up." Then you could stop.

When you led your own group, did you also have a sense of how Monk's music could help you develop your own concepts?

Yeah, there was something—it was freedom. We were trying to get away from the standard repertoire. We wanted to get our own sound, and we were looking for a certain freedom on the other side of discipline—to get through those structures and to be able to play them freely. We thought it would sort of promulgate a new style—and it did.

The thing that interested me most was the relation between the given and the gotten, between what you're playing on and what you come up with. And when Monk played that music, it was very consistent. In other words, the tune came and then he played, and it was all one thing really. And the language that he improvised in was the same as the language he wrote in. So, there was like a homogeneous quality to it. We were after a similar kind of thing—not playing like him, but playing music that held together that well, trying to come up with a style of improvisation that both fit that music and was our own, and was free.

Your varied approach to the soprano would seem to fit in with that kind of search.

Well, I've tried to play it every which way it can be played, and I'm still trying to do it. If you live with something a long time you begin to see its different aspects. You turn it around and one day you stand on your head and look at it. So you just keep turning it over and over and over again. Eventually you see quite a few things.

You've been quite adventurous in your collaborations, with so many different types of musicians in different countries. Are there some unusual collaborations that come to mind, either past or present, that perhaps were different than what you expected?

I can think of quite a few. For example, playing with Indian musicians, Moroccan musicians, and Japanese musicians. And playing with amateurs. And playing with European musicians—German, Dutch, Italian. It's all good. I mean, even if it's no good, and you don't do it again, just that one time where you suffered and it didn't work out at all, you learned something from it. At least, learning not to do that again or to do it differently or something. In improvisation and all that, the spirit is all. And I think you can find the right spirit with anybody. You get with an Eskimo in an igloo on the right day and you find the right spirit, you can come up with something, I'm sure.

When you're working like that with musicians from different cultures, how do you manage it so that they aren't just a background or you're not instantly trying to learn their whole system of music?

Well, it's the place you put yourself in. You try and stay level with them. In other words, you try not to play above them or below them or on the side, but right straight on. And sometimes you have to actually move around the space to find the right space where you can get this connection. And it's not easy sometimes. Sometimes it's impossible. Because in most cases like that, they play what they play. They're not going to suddenly learn . . .

And I can't do that, it would take me years and years to get that music in my blood. So, we're doing different things at the same time in the same place. It's a question really of just finding some fragile thread, just to get the connection to it. And it won't last, it's a temporary thing but it can be wonderful.

In your own group, all the musicians are strong individuals with their own sounds. When you work in other groups like Company, is it a way of offsetting what you do with your own group?

Yeah, absolutely. You can't do what you normally do. So that's good for you.

So you don't have to be burdened with your own identity for a change.

You must drop it. You must really stay on your toes and try and get with the current situation there, and forget about what you normally do. Because it doesn't work in the situation.

Is it a way of staying flexible?

Yeah, stay alive. All these situations keep you alive. And if it's the wrong situation, and you stay in it too long, it'll kill you.

In a solo situation, in a sense you're confronting what you've got more directly.

Yeah, but the way I see it, solo playing for me is only possible as a contrast to playing with a group. In other words, if you only do solo playing, it's no good. It gets worse and worse after a certain point. Unless you're in tune with other musicians, you will not be in tune with yourself. So you have to go back and forth and change the situation you're in. A solo is interesting to listen to because it's different. And when it is not different, it loses its interest. Change is what interests me.

In a lot of your solo playing, you do tunes that you also do with the group. Are there tunes that you don't usually do with the group that you do solo?
Yeah, stuff we haven't gotten to yet. Sometimes it's nice because I can try out stuff that we won't get to for years. It's already written, but it's just not in the book right now.

So, the solo pieces are structured in the same sense as the group pieces.
That's right. They're all group pieces, I never wrote a piece just as a solo. I have enough stuff that was written for the group originally that I can do solo. They're only known as solo pieces, but eventually they'll be for the group. Some of them even have words, they're songs that we haven't even touched yet.

What about your work with texts? Do you also write lyrics for your songs?
Sometimes. I have about five I wrote the words to, but mostly I use other people's texts. The first song I did was for a movie about parachute jumping and I wrote the words myself. I did a little research on the language used in parachute jumping and wrote something like a rock 'n' roll tune.

This was around '66 and I was already working on the Lao Tzu stuff by then. It was the time of the Vietnam War and there was a lot of protest in the air. We used a political choice from Lao Tzu about war, rulers, and politics. With synthesizer (Richard Teitelbaum), voice (Irene Aebi) and saxophone, we did this improvised polemic called "Chinese Food," and that was one of the first ones we did. After that I started writing settings for some other things by Lao Tzu. Gradually that grew into *The Tao*, a cycle of six pieces from the *Tao Te Ching* which is something we're still working on. Then I got into all kinds of poets, using texts in French, English, and Italian.

What inspired you to start setting texts to music?
First of all, the voice had sort of disappeared in jazz. There was no voice with Coltrane and all that. Or if there was, it was unsatisfactory to me and I really wanted to hear something. So you have to do something yourself so it can exist.

Then there were certain inspirations like Harry Partch, who set a hobo letter to music in one of his early pieces. When I heard that I realized that anything can be set to music, which gave me the impetus to try various things like Lao Tzu, for example. One of the first things I did was a Buckminster Fuller piece, a very dense piece that goes on very fast ["The Sun," recorded in 1990 on *Itinerary*]. We set it like a priest's litany in which a certain pitch is improvised. That's a piece we've done several times, but have never definitively realized as yet. And experience with these things led me on to other things.

Were these earlier pieces with voice improvised as far as where the voice comes in?

At first, yeah. But only at first. I just didn't know how it was supposed to go, so it was improvised. Now we've gone the other way around. There was one situation where I fixed a melody for a lyric, Irene learned it, and then she had a record date with somebody else. They didn't want to hear about my piece, so she improvised it. But because she'd already learned the melody, it came out great.

That's something we used to do with Cecil Taylor too. Sometimes we would even have parts which you learn but never play. Instead of doing that you improvise something, having already learned this and not playing it. So that kind of thing was very interesting.

How do you select the texts you use?

Well, the first consideration is whether it is something Irene can sing. Everything I wrote was for her; she showed me the way the voice works and all that. We've been together for fourteen years and she is the voice in my life. She's a person and certain things would sound incongruous coming out of her mouth. You've got to be careful about that. It's like writing music. You wouldn't write some kind of vulgar phrase for Steve Potts to play, because it wouldn't fit.

The second consideration is whether I can set it. You know, do I like it? Then I might mull over something for a long time, sometimes years in fact. I first came across the Chinese stuff in the late '50s, but it wasn't until '67 that the melody was fixed and then it took another eight years to find the bass part, etc. So these are long processes. But now, having written maybe a hundred different pieces with words, they can be done much faster.

How do you relate the musical sound to the meaning of the text so it does not seem superimposed?

Well, music and words is a very tricky thing. The music is the way of delivering the words, like the van that delivers the words—the *livraison*.

Why set the words in the first place? The idea is to have a melody that can be repeated an infinite number of times. In that way it will live and be more easily deliverable. And it has to be right, it has to be singable and catchable. It has to hold up so eventually it can be picked up by the concierge or anybody and sung. The idea is that when I'm gone, people will still be singing that stuff.

Now I'm not anxious for that to happen yet, in fact quite the opposite. We keep it in the family until they're realized. Eventually, I hope people will start to hum these things and pick them up but that can take twenty, thirty, forty years. I don't care, but that's the idea anyway. It's like Canetti said, "Music takes the sting out of words." I really think that's true. It's like when I read the Buckminster Fuller piece, I thought, "Man, this stuff is fantastic, it sounds so good." Shakespeare is also incredible—so rich and full of information that goes by so fast. We just have to get into that.

You're now working extensively with poet-painter Brion Gysin. How did you come together?

When I met Brion, I was working on a set of pieces called *Clangs* based on short texts by artists [recorded long after in a version for double sextet, in 1992]. I had something by Gaston Chaissac and wanted to use texts by Schwitters and Apollinaire. I was also looking for some others. I asked Brion if he had any lyrics written and then we started to talk.

What we do is like a demo of some future version of the group. There are things with the group and also some things he does himself. He does what he normally does in a poetry reading, but it's bent a little bit by the evocation of the eventual musical setting. We both bend. I soften the metric thing. It's just like we stay together in a way. I think we're going to make a record with Brion soon. Some pieces will be just him with accompaniment, others just him and me. We'll also do something like the group singing the Brion Gysin songbook or something.

Do you have any plans to do a whole record of your songs?

Yeah, there's one in the can for Saravah [*The Owl*]. This record goes back to '77 and has been redone and remixed several times. The final thing now is to get permission to use the texts, which is tricky. There's stuff by Picabia, Dalí and Apollinaire, and they have to contact the heirs.

The last record that Hat Hut put out, called *The Way*, has got the whole Lao Tzu cycle on it. Then another album, *Troubles*, has got quite a few songs on it, including pieces based on Japanese poems from the *Manyoshu*, and a text I wrote called "Wasted."

There's one piece of yours, "No Baby," which you've built up more and more over the years. On earlier albums you did it unaccompanied but now everybody plays it. Did that piece come about because of the rhythm of the phrase?

Well, yeah. Actually that piece is a homage to Sidney Bechet, and it's based on my analysis of his character. And with the soprano, it was the idea of somebody jumping up and jiggling . . .

I think a lot of what I do comes from language. I've always been a language freak. When I was a kid they called me "the walking dictionary." I just love language, grammar, mathematics and all that. I've always been interested in speech. Even before I was into music, I was into the word.

What about the titles of your compositions? Is there a certain concept behind such titles as "Stamps," "Crops," "Snaps," etc.?

Yeah. These are things. They're all specific stories, each one of those pieces. Every piece I write has a reference to somebody as well as the things which have to do with the person. Take for example "Stamps," which is about Miles Davis. The pieces are on many levels really. "Stamp" can be a language or the stamp of an animal, a postage stamp or the mark somebody leaves on something. Stamps can be Miles's way of playing, the way he uses harmony, the touches. And "Stamps" also is the first piece we play with the group every night. It's all based on the open strings of the bass and the cello, and it's a way of warming up and breaking the ice, accustoming the public to our sound that night. And so it contains the basic open tuning of the whole group. It's our stamp on the evening.

You're one of those musicians with one foot in Europe and the other in America. Have all the years you've spent in Europe added some sort of European musical sense?

Well, yeah, it's mixed up and the longer I stay here the more mixed up it is. What I do has a lot to do with America, and it has a lot to do with Europe. It also has something to do with Japan, China, India, and even Africa. So I might as well be here as anywhere.

In Europe it's more broad-based and goes back further. If you're in New York, on that little island there, you don't really care much about anybody until they come on that island and stand right next to you. I mean, you've heard of Europe, but it doesn't mean too much in New York. So I think in America you're more out of it than you are here as far as the world goes.

Songs: Steve Lacy and Brion Gysin

interview by Jason Weiss

The sextet's first record, made at the beginning of 1981, was a collaboration with the poet-painter Brion Gysin (1916–86), *Songs*. Best known as an old friend and collaborator of William Burroughs, Gysin was a multinational, multifaceted artist and performer whose influence reached far and wide. Lacy's group subsequently performed another set of Gysin songs as a ballet, *Stuff*, in France and Italy, but that music was never recorded: the lyrics were part of Gysin's screenplay of the Burroughs novel *Naked Lunch*.

The following interview with Lacy and Gysin, on the occasion of their album, took place in May 1981 in Paris. It was published first in French translation in *Jazz Magazine* (September 1981); the original, English version appeared later in Ishmael Reed's literary journal *Quilt* (November 1984).

Steve Lacy, you were setting painters' texts to music and through that you found Brion. How did you know of him?

Lacy: I guess I knew he was a poet-painter.

Gysin: We met through Victor Herbert, and then again at the American Center in '73.

L: In '65 in London, I had heard recordings—they called it electronic poetry—and some of Brion's stuff was on there.

His permutation poems?

G: It must have been Henri Chopin's record, *OU*.

L: I thought it was amazing, I really liked it. I had been thinking in . . . not with electronics, but some of the results achieved.

Did that tie up with any jazz roots for you?

L: Well, jazz is speech rhythms. It's like *parlando* music. And it all comes from phraseology anyway, it's just a language. So, when I heard that stuff, I found it exciting.

G: My opinion is that Dizzy Gillespie hasn't been recognized as a great sound poet.

L: Absolutely. No question about it.

Your whole interest in that seems unique for a jazz musician.

L: Well, you could find little snippets of that in many people, back to Louis Armstrong. You can think of Fats Waller and Billy Strayhorn and Ellington, and then to people like Red Allen and Roy Eldridge. Well, many. I think what I did was dig a certain vein a little bit wider or deeper than is customary, but it was nothing new on the scene really.

What was your first collaboration?

L: The first thing was "Dreams." The music was written in '69, and I asked him to give me the lyrics in about '73 or '74. By that time I knew he was the inventor of the Dreamachine. And that really struck me. I had this piece called "Dreams," and it was a melody that came to me in a dream in Rome. It was written to Italian lyrics by Falzoni, but it never got off the ground. But the melody was haunting. So I thought Brion, being an expert on dreams, might be able to supply me with the necessary lyrics, in English. And he agreed. He came up with the most fantastic thing, really, the lyrics are out of sight.

The music was what it is now?

L: The melody was identical. But the bass line and some of the inner voices took a while to work out, quite a few years.

Brion Gysin, when did you first start noticing jazz?

G: Oh, I always noticed it. I used to be very snooty about it too. I remember saying, "Well, it's all very well, but they're improvising on tunes that don't interest me in the first place." That's where I stood, on the wrong side of the street. But I knew I was hearing both sides of the street.

Later, in Morocco, Paul Bowles and I were sharing an Arab house with a high tower where you could get very good reception. He had a good radio and we used to play nightlong games of listening to German jazz, Japanese jazz, Australian jazz, and all sorts of things you could get on short wave.

Also, in New York, [John] Latouche did a rather disastrous show together with Duke Ellington, *Twilight Alley*. I went to Duke Ellington's house and *saw* how that whole music machine worked.

Was there a musical imprint that you intended on your new record together, *Songs*? It seems on the edge of various styles. There are strains of Kurt Weill, for instance.

L: Well, I'm aware of all these people and what they've done, and Weill was a big influence in my own work. But one thing that's been a strong factor in this is my own desire to insert serious lyrics into the jazz fabric. It's like a search for quality. To raise the level of the lyric, so you have something good to play on. Because we play with those words. When we play those tunes based on Brion's words, all the music comes out of the words. I've been lucky to have Brion's stuff to work with. For me it was a miracle finding stuff already made of that quality. Like when he gave me the words to "Dreams," it came out perfect. Then I wanted to see what he had already done. He showed me this stuff and read it for me, and I thought it was great. Because it seemed like it was already set. Just the way he would read it, I could hear it in a certain way that it was already pitched. So I just had the fun part of mulling it over, listening to tapes of him reading it, and finally fixing the pitches and everything myself. And then to getting them realized is a long step and that involved, well, learning them.

G: That's right, I was just knocked out, in this photograph taken by Hart Leroy Bibbs during the recording session I'm just in a state of sheer ecstasy. And it's because, when it was all put together like that with the sextet, I heard my own voice coming right through there in the whole thing.

How far back does the earliest song date from?

G: Well, in the '40s, I had a project for making a musical out of the biography that I wrote of the man who was the original Uncle Tom, Josiah Henson [*To Master—A Long Goodnight*]. And the only one from that period is "Nowhere Street."

What had you written of that project?

G: I wrote the story and the lyrics. The story was as it really happened, not the way Harriet Beecher Stowe saw it. In other words, how it led him on to all that and how he got kicked in the ass in the end by his name becoming the most pejorative one of all. He never thought this shit was going to fall on him like that. That was the way the musical was supposed to go. And "Nowhere Street" was . . . there's a separation with his great love, he's decided to make it north and she's left in a kind of deserted town like Cincinnati, a suburb of Cincinnati in 1850, where "Nowhere Street" was. She comes on stage and the leaves are falling and lights are coming on in the houses and going off in others, mysterious, a kind of haunted house sort of thing, and frogs croaking.

How much of that did you see when setting the music?

L: I never heard this part about Cincinnati before. But Bobby Few is from Cincinnati.

G: No shit!

L: But it's apparent in the lyrics. They're so vivid in their painterly abilities that the whole thing is right there for you.

Do the Jajouka musicians of Morocco seem to be any point of contact between you?

L: Yes. Brion hipped me to that whole thing—the music I've heard, meeting some of the people, and playing with the President. It's been sort of a good glue between us, reinforcing other things. I've gotten into it as far as I could in the time. But it's a trip. I would have to go there and give up everything else . . .

G: Like me. Like I did.

L: . . . And get to it. And I'm not about to do that.

G: He's scared.

L: I'd like to go in a helicopter, stay for a few days and get out of there, you know, when I could.

G: Like me. I stayed all the time there because of that.

L: It would have been wild to hear Trane play with them. But maybe in another life or something, in another world.

When the two of you perform together, what establishes the time?

L: Well, what we do is like when the songwriters do a demo of their tune. The lyricist sort of says it and the other guy sort of plays the melody, but shifting a little. So it's not strict time. Sort of collapsed here and stretched out there, so it gives you an idea of how it might sound.

G: Here's the poor author standing in the crook of the piano.

L: Like an *art pauvre*. No, sometimes it really comes out perfect, where it's not exactly sung but heard. A kind of delivery.

G: This is where you're standing out there in front of twenty prospective backers and their girlfriends.

L: Yeah, they got the singer next to them and the money in their pockets. "These guys wrote this song. Honey, you think you'd like to sing this? I'll buy it for you." . . . But where we usually do it is poetry festivals, where any kind of a musical phenomenon takes it out of the level of the ordinary there.

What is the role of improvisation between the two of you?

L: In his work, I found it to be very jazz-like, in that he was living it. When he delivers it, he's playing. It's different each time. It's delivered in a free, improvisational manner, and that leeway is written right into it.

G: And things that I've written *sur commande*, like "Hey Gay Paree Bop" [written for the Lacy sextet's tour of North America in the fall of 1980], I sort of commanded myself into song. So in those, there are all kinds of points written where you can go off, do anything you like, but come back to them.

L: Yeah. The more we do that, the freer it's getting. And I imagine if we do it for a while, then somebody else'll pick it up there and do it another way. And that's got to be.

G: I would certainly hope so. Because if we're all going to space, what's going to space with us will be music.

L: Especially little tunes you can remember.

15

Unrecognized Giant?

interview by Xavier Prévost

Throughout the 1980s Lacy's sextet became the prime engine for his musical thought. After *Songs* with Brion Gysin, the sextet recorded the extended suite *The Four Edges*, which together with another, the solo work *Hedges*, made up the album *Ballets*. Amid many side projects for Lacy, his band recorded about one album per year during that decade: *Prospectus* in 1982 (augmented by the trombonist George Lewis, who worked intermittently in Lacy's bands for the next twenty years), *Blinks* in 1983, *Futurities* in 1984, *The Condor* in 1985. However, after some three decades as a professional musician and despite an extensive catalogue, Lacy still had trouble finding enough work for the band, as he explains in the following interview from *Jazz Magazine* (September 1982).

What led you to modify your group, Steve Lacy, to make it a sextet and by so doing bring a piano back into the band?

The quintet reached a point where it had to change. Many things have changed in the last two years: the 1980s are a period of change for us too. For a long time I wanted to play with Bobby Few, but it wasn't possible before. It's the second year we've been playing together as a sextet. I've had many occasions to play with Jean-Jacques Avenel, for over ten years; with Bobby as well, a number of times, but now it's regular.

Has that obliged you to modify your repertoire?

Of course, we had to change a thousand little things, and big ones too. It's much better, it's . . . how I wanted!

Irene Aebi sings in French in this new repertoire . . .

Yes, some poems by Samuel Beckett, and also a text by Blaise Cendrars, "Prospectus," and then "Clichés": that's the text of a postcard from Africa sent to me by a friend, Aline Dubois.

Do you have more opportunities to play than you used to?

It seems very difficult now, everyone has ideas. I have a lot of work, personally, to do all sorts of things, but what I would like is to play with this group, and it seems very difficult to get enough gigs in order to develop the group musically. We don't do enough concerts in a row and so we're obliged to do too many rehearsals: there are too many rehearsals and not enough *performances*. That's the problem right now, because I don't have a manager, I've never found a good one, I only have some friends who find things now and then, but it's very irregular, and very frustrating. But I'm not an organizer, I'm not good with business matters.

What projects do you have for the sextet?

We're preparing some ballets, we've already done several . . .

Do you plan to include some Monk tunes in the repertoire for the sextet?

We're supposed to take part in a festival in September, in Austria, where they've asked us to devote half the program to Monk tunes.

Will you play tunes that you're particularly fond of, like "Skippy"?

No, that's too hard. I haven't thought about the program yet . . .

Alongside the sextet, you often perform solo, as a duo, as a quartet . . .

This group is exactly what I've always wished for. When there's an organism, a group, there are always people who want either to block or destroy or divide what exists. Most organizers of concerts or festivals have ideas contrary to mine: they want me to play solo, in duo, with other bands, with local musicians, to play Monk tunes, all sorts of things, but I would like to do what I'm doing now, so it's a struggle, and it's not easy . . . Now we're starting to play some in trio too, it's a new formula, half the sextet . . . But I would like to have the whole group playing in order to develop it on the musical level. It's too difficult as it is, I'm going a little nuts.

What about the festivals?

I have practically no opportunities to play in the festivals, except for one or two small festivals, the others, no, and it's a scandal! I don't ask them, they don't ask me, no one organizes that for me, so it's zero . . . Me, I can wait, but that becomes difficult for the group. These are problems of work, unemployment, universal problems . . . People imagine you can form a group, it's very interesting a group, but these are people who have been working together for some time; we've been working together for over ten years, since 1971. There are only two or three groups in the world who've stayed together as long, my music has developed, things are happening, but it's harder than ever . . . Why? Others come and go, pass through, new ones arrive, and we're still struggling. I hope that will change one day, for the moment I'm not happy about it. Only the public is with us, always, more and more, for a long time now: that's what reassures me. It's the quality of the music that directs me and nothing else. I'm sure we'll get there one day, it's the public who sustains us, we play for them and they come for us. Made for each other, you know?

Futurities

interview by Isabelle Galloni d'Istria

A Guggenheim fellowship helped fund Lacy's largest work at the time, *Futurities*, a spellbinding, evening-length show with songs based on twenty poems by Robert Creeley, which had its première at the Festival de Lille in France, on 15 November 1984. The work featured nine musicians, two dancers (Douglas Dunn, Elsa Wolliaston), and a large, chevron-shaped painting by Lacy's longtime friend Kenneth Noland, set like an altar in the middle of the stage, its translucent colors brought to life by the lighting designer John Davis. Originally centered on the single voice of Irene Aebi, *Futurities* was recast some twenty years later in a concert version for five voices including Aebi (plus instrumentalists), and performed at the New England Conservatory of Music after Lacy's death.

The following interview, conducted when *Futurities* was still in preparation, appeared in the French journal *Pour la Danse* (October 1984).

You have often worked with dancers.

For a long time, yes. With Simone Forti, the Théâtre du Silence, Pierre Droulers, Dominique Petit, Sheela Raj, Sheryl Sutton, Shiro Daimon . . . with all sorts of dancers and in all sorts of combinations. In dance halls, with striptease artists, and with imaginary dance too. Really, everything we do is for dance.

You came up with the idea for this show. Was it a vision? Can you say what it was you imagined?

A vision, exactly. A vision of a sort of marriage, a sort of marriage ceremony in jazz between the words, the music, and the dance. It's an old story, no? I imagined a show and I've been working on it for the past two years. Everything came from the texts and everything begins with the poems. I had heard about Robert Creeley and I met him thanks to a friend. These poems are very simple, very clear, and they're all about love. There are hundreds of these poems and the first thing I had to do was choose the ones I could set to music. Putting things in order, I've been doing that all my life. I imagined a couple of dancers but all that came after composing the music. For several months I didn't know what I was in the process of making. One day, I saw that I had eighteen songs and that they went together. It was fantastic. I tried to put them in the right order and that took me a year to find the key. Now there are twenty of them and a line going through those twenty. The show is that line.

Who is getting married through this jazz work?

There are a lot of marriages. For example, marriage between the poet and the painter. They knew each other a tiny bit because they both come from Black Mountain College. They respected each other but had never dreamed of working together. I made the marriage between them. Also Douglas and Elsa. They had never worked together, and that's a curious sort of marriage, no? [He is thin and blond, she is large and black.—Ed.] There's also the harp. There hadn't been a harp in our group. It all follows like that. The ensemble is very mixed but the line, the structure, the consistency, is the poems. For example, the first one, "Sad Advice," says: "If it isn't fun, don't do it." That was our guide for the whole show.

The other day, regarding that idea of marriages, someone pronounced the word "polygamous." Well, in botany, they say a plant is polygamous when it carries male and female plants on the same stalk. I'm thinking of Douglas and Elsa, who show the characters they are as well as the opposites that they carry in them.

Personally, I've never used the word "polygamous," but I find it interesting. The music that we do, we called it "post-free." Then, "poly-free," because at any moment, one can change their point of view. It's a somewhat advanced sort of freedom. We break the barriers, we work, and at that moment we can change the system. But these are old words, the labels serve for a season or two, later they're worn out.

Let's get back to the poems.

They're very deep and very simple. They contain universal truths: love, death, the rhythm of life. Moreover, one of them gives the show its subject, "The Rhythm." Of life. Of death. Of tenderness. Of growing old together. Of children. Of time. Of the moon. Of the seasons . . .

You gave the "protagonists" some words, ideas, poems. You spoke together. What does one speak about in such cases?

I explained my idea and I gave them the poems. My work was already far along. Something existed that they were able to see. So I could speak about the project and it was convincing. The hardest thing in this type of show is bringing the people together. Dunn and Noland come from the United States, the harpist from Brussels, it's difficult to have everyone at the same time. Difficult but possible.

And Kenneth Noland?

That's another marriage. Noland and theater. A first for Noland. I liked his work a lot and I thought his paintings were so beautiful one could look at them for hours. I wanted to make a ballet with colors that were so beautiful, so incredible and sublime. I convinced him. I don't know yet what he's done for the show, I haven't seen it. I think it will be an object, a sort of abstract altar, a very big object, huge and painted. An object to catch the light. And there's another marriage: John Davis's lights and Noland's painting. I introduced them and it worked. For Noland it was a revelation to see the lights on his canvases.

You made the choice of a mixed duo. Why Elsa?

I don't know why. That's who I wanted. I think she's fantastic.

At first you had in mind two black dancers. The contrast that Douglas Dunn brings in, from every point of view, is really fascinating. How did the meeting take place?

I was thinking of Harry Sheppard in fact, but he wasn't available. Irene Aebi always wanted Douglas. Me too, but I couldn't imagine it would be possible. Irene insisted and we phoned New York. Douglas said okay. He likes Creeley a lot and that's another marriage, Douglas and Creeley. Douglas knew the text already and he understands all that perfectly.

One feels a great serenity in the relations between this man and this woman. Where do you think that serenity comes from?

I believe it comes from their great experience. When it's possible for two artists of that stature to understand each other, it's serene. One no longer does stupid things at that point. Douglas has already had numerous experiences, Elsa too. So the work can be fun.

In the translation of the poems made by the dancers, are there things that surprised you?

Yes, of course, but that was the idea from the start. To inspire me. I find a lot of pleasure in that and a lot of ideas, and I learn numerous things in such an adventure. The surprise is almost obligatory. When I work with dancers, it's in order to be surprised and also to play better. They oblige me to play as well as possible.

Have certain things pleased you in particular?

The fact that it's worked. Up to the last moment, before this unusual couple set out to work, I didn't know. It's like a couple in life, they meet for the first time, he's handsome, she's beautiful, but it may be they're not in love. It's always a risk. There, it worked.

I think that both of them refuse to be swayed by the usual forms that govern conduct as much in life as in dance. They seem to be beyond that and by what they invest of themselves, they're in tune with each other.

They give a lot of themselves, it's true. They've plunged into this thing like heroes. Douglas is very courageous and Elsa too. That may be what has pleased me most: their courage and the daring things they've found together.

Now that the choreography is practically in place, is this duo what you wanted to see?

Yes, I'm not worried about that part anymore. I must concentrate on the preparation of the music. It's complex, there are eight musicians and for Irene, the voice, it's a tour de force.

Do you think this duo exposes deep truths about the state of being together as a couple?

Perhaps, yes. We'll see. It will perhaps illuminate the act of love a little bit. The nature of love. Because the poet offers this information in the text.

Do you imagine dance when you're composing?

Like I was saying before, everything I do comes from dance, applies to dance, is concerned with it. Jazz is a music for dancing, and the music itself dances. I've never forgotten that even when the jazz became too complex. I knew that it was temporary.

The average age of the people expressing themselves in this show is above forty years old. In your view, does that mean something?

Yes, precisely, it's good you pointed that out. The poet is about sixty years old, the painter fifty-eight, the dancers forty, and me, I'm fifty. Perhaps simply because one cannot understand the rhythm of life before that age. But I hope that the audience will be young and mixed and that the kids can have fun too. It should be a good show for the kids.

The Solitude of The Long-Distance Player

17

interview by Gérard Rouy

By the mid- to late 1980s Lacy's production—of recordings, large-scale projects, collaborations—increased significantly. As a correlative, added recognition was coming from new quarters. The Rova Saxophone Quartet became the first musicians to devote an entire record to Lacy's music (*Favorite Street*, 1984). Peter Bull's documentary on him, *Lift the Bandstand* (Rhapsody Films, 1985), caught the sextet in top form with an extended performance of the song "Gay Paree Bop," by Lacy and Gysin, live at the Public Theater in New York. In 1986 alone Lacy made ten records, most under his own name or as a co-leader. Among the more unusual releases that year was a concert in Tokyo where he was reunited with Don Cherry in a quartet led by the drummer Masahiko Togashi, with Dave Holland on bass (*Bura Bura*). Also, Lacy had two particularly distinctive solo records: *Hocus-Pocus*, a set of exercises and studies for the saxophone written for his own use (this being book "H" of a larger series of studies, "Practitioners"), and deliberately made to be difficult; and *Outings*, two long pieces drawing on Mediterranean archetypes ("Labyrinth," dedicated to Giorgio de Chirico, and "Island," dedicated to Max Ernst), instigated and produced by the Roman musicologist Gianfranco Salvatore.

In the following year, 1987, the composer Gunther Schuller, a longtime friend and supporter of his music, published Lacy's book *Prospectus* (Margun Music), a collection of scores to sixteen pieces written mostly in the 1970s. Among other ventures at the time, Lacy also performed in Italy, accompanying silent films by Georges Méliès, Buster Keaton, D. W. Griffith, and Fernand Léger. Later that year, with the release of the sextet date *Momentum*, Lacy at last entered the roster of a big record label, in a nonexclusive arrangement with the new Novus series at RCA, which endured for five albums in about five years. Toward the end of that same year, he also recorded *Paris Blues*, a duo with Gil Evans, which was to be the veteran bandleader's final album.

Though still relatively young and going strong, Lacy already had a long career behind him, as reflected in the following panoramic interview, which originally appeared over four issues in *Jazz Magazine* (November 1987–March 1988).

You started frequenting the jazz milieu by photographing musicians . . .

It's true, but I lost all those photographs . . .

Were you a professional photographer?

Yes, I did portraits of musicians and sold them at concerts. That's how I was able to get in and how I began to meet musicians. That's also how I found my first teacher, Cecil Scott.

And then it was through him eventually that you started playing in various Dixieland bands?

Yes, it was really a miracle that I was there at the right moment. I played with Henry "Red" Allen, Buck Clayton, Dickie Wells, Buster Bailey, Pee Wee Russell, Jo Jones, Joe Sullivan, Max Kaminsky, Sandy Williams, Pops Foster, Zutty Singleton, and a lot of others. There were two concerts each night on the weekend at the Stuyvesant Casino and the Central Plaza, and I worked at both places. Each one had two groups per night and sold lots of beer—it was Dixieland and beer. All the great pioneers were there, even James P. Johnson—I didn't play with him but I saw him. I worked with Willie "the Lion" Smith. There was Vic Dickenson, Jimmy Rushing, Walter Page—it was fantastic. I loved that music like crazy. I read everything, listened to everything, I tried to learn everything.

What hooked you on the soprano?

It was obvious: I was born for that, it was made for me. It was like a marriage, I fell in love with the instrument, and when I saw that no one was playing it, that really made me want to do something, the path was open. There was no one. I hate being in competition with others, and I wanted to find an instrument that wasn't used much. That was truly the case with the soprano.

After your experience with Cecil Taylor, what were the first manifestations of the avant-garde in New York?

The arrival of Ornette Coleman! The door was ready, everything was ready, and when Ornette came knocking at the door, it opened. I had already heard his records and liked them a lot, I had no problem with that, I liked it right away. I played a little with Ornette and a lot with Don Cherry, Billy Higgins, and all the others. Ornette showed us certain things that were fundamental: space, time, how to treat time in space and space in time, that is to treat the material like something malleable, not like something predetermined. At the time, it seemed to me that everyone was playing the same piece in the same way, the same chorus. It began to resemble gymnastics—it was more athletic, the speed, the scales . . . I always resisted that, and I think that jazz is against formulas. It's an anti-formula music.

Were you connected with the Jazz Composer's Guild in the 1960s?

I was a bit involved but I wasn't a member. I didn't consider myself a composer and I thought it was reserved for that. On the other hand, I took part in Carla Bley's bands and those experiences. There were a lot of people: Milford Graves, Bill Dixon, Archie Shepp. That was around '64, things were beginning to crack open, to move a little, for me it happened when I was in Europe at the end of '65. Everyone had the same experience at different moments and in different places. For example, Don Cherry was already there at the beginning of the 1960s and he was completely free, he had no problems of that nature. It took me five years longer after all sorts of experiences, to be able to drop the theme, the melody, the harmony, the rhythm, tonality, everything. Not before the end of '65 and even '66. That was the year of free jazz for me, '66, and it lasted about a year, a year and a half.

And Albert Ayler?

He too was there before us, he had his trio with Gary Peacock and Sunny Murray in '63. I heard him in '65 in Paris at J.-F. Jenny-Clark's place. We listened to that together and we too wanted to play free. It took us another year.

Why did you come to Europe in '65?

I had a gig in Copenhagen for a month, with Don Cherry and Kenny Drew at the Montmartre, and after that, I didn't want to return to New York anymore, I wanted a change. There was no work in New York—it was cruel at that time. And then I was at the end of a marriage, I wanted a divorce, and from New York as well—I was born there, I had lived there for thirty years, and I had had enough of it. I had understood everything, I didn't need New York anymore. I saw that there was work for me in Europe, not only work but also good musicians. I had no more respect for New York, I had had to accept nonmusical jobs, at record shops, book shops, at an airline company, all sorts of stupid things in order to survive. I really wanted to live as a musician and nothing else. I wanted to be alone in Europe and be able to roam around there for the first time. After Copenhagen, I didn't know where to go, I had no engagements, I had nothing anymore, just my sax and my passport. I had met a woman who was on her way to Paris: I decided to come to Paris. Right away here I found Don Cherry, Jean-François [Jenny-Clark], Karl Berger, Aldo [Romano], and the Chat qui Pêche. Madame Ricard was happy, she hired me right away. Then Francis Paudras brought me to the country and I spent a whole summer at the "Bud Powell Club" in Normandie. Bud was in Paris at the time, I had known him a little in New York. I liked Paris right away, I fell in love with it—there was jazz, a public and musicians, everything I desired. However, I couldn't stay.

Do you think you'll ever return to New York to live?

No, it's no longer like it was, it's harder and harder, too much so for me. It's too expensive and it's not *free*, I don't feel *free*, even to go sit in a park, I feel like a current of air. And there are too many musicians, they don't need me. France was a cultural refuge for me, they understand certain things a lot better in Europe because they're older, the culture there is a lot more vast, richer and better known, better understood, even the jazz musicians are better understood here than over there, more studied and loved. In America, there's a confusion between cinema, baseball, rock, jazz, there's no distinction. What also keeps me here is my group. I found these musicians here, Oliver Johnson, Steve Potts, and Bobby Few—who is one of the reasons why I came. I had heard Bobby at the festival of Amougies in '69. I had gone to take part in that festival and make a record for BYG, and when I saw all those musicians who were in Paris and me in Rome, I felt isolated—I was working with amateurs. So, I decided with Irene to come to Paris. There are good musicians here but not too many. In Rome, there weren't enough.

You studied composition with Gil Evans?

A lot. I've had a good relationship with Gil, and it's not over. I was supposed to play with him in London this year, for his seventy-fifth birthday—a concert at the Hammersmith Hall. I've worked a lot with him in all sorts of bands, in small groups and even as a duo. I adore him, he's the best, the greatest magician of images. I think that all those who loved Duke Ellington—Monk, Cecil, Gil—were in the magic. Miles Davis too.

Which records of Coltrane impressed you the most at the time?

There are a number of them. *Om* was a lesson for me, and *Ascension*, but also *Giant Steps*. When I worked with Monk in 1960, at the Jazz Gallery in New York, Coltrane was playing on the same bill with his first quartet, he was already playing soprano. I was working on soprano with Monk, and there was something going on, that's for sure. I believe a lot in the physical aspect of transfers between musicians, those who work together—it's not a matter of influences from records, but of something given personally, from hand to hand.

You told Philippe Carles in 1965: "I like Coltrane on soprano, but not from a musical point of view, it's . . . very amusing." What did you mean by that?

It took me a moment to understand him, and it took him a moment to understand the instrument. I think it was two or three years before he was really comfortable on the instrument and able to do what he imagined. He told me several times that he was having trouble, he asked me for tips about mouthpieces and reeds, how I did certain things . . . It's not an easy instrument, you have to struggle with it, but since he played tenor with such an enormous technique and such breath, by comparison he was playing the soprano in a small way, handling it like a giant playing with a little thing.

In 1976 you said about your work: "It's not easy to sell, it's not commercial. Maybe it will be some day, I don't doubt it. If the music is good, it turns into gold. But that takes time." Has the time come now?

Yes, but it was already on the way, I knew. It's always like that: each time I look to move forward, it doesn't budge, but at the same time it's like a tree—slowly it rises and goes toward the gold. Yes, the gold and silver are beginning to come in a lot better than before . . . Now they're starting to play my pieces, a little bit here and there . . . Monk told me he wrote "'Round Midnight" when he was eighteen years old, it took about twenty years for Miles to record it. After that, he was launched, but it's something that's long lasting, like wine—new wine is only for the experts, you have to wait for it to be good for everyone. It's exactly the same for music. I wrote my first pieces twenty years ago and slowly it's on the way.

Do you like going back to play your old compositions?

Yes, it's delightful, interesting, exciting . . .

Do you change them?

It depends. Sometimes I see them better now, sometimes I set them in another context. There are some things that will never change: the melodies, the words, but the costume, the context, the setting can change. I can also adapt them for other combinations of instruments—I did that for a string quartet, the same piece for a saxophone quartet [both the Kronos Quartet and the Rova Saxophone Quartet played Lacy's "Precipitation Suite"]. It's a piece that I've readapted several times, and it's not over. If things are good, they'll be even more so later. I have a lot of experience in that domain, because the first years I was composing, I threw everything into the garbage before it began to be good. Only time can say if a thing is good.

Your career these days is divided in three: work with your sextet, solo, and encounters with different musicians. Do you still complain about not working enough with the sextet?

Yes, it's more difficult to work as a sextet than alone with a local rhythm section. And then the organizers always have ideas: "I'd like you to come play with X, it would be fantastic, I want to hear that," and sometimes I regret having said yes. But on the other hand, I love the encounters, I like working with Dutch musicians, German, English, Japanese, French, Italian . . . It's always interesting, and I learn a lot—there are good musicians everywhere, you have to adapt the instrument and yourself, change your point of view and learn other music in other situations, in order to progress . . .

Let's try to examine a few privileged encounters: Misha Mengelberg . . .

I've been collaborating with him for a long time. Sometimes we're opposed, he's hardheaded, so am I. It's the Dutch school, but I think we play very well together, people really appreciate it. I've learned a lot with him. With Derek Bailey too, it's music that makes not the slightest concession, he does only pure improvisation, and for me, that's a step outside, into the void. I have to constantly take risks with him and I like that, it obliges me to play things I don't usually play, it's a push toward the unknown. Gil Evans did the same thing with me, he pushed me into the blue. I was lost but he liked that. You have to have the courage to swim in the blue, in the unknown.

You also worked a lot with the group Musica Elettronica Viva.

That was terrific: Richard Teitelbaum and the Moog synthesizer, electronic music and improvisation, other ways of working, other values. Contemporary music is something else, those guys had one foot here and one foot there, me too.

You even transposed Webern's pieces for soprano voice . . .

I transposed all of Webern's pieces for the soprano saxophone, I think that was in '59. You couldn't find anything in stores for the soprano, no exercises, no pieces, and I was obliged to look for music that interested me and that I could play. That's how I found Monk's music as well as certain things by Kurt Weill, Duke Ellington, Billy Strayhorn, and when I heard Webern's music, I found that fantastic for the soprano, it was made for the voice but I was also a soprano. I only had to transcribe it into another key and I had exercises of an amazing difficulty. I remained a week or two on each measure, just to decipher, to feel it. That was a profound influence, his rhythm and the intervals, the dynamics and the ways of using the soprano's register. Webern was one of my best influences, his compositions were sublime, of such perfection, like Monk. I was obliged to invent everything because there was nothing for the soprano. There had been Bechet but that was too old, I had to look for something current as well as a repertoire. For a long time I've been concerned with the idea of the repertoire.

You often play with Mal Waldron . . .

That's a long collaboration and a great friendship that dates back to '56, when we got together with poets, "Jazz & Poetry," in New York. We worked at the old Five Spot to record Monk tunes for my second album, he's the one I called, I thought he was the best for that. I saw him several times with Billie Holiday, then we lost contact. I found him again in Europe. We started to play together again in the 1970s, and now we have a duo that works very well. He's one of the best accompanists in the world.

What do you think of the evolution of the jazz saxophone in recent years?

I'm a bit disappointed. It moved so much with Trane, Pharoah [Sanders], Ayler in the 1960s. Now the young seem a bit timid, as if they were afraid of ruining their instrument. Yet it's a long, hard battle with the instrument. They make very nostalgic music, a return to bebop and even to impressionism, it's a pity. Still, there are exceptions, I've heard good saxophonists, but they're not so young. I've heard John Stubblefield, I've heard John Gilmore, he kills me, and Pharoah too, and Archie when he's well. I ask for the saxophone to be played in a *current* manner. I've heard so much sax and I do so much myself: too many saxophones, I find it a bit tiring. The first time I heard Peter Brötzmann, it was a shock. And that's what I ask for: a slap. I'm always searching for the magic, something different from everything I've heard.

You work a lot with dancers . . .

The two poles of our work are song, the songs, and dance. The music is always between the two. Jazz for me is always a dance music—long ago we used to play a foxtrot with dancers on the floor, with Cecil we did that kind of thing a lot, myself I played a lot at dance parties. In New York they danced to Horace Silver and Art Blakey up until '54, that was music made for dancing, then it disappeared, but not for me. I've always wanted the dancers to come back in one way or another. In Rome we worked a lot with modern dancers, and in Paris we've done that since the beginning. We played with the Théâtre du Silence from La Rochelle, the Groupe Chorégraphique of the Opéra de Paris, with Pierre Droulers, the actor Shiro Daimon . . . It makes the music move in another way, you have to put the music at the service of the dancer, it obliges you to play in a different way. We've also started working for the cinema—

we've done several documentaries, there's a feature length in sight—and for video.

At the recent funeral for Michel Salou, you played a piece by Monk. What kind of relation did you have with him?

I had known him since my very beginning in Paris. He's the first agent who helped us when times were really hard. He was a friend. He was very ill, he wasn't supposed to work anymore but he tried even so . . . At the time, he was the only person who helped us, he wasn't the only one who liked us but he was the only one with a bit of power who could call the Maisons de Jeunes, the Maisons de la Culture, and insist that they hire us for concerts.

On Practicing, and Exploring the Instrument

interview by Kirk Silsbee

The following conversation, which appeared long after the fact in *Cadence* (October 2004), took place on 26 March 1988, at the club Catalina's in Hollywood, where Lacy's sextet was performing. Late that spring Lacy returned to Japan, where he recorded the trio date *Voices* in concert with Togashi and Avenel, and in the summer he made his second album for RCA Novus, *The Door*, a reframing of the jazz continuum past and present; it was the last record with the drummer Oliver Johnson in the band.

18

What is your philosophy about addressing your instrument?

I don't think there's enough scientific exploration of instruments going on. From the level of musician that I hear around, people are not thrashing with their instruments anymore the way we used to do. It's a battle. I guess I learned that from Cecil Taylor. He battled his instrument, throttled it, and his neighbors were pounding on the walls and he went on playing anyway. You have to have a certain warlike nature and a kind of a thirst for violence, in a way. It's sort of a violent approach to your horn, but I think it's the only way. I think you must spend some time in your life doing that. You don't have to do that all of your life but you have to beat it up for a while to get to the bottom of it, to tame it. Otherwise you'll never tame your instrument. It'll always be out of control. You'll be at its mercy, subsequently.

In general, there's a fear of really grappling with your axe to many people all over the world. There's a kind of a "soft shoe" approach to practicing and people don't really come to grips with their horns and they don't get to the bottom of them. They never get the material to vibrate enough so as to get something happening. I think the fundamentals, the overtones are really very important and a good way to get the brass vibrating is to dig in without the octave key. The overtones, from the bottom of the horn all the way to the top, are there if you want to get to it. It'll take you years to get to it, but it's there if you want it and it's on every note. But as you rise, the notes get weirder and weirder and more and more out of conventional tune. And if you don't have those, if you never let them out of their cage, the fundamental, the bottom note is never really as rich as it could be. You have to be very patient and fish them out like fish, one by one, very slowly. You must never try to go too high immediately. You must just go as high as you can, until that strengthens your lip. Then you can push it a little bit further when your muscle gets a little more developed, then go back down and stay there for a while. You build it up very little by very little until you can go to the moon.

Is it a matter of pressure or is it in the mouthpiece?

No, I think it's more in here [points to his head] and in here [points to his throat]. First of all, you've got to hear them. Sometimes you can play them and then you can hear them later. And the reed has a lot to do with it. I use a very soft reed and a very wide mouthpiece but it took me years to build up to that. Sometimes that could be easier with a smaller mouthpiece. Anyway, it's merely a material exercise; it's not to do with music, necessarily. It's just to expose the fundamentals, the components of your sound. That's what's in your notes, that spectrum.

At first, they sound terrible and they'll drive you crazy and your neighbors will pound on the wall. It's just awful to try and fish those things out at first. It takes a long time to even start and it's painful because it sounds terrible and makes you feel like an amateur. Some of them—when you play higher—will sound terrible. They make very funny scales that you'll never hear any other way. So it's good for that too. It's good for your lip, it's good for your ear, it's good for your saxophone. And those sounds want to come out but everybody suppresses those things. They used to be called "squeaks," but now we dignify them and call them "sound components." But it's well worth studying and it really helps everything about your playing. But go very slowly. If you can achieve four overtones on every note of your horn, you're really doing something.

What are the mechanics of this exercise?

You have nothing to go by. You have to fish them out in the dark and you'll have to employ everything you have: the diaphragm, the air column, the lip, the ear, and patience. But I couldn't tell you, technically, how it's done, you just have to do it. I don't even know how they're done. I can do them because I've been doing them for years.

Other than the obvious way it builds your lip and stamina, how do you apply that to your actual playing?

In the '60s there was a movement: what they called *the free revolution*, *the breakthrough*, *the new thing*, whatever. Albert Ayler and a lot of us other musicians sort of stopped playing tunes and broke the beat and dropped changes and everything and started using this kind of language, this kind of a free, stratospheric exploration mixed with normal music. And we still play that sometimes, but it's really a sound of the '60s to me. All the really great saxophonists can do that. I even heard Stan Getz do that one time for a couple of seconds, as a joke. He played a free cadenza at the end of a ballad or something. It was incredible. To him it was a joke, but to me it wasn't funny at all. So the stuff is there if you want it, but it's all mixed up like that or you can do it scientifically. Another way to mix them up is by emphasizing certain of them and they're very useful as far as coloristics, certain expressive effects. They're wonderful effects. I use them all the time. Instead of a certain note, I'll use the harmonic, which sounds like that but it's a little bit sharper than the normal note and I get a certain expressive effect I want. If you have them in your pocket you can deal them when you need them.

When you compose, do you write such things in?

Yeah, once in a blue moon. Mostly I play with Steve Potts and he knows what to do. It's never indicated or anything. I just let him grow it for a while. And I know that after a while it'll come out like him and like I would have loved it. Then if I'm working with a stranger, I wouldn't dare limit him like that either. We want as much freedom as we can buy. The tunes are written for that effect, so as to promote a certain quantity of freedom. There's a slightly different area in each piece, that's all.

The soprano saxophone is so susceptible to temperature changes, how do you keep it in tune?

It's a constant struggle. Every night, every day, every moment. There's a rare few minutes here and there or a half-hour or a set or two where we're really mellow and don't have to worry about being out of tune. But the rest of the time it's a losing battle. For example, last night the piano was flat as a board and we had trouble getting tuned. It's a compromise. I'm supposed to be the leader but the leader is sort of a mythical "A," the ideal "A" between us all. It's not even the real "A" that the piano's got. It's the "A" that should be. So we try and tune to that and if the piano is too far away, well, we make a compromise and go a little bit more toward the piano. But it changes in every town we play and every night, and I think the moon has something to do with it too. And certainly, a reed will change your life. A good reed or a bad reed. That will kill you or bring you back to life. I usually break them, or sometimes I save them for wartime. I have a big box with a "W" on it for wartime. I discovered these a few years ago. They're the most wonderful reeds for the soprano called Riviera. It's a very small model, very obscure. It's one little family in the South of France that makes them, in their farm. I order them by mail because they're hard to find but, jeez, they last long and they go higher than any other reed I've ever played. They gave me half an octave more than I had before.

What brand of horn do you play?

Selmer. One reason I like to live in Paris is because the factory is there. I just evolved one horn to another: a King, a Conn, a Selmer, and another Selmer and another Selmer and finally I realized that that was it. I tried the other ones and I didn't like them as well. So when you find your marque, there's no sense changing any more, you better stay with it.

What's your general attitude toward practice?

It's what I was saying before about grappling: you have to really treat your instrument badly. You have to really beat on it. You have to hit on it and insist on certain things that it doesn't want to deal with. You have to stay on some low notes until the instrument is crazy. Another thing I would recommend to you is tight corner exercises where you limit what you're working on to just one or two notes and you stay on it a long, long, long time. You take a half step and you play this half step for a while. Just go back and forth on this half step. If you keep that up for a while it starts to get very boring. When you get beyond the boredom, it starts to get interesting a little bit. If you stay on it after that, you get into the realm of hallucinations and there's where the fun begins. There's where the interval starts to get bigger and bigger and you start to get smaller and the interval gets bigger than you are. You're a little person in this big interval, which is a half-step really, and it's so big that it's incredible. You're hallucinating. You can do all kinds of things that you never dreamed of with that half-step. It becomes a room and after an hour in this room, it's like a trip. You have a rest and everything is transformed. Your horn and all the elementals will never be the same. Your ear is changed. A trip like that changes your whole life. Well, there's a thousand trips like that possible. I would recommend that you start dealing with things like that if you're interested in digging what can be dug out.

Why is it that saxophone players seem to have more fluidity in their harmony than, say, guitar players?

What about Wes Montgomery? I don't think you can get any more fluid than that. The saxophone is a liquid-type instrument. There's another thing I'd like to point out, something I learned from a little book I read years and years ago—you can't find it anymore—called *The Art of Melody*. It explained that one of the characteristics of melody is that the highest note in a melody is the most prominent and the lowest note in a melody is also memorable in a certain sense. The highest and the lowest stand out from the body because inside the notes are crisscrossed in various ways. Sometimes when you reach a high note, after the melody is over, you remember that. So you must be careful in your melodious conception not to overdo the high notes because you cancel yourself out if you do and if you achieve these high notes you'll soon realize that they can be a drawback and a drag and you can hang yourself up and do some ridiculous things that sound just awful. The more extra baggage you get, the more awful you can play. Be careful of high notes; don't overdo them. They're very effective but only if done sparingly.

When your band tunes for a concert, does it tune to a piano?

We have a group with two saxophones in it and the front line is those two saxophones plus the voice and violin. Basically the two saxophones are the lead players so they have to be in tune. If the piano's out, we have to make a compromise. If the piano's in tune, we all tune to the piano. We used to have an opening piece that we did called "Stamps" that we played for many years. It was built on open strings of the bass and cello and it made an A minor scale. We used to play this so as to tune up and also to tune the public up and break the ice. But we played that tune to death; we don't play it anymore. Now we've got a new one but it's not for tuning up. We just try and tune up before we play and hope we're in tune.

Do you write nonspecific pieces or are they written for your band members?

The pieces are written for the players. I'm lucky enough to have the players and the vocalist so I can write for them. It's like Monk told me a long time ago: the reason he made those tunes so interesting and so difficult was to get the musicians interested enough to come to rehearsals. He made the tunes very interesting. We try to do the same. I have a horror of boring my musicians with something beneath them or something not worth doing or something that wouldn't turn them on. And we've been through several episodes where pieces just didn't turn the players on and so we dropped the pieces. We don't drop the players. In the pieces we do, there's a lot of different ways we improvise on them. Some of them are wide open and some are quite closed and many of them are built on scales. Some are a set of changes, and many are a kind of vamp and the vamp is expressed in the introduction of the piece. It could be four bars repeated four times with a hold on it or maybe a sixteen-bar introduction or something like that. And that's where the improvisation grows from later on, after the tune is stated.

Do you write lines for [the bassist] Jean-Jacques Avenel?

Usually what I write for him, he could stay on infinitely. I try to make it so interesting that it isn't boring to be just doing that. He likes freedom.

He's got ideas and he's got better ideas than I do. He comes up with some stuff I couldn't imagine and it's much better than my line. It starts from there but he embellishes it and he takes it further and it becomes his thing. My idea was just the boiled-down, bare bones of the thing. He starts there and takes it to his own domain. That's what I want. Duke Ellington showed the way to do that: how to feature certain attributes of a soloist, how to bring out certain qualities of his players. The player has a romantic side, a cute side, a mean side, and he can play like that too. And you want to bring out all of those: the savage side and the jovial side, whatever's in the soloist. The soloist has many sides.

What is your estimation of [the drummer] Oliver Johnson's role in your ensemble?

That's a good question. It's the fundament; it's the *batterie*, as they say in French. It's the battery. He's the stoker, really. Without him there ain't nothin' happening. I would say the drummer is the number one principal in the jazz band. Even when I play solo concerts it's only because I've played with a lot of good drummers that I'd even dare to do that. I only do it once in a while and I go back and grab onto my drummer again. Drums is it.

Do the drums support the bass or does the bass support the drums in your band?

That's a chicken/egg type of thing. They're locked in eternal harmony together 'til death do they part. It's essential that the rhythm section function together; it's a group exercise. It's like a punter with the boat and the captain and all: they have to work together. It's got to swing together; otherwise it's going to sink together. And that, like intonation, is a constant problem. Rhythm sections have always got to be worked on, worked out, and worked in. They have to be fed interesting things to grow on, to develop. You have to cook and stew a rhythm section over many, many years before it becomes really good. I'm very lucky. I have a fantastic rhythm section (Bobby Few, Avenel, and Johnson), these guys are amazing. They've been playing together for so many years but in the last couple of years it's gotten even better. It's really just right now. I'm there to learn from them. I mean, they got more rhythm than I do, that's for sure. Monk gave me some good advice many years ago: make the rhythm section sound good with what you play. You know, that's what Miles brought in: how to delineate a rhythm section, how to effectively set off and be set off from a rhythm section. That stuff he did with Philly Joe Jones when they had that rhythm section was of capital importance in that sense. It set up the next ten, twenty years of activity, of how musical business should be conducted. His style had a lot to do with boxing. They were all interested in that. It was a boxing rhythm section: incredible, unforgettable.

Do you see avant-garde music as the culmination of what jazz was supposed to be?

No, that's part of it, that's an episode. To me it goes way back and it's all one thing. My heart is always with the old stuff: the New Orleans, the Kansas City, the Chicago schools. I was steeped in that; I was brought up in that. I started playing that music and my heart is always there. So you can avant all the gardes you want, but what Louis Armstrong and Earl Hines did in 1929, it doesn't get any better than that. It doesn't get any freer than that. Those are the standards. Whatever we do now has to be at least as good as that. Or better. It can be better.

In Jazz, since every chorus can be improvised differently, it can be hard to quantify what a band is trying to get at.

Look, why improvise? Improvisation itself is nothing. It doesn't impress me. To me, I don't value improvisation per se. A great composition or a great improvisation, they're equally great to me. Music should just be good. I don't really care how it's done. And I think most of the public doesn't give a damn who is improvising where. That's for the experts. It's like in a restaurant: you don't want to know what's in the food, exactly how it was done, and all that. You just eat the stuff and it's great.

19

Art Is Made to Trouble

interview by Christian Gauffre

The year that Lacy was made a Chevalier of the Order of Arts and Letters by the French Ministry of Culture, in 1989, he gave the première of a work commissioned by the ministry in honor of the two hundredth anniversary of the French Revolution. *Anthem*, his third album for RCA, placed that work as its centerpiece and came out the following year; it marked the first appearance on record of the band's new drummer, John Betsch, who would become a mainstay in all subsequent Lacy groups. This interview was published in *Jazz Magazine* (June 1990).

How did the project come about that ended up as *Anthem*, commissioned by the Ministry of Culture and recorded for RCA Novus?

1989 was in every sense a revolutionary year. Everywhere that's all people talked about, revolution. We didn't want to let events pass us by. The text that we use dates from 1918. It's the work of a Russian poet, Osip Mandelstam, who is speaking of the Bolshevik revolution. I've been mulling over the text for years. Suddenly, last year, it all took shape when I received this commission. We've made a revolutionary hymn, which also became an echo of the revolution that jazz went through twenty years ago. This record, with its great diversity, is an excellent introduction to the 1990s.

A "revolutionary" musical work having a text as its point of departure . . .

I always start from the text. But the words imply a long period of reflection, which can stretch out over years sometimes. It can happen that I reflect on something for ten, twenty years, before I know what to do with it.

Is it more difficult, in the end, than to "simply" write music?

Music is what makes the words take wing. It's a true alchemy, where everything seems rather mysterious, but first of all it's the time that matters, the time, but also what the musicians want to do, what the singers want to sing, what the public wants to hear . . . What the people who offer the commission accept to pay for! It depends too on what the author of the text will permit. We must be respectful toward the one who wrote the words. So many considerations enter into play that we have to examine a long time before launching into a work of this type.

Do you prefer studio recordings?

Yes. A good live recording is a miracle. The music we make is too difficult, too precise. It may suffice for a concert, but not for a record: the more you listen, the more you hear the mistakes.

In your concert at the Queen Elizabeth Hall in London, Bobby Few was not able to play: how did you feel about that forced return to a past format?

Without the piano, the color is very different. The music is drier. The piano is a liquid component in our music, very important for filling in the space behind the voice. We worked for a long time without a pianist, as a quintet. Then, about ten years ago, we found in Bobby Few the pianist that we were seeking. That's to say, his presence fulfills us and so his absence troubled us.

Things seem to have evolved favorably for you, these last two years . . .

Oh yes, it's much easier. And what makes the difference is my entry into RCA/BMG. There are people now who distribute my records, publicity teams who promote us, who support us. When we have a concert, they help us. The records come out well, they're well distributed, it's very important. Vital even.

Have the record companies changed their attitude toward your music?

Yes. Before, it wasn't interesting for them. It has become so. You need about twenty years for something to become interesting. We don't sell great quantities, but regularly. Some records made twenty or thirty years ago continue to sell!

Does the soprano saxophone profit from this evolution?

The instrument is in full development. Good musicians are taking an interest in it—I'm endlessly being contacted by people who would like to study with me: Italians, Germans, French, Canadians . . . If interest in the soprano is growing, that's because it has been clarified: the instrument's voice is known now, it's clear, recognizable. It's become a "normal" voice. That which was not possible has become so.

You told us recently that you're very attracted to Brazil . . .

Brazil is the music, first of all. We learn each time we play someplace new and I'm convinced that would be even more the case in Brazil. The music evolves, it moves. A few weeks ago, we were in Istanbul: Turkish music is so different, the Turks have such an unusual ear that our music responds to their reactions and so on . . . It's a movement that's internal to the music, important so that we can progress. I've always dreamed of playing in Brazil, out of curiosity, for the pleasure of seeing what would happen . . .

Are there particular musicians in Brazil that you would like to play with?
We already played once with Hermeto Pascoal . . . But I would like most to go there with my group, and play for them.

Shop Talk

interview by Mel Martin

With greater interest in his music, Lacy began touring the United States more frequently, about once a year by the end of the decade. In addition to more albums for RCA in these years as well as other ongoing collaborations, he also managed to record a cherished project, the song cycle *Rushes*, based on ten Russian poems (Tsvetayeva, Mandelstam, Akhmatova), for a small Italian label; the work was performed by the trio of Aebi, Lacy, and his old friend Frederic Rzewski, the pianist and composer. This opened a new front for Lacy in later years, centered directly on the songs, with the music sometimes stripped down to the essentials.

The following interview by the saxophonist Mel Martin, which originally appeared in *Saxophone Journal* (November–December 1991), took place on 13 April 1990, the day after a concert in Oakland, California.

Why don't we start with you telling me the set-up you're currently playing.

I have a Super Action Series I Selmer that I've had about six years. Before that I had the previous model, the Mark VI. It's like a car. You stick with one name brand, and trade in the old model for the new one when it comes out. I'm waiting for the newest Selmer to come out. I'll probably take that and give them my old one. But I love the old one; it's been great.

You were saying that you feel they have made certain gains but with these come certain losses.

By now I've gotten used to those losses, and they don't even bother me any more. They were small things but they really are important. For example, the left-hand pinky action. The difference between the Mark VI and the Super Action was radical and unnecessary. The Mark VI worked perfectly well. But in order to conform with the other members of the family, the tenor, the baritone, etc., they changed all the fingerings on the left hand, including the pinky. For soprano it didn't make sense to match the roller mechanism. The older ones were a lot simpler and worked much better. It's like the old thing, "If it ain't broke, don't fix it." But they fixed it! The overall gains were much more important and I go along with Selmer and their tooling philosophy and all that. I've tried the new soprano model which is in preparation now, and it's pretty good.

Do they take your input in developing the instruments?

Yes, they call me before they go into production, when they have a prototype, and they call legitimate saxophonists, too.

As opposed to the other kind [laughter].

Really, they call all kinds of so-called experts who test them out and give them their opinion and advice. Selmer and I are very much in tune, and that's important. Another important thing about living in France is that the reeds come from the south of France. This is very interesting. Recently I visited the factory down south, where the reeds I use come from, and I got to know the process in person. It's a small company called Marca (distributed by Leblanc). It's a family concern, and they sometimes supply the cane to Vandoren.

I don't know if you're familiar, but over here there's been severe reed problems for a number of years now. Most of the professionals and students alike are crying the blues pretty badly over lack of good cane. Many well known products seem to have fallen down badly. They are cutting them fine, it's not that they don't have good quality workmanship, it's just that they're not getting good cane.

It's a vicious circle. Like it was explained to me, reed is a weed which grows wild all over this region called the Var in France and only the wild variety is good—the stuff growing by the roadside and all that. If you try to plant it, it's no good.

That's what they found. They can't duplicate that natural chemistry.

Let's call it spirit, because to me, there is spirit in a reed. It's a living thing, a weed, really, and it does contain spirit of a sort. And they say these areas make sound when the wind comes. It's really an ancient vibration.

Apparently, part of what their problem was in obtaining good, wild, French cane is that land developers have moved in on a lot of that land, and also severe winters hit the cane crops quite badly. Even Vandoren doesn't get all their cane from France anymore. They seem to have always had the better quality of cane, however, I don't always enjoy their cuts. Are there such things as bamboo reeds?

No, cane is not bamboo. Bamboo is different. Cane is rushes, or *roseaux* in French—*junkus*.

When I went to the Roy J. Maier factory down in Los Angeles, I thought that was bamboo they cut the cane out of.

They are stalks like bamboo, but it's a different plant. Bamboo is not a weed, it's a flowering plant, but these are weeds that grow wild to about twenty feet. They're not like bamboo, which can make a forest and bloom once in a hundred years. Bamboo is a magnificent plant. These are crude weeds, this is what they make baskets out of.

Ah-ha. So you are able to get good French cane, but from a small company.

I order directly from them. I've seen them in Japan, and I believe you can get them in places like Charles Ponte in New York. Specialized places probably know about them. But I use very soft ones and I must order them directly.

You use a pretty open mouthpiece, too?

Yes, Otto Link made three identical mouthpieces for me a number of years ago and I use them. It's a number twelve, and larger than their usual sizes. They normally go up to a ten. I had an eleven which got stolen, so I asked for one a little bit bigger and that was it.

I heard you play into the stratosphere. Notes that are up there and I'm wondering how you do that on a soft reed on an open mouthpiece.

It's in the reed. There's a lot more flexibility with a soft reed, so you can go much higher. A hard reed is limited. After you reach a certain point, the door is closed. I arrived at using the soft by going through the hard. I used to play hard reeds, and plastic reeds, and metal mouthpieces, etc. I went through those phases over a period of thirty years before I gradually arrived at the best solution for me. I can have the maximum flexibility and sound possibilities. I can release all the harmonics in the horn without killing my lip. When you go to the moon like that, it hurts, and you can't do it that often and it's got to be controllable.

I've noticed in the past, and especially hearing you last night, how you make great use of the low register. Obviously you also have great control of the high register, but you were playing the low register in a way I hear almost no soprano players doing, which was intriguing to me.

Yes, I find the low register very fascinating in the soprano because the low register of the tenor is too low to dwell too long on. But the low register of the soprano is very mellow and right in there. The soprano has all those other instruments in it. It's got the soprano song voice, flute, violin, clarinet, and tenor elements and can even approach the baritone in intensity. It can sound like a baroque trumpet, too. It's used instead of the baroque trumpets sometimes for the Bach concertos.

You've lived in France since 1970. I still see you as being very vital and creative and what you call "on the cutting edge" of the music. There is often a viewpoint from this side that people living in Europe tend to lose that edge a bit. How do you feel about that?

It ain't necessarily so [laughter]. You must go where you don't lose your vitality. In New York in the '60s my vitality was being sapped and stifled and stymied and subdued, and it was terrifying. It seemed like it was hopeless. Then I went away for a couple of years, came back, and it was worse. It seemed to open up and get a little better in the '70s, when I started peeking back. Since then I go back more frequently.

I think the '70s were a bad period for jazz.

I think it was a period when it was best to be busy doing your own thing, because you couldn't count on any community support. It was a very tough time, yet glorious. That was when we did the research that was necessary to refine what we did in the '60s, the breakthrough period, a revolutionary period in jazz. The '70s was the time when you couldn't continue what you did, you had to make it go into a more modern direction in a more acceptable way. What we had found was too chaotic, we had to start shaping it.

If you can describe it to me, what ways did you personally find to shape your music?

Composition! By finding the appropriate structures to contain the type of improvisational material that we had discovered. What Monk had was the appropriate containers. He wrote the lines that made the guys sound good and that they liked to play. They developed a language and improvisation came naturally out of that material and it was a coherent whole. That was what I was after. The saxophone is a very interesting machine, but I'm more interested in music. Saxophone is part of that. I was spoiled by Monk's music because it was so good, so complete. You could play them over and over again, even just the heads. You could play them badly and they sounded good!

Were there a lot of problems when you first moved to Paris?

I would not recommend anyone coming to Paris and hoping to crack it. It's a rough place. It took me five to ten years before we got to the place where we could swing a bit over there. We had to start from scratch all over again which took a while in a strange place to cope, adhere, and to surface above the water. You say the '70s were hard for you, well they were hard there too, and that is why you really have to invent work. In the '80s the work was coming in, and it still is. But before it comes in, you have to invent it. If you have music you want to play that no one asks you to play, you have to go out and find where you can play it. It's called "do or die." In the '50s we rehearsed many times with Cecil, but only performed a few times. When I had a band with Roswell in the '60s doing all Monk, nobody wanted to hear about that. Nobody would hire us. So we went block by block canvassing to find places to play. We played for peanuts. But we did what we wanted to do, we heard what we wanted to hear, we performed what we wanted to perform, we learned what we wanted to learn. Of course, years later the record from that will sell forever. You have to go through hard times. People don't want to suffer. They want to sound good immediately, and this is one of the biggest problems in the world. I think it's very important to go through periods where you sound just rotten and you know it and you have to persevere or give up. The next day you still sound rotten, and it goes on for quite a while until one day it starts to get a little better. Something is really happening in a phase like that.

That's really developing a drive that people don't usually have.

You have to sound sad first of all, then maybe later you can sound good.

Do you have anything you would like to add for the readers of this magazine?

The potential for the saxophone is unlimited. I've been working on the soprano saxophone for forty years now and the possibilities are astounding. It's up to you, the only limit is the imagination. Circumstances can be very important. Find the right people to work with. You can work on the saxophone alone, but ultimately you must perform with others. I've performed solo for twenty years now, but I don't do much of it, and I don't do it too often, because it's an exceptional thing to do. If you only play alone, you go crazy and out of tune and play foolish music. Jazz is people's music, a collectivity. Also, never play anything boring, but play difficult and interesting things. If you play boring things, you risk losing your appetite. Saxophone can be tedious with too much of the same, so you must keep stimulating yourself with good materials to keep your appetite alive.

It's Got to Be Alive

interview by Ben Ratliff

Increasingly, for many of Lacy's larger projects, he drew on the sextet as his foundation, augmenting its sound with other instruments and voices according to the colors with which he sought to infuse each work. For a week at the end of November 1990, in Vienna, he had the rare opportunity to perform his music with a big band in a festival called "Listen to Lacy" (in which he also performed with the dancer Shiro Daimon and the pianist Frederic Rzewski). The marvelous result of that experience can be heard on the album *Itinerary*, which came out the next year. On it Lacy is joined by sixteen musicians (among them another intermittent collaborator, the trombonist Glenn Ferris), at the heart of which his regular sextet sounds as if expanded through a prism; the recording was dedicated to his orchestral and coloristic mentor, Gil Evans. Most of the music was written in the late 1960s, including "The Precipitation Suite," and reworked for the new occasion. Another old-become-new project that experimented with variations on the sextet was *Clangs*, a set of songs based on artists' texts and recorded by his double sextet early in 1992. But these were ventures beyond the sights of the big label back in New York; in the summer of 1991 his sextet recorded what turned out to be the last of his albums for RCA, *Live at Sweet Basil*. The following interview took place in New York on New Year's Eve of that year and appeared in *Cadence* (December 1992).

Why don't we start with the question I asked you earlier, about how it's getting harder to be a musician in New York, and the air of mediocrity that you see creeping into culture?

Ah . . . ah ha. Well, there's a word for that: you can call it "pollution." And it's just harder to get through. As I just explained it to somebody last night, it's the door—everybody's trying to get in the door, but the door is no longer a clear-cut door. It's all overhung with, I don't know what, with plastic drippings, it's no longer a square opening there, it's all covered up and there's only a small place to get through the door! It's like the door is closing, gradually.

I'm talking about junk music. Junk music. Like junk bonds, and junk this, and junk that. Bunk rotten stuff, I mean plastic machinery, synthetic nonsense . . . the marketplace is so glutted up now with all kinds of gunk, that if somebody's really trying to get through with something, with a real product, it's harder than ever. Because, years ago, you had to compete with other people playing instruments, there was a reality about the scene; you could get out there and grapple musically. We used to fight musically, we used to . . . joust. When I was playing with Cecil [Taylor] in the '50s and all that, things were more clear-cut. Everybody was against us, but at least we had a possibility of fighting. And we did get through, and Cecil got through like mad. It may have taken twenty years, but it was possible. But now, if somebody wants to make that twenty-year commitment, I don't know whether I'd recommend that he do that, because at the end of twenty years he might still be on the outside, because of all the, ah, how should I say . . . the late arrivals, all the people who just, like, go out and buy some hardware, and punch up some stuff. You know, music takes place *in time*, and there's only room for so much. So if there's so much around, and you come around, you feel pretty foolish with an outside product, because there's so much going on there already.

But don't you think there are new directions in which musicians can go?

Oh, yeah! If you have the imagination, there's no shortage. There's plenty of stuff that hasn't been done yet, and plenty of stuff worth doing. That's not the problem at all. It's just the possibility of living off that that is harder. The marketplace is hard.

It must have been especially hard when you were starting out in the '50s.

Yeah, but it's worse. In my opinion, it's much worse now, because the quality has gone down, and people consume junkier stuff than before, really. The standards have lowered. Airport music, and stuff that you hear around, and what's on the radio. You know, if I come to New York and switch on the radio, it's appalling! I find it appalling. In France, where I live, in Paris, you can go across the dial, and you find good music! And some popular stuff, and some junky stuff, but there'll also be some top-quality jazz, and some good contemporary music, and some classical music, and some French songs. You can find a variety of quality stuff. But in New York, man, it's mostly gremlin music and stuff like that. Soul music. I can't *stand* soul music, so-called "soul" music, wow. They call it soul music because you *sell your soul.*

Are there any younger players that you at least find promising? For example, of the more popular ones, there are the M-Base musicians, Steve Coleman, Cassandra Wilson—you've heard them?

I've heard them; I think it's promising, what they're doing, but I'm afraid for them. I'm afraid for them because they're worried about PR, and media, and all that. Man, this is *not* what you're supposed to be thinking about at that age, marketing yourself, and all that. That's impossible!

What kind of a deal is that? We didn't do like that. Bird didn't do like that. But, now is the age of Mr. Marsalis. You have to have a nice wardrobe, and a PR office, and everything like that, and you better have your P's and Q's together—otherwise, you're gonna get wasted. And the scene here was always such that some good musicians got wasted, but now—it's not hopeless, but it's hard. It's really too hard.

Did you see the recent *Time* magazine article with Wynton on the cover?

Well, they never put Miles on the cover of *Time*. So, there it is right there. Mm, mm, mm. No, that's discouraging, all that whole kind of thing, really.

Do you have a sort of general philosophy about brevity or succinctness in art?

Ah, yeah, yeah, I would say I'm a nutshell man. Boiled down. You know, Monk taught me a lot of that kind of economy, and Stravinsky too.

When you dedicate pieces on your records, is it because the piece always says something about the person you're dedicating it to?

Yeah. To me, music is always about something or somebody, or from somebody or something. It's never in the blue, never abstract. You have to dig into it to see what's happening, you have to question it. Sometimes I don't know what it's about or who it's about until it comes out; after a while, I question it, and I see—"ahh, that's who that is."

For instance, your piece "The Rent" [on *Anthem*], which was dedicated to jazz critic Laurent Goddet.

He was a good friend of ours, and a champion of music, one of the first people that helped us when we got to Paris. Well, it's a description of his life and death, really, that piece. It's a cha-cha-cha, and sort of a grind. He killed himself, for what I thought was a ridiculous reason, and it left a rent in my heart. And, it's also a play on his name "The Rent," *Laurent*. And, the rent is a phenomenon that we're all forced to deal with—we have to pay the rent, you know?

That wasn't the reason he killed himself?

No, he killed himself over a girl.

It's a very sad piece, too.

It's sad, and it's fun too. The cha-cha-cha part is very light; the other part is sort of grim, yeah.

And there's a piece on your new record dedicated to Bob Marley?

Oh, "Retreat," yeah. That was actually done on an old record called *Prospectus*, with the words. The text is by Gainsborough, the painter, in French, about the desire for retreat, "I don't want to paint any more portraits. I'd like to just take my viola da gamba, and my paints, and go off into the country, and paint landscapes, and just live out the rest of my life in peace." It's complicated, because it's from an English painter, in French, and it's got a Balinesian-Japanese scale, and it's dedicated to a reggae musician. It's got a bunch of flavors. It's like a cuisine. You have a spice from here, and you have another ingredient from there, and it's got to be blended, these things. It's all in the cooking, really.

You're one of those musicians who keeps going back to your old work, and changing it, and reinventing it over and over again. Is that something that you really enjoy doing—say, more than composing?

No, no, they're both necessary. I mean, you have to make new things, but you have to let them grow old. I think that the best things are the oldest things, when the music gets to be a certain age. The new things we do are very interesting, but we have to do them over and over, we have to let them get a little bit old before they're *really* interesting.

So you often wait for a few years to record something?

That's right. Well, very often, we recorded things, and after we recorded them, they started to get much better. And then the difference between what we're doing, and the old record, is so that we have to record it again.

What about the stuff you did with the big band (in a recent Steve Lacy Festival in Vienna)?

Most of that is a cycle about the weather. It goes back to '69 and '70—it's called "The Precipitation Suite," and it's really about the wind, clouds, and rain. Afterward comes the sun, and then—moon. It's like a cycle of elements. And then there's a piece called "Sweet Sixteen." So this is stuff that's twenty years old but has been reworked in solo, trio, big band, quartet, sextet, rewritten, reconsidered, reworked. But it's still about the weather. This is real program music. It's a program of three minutes of wind, and six minutes of clouds, and seven minutes of rain, and the piece called "The Sun" has a very important text by Buckminster Fuller. It's a litany, a technological litany, very interesting piece. That's from '68, and we never really recorded it until now. I think it came out very good, really. It's hard to describe; it's just like the sun. It's really such an optimistic message, just shining like the sun, really.

It was all written out, there were no solos, no improvisation. There was improvisation in the manner of delivery, but the elements were given. All the elements were furnished. It's a sort of elemental improvisation, where I give you a certain amount of notes, and I give you a certain amount of time, and you have to do it your own way. It took me a long time to prepare that, but it's something I've been thinking about for twenty years. I love big bands, but it's a question of economics.

Do you still practice a lot?

Ah, yeah, yeah. I better! [Laughs.] Last night, for example, yesterday, I practiced an hour or so before the concert, got a good warm-up. And then sometimes, when I'm on the road, if I find a good place to practice, I'll practice a couple of hours there. At home, I'll try and get in an hour or two every day.

Is it especially necessary because your instrument is so sensitive?

Yeah, I have to keep my lip up, and I keep the instrument happy. And before a solo concert, I have to really warm up well.

When you're playing a solo performance, is it harder to take risks when you get to an improvised part?

It is such a risk to begin with. Just to get up there and do that is a risk. And to stay there, man—it's nothing *but* risk. I mean, really, that's like walking on a high wire. Especially in New York, man, with all those musicians out there, and the critics, and old friends and fans, they all come out, and you better come up with something! In New York, if you get up there and you falter, people say—you can hear them do it!—they start to grumble. And you'll be wasted, you better give up. No, you have to have yourself together, really.

So that makes you want to take more risks.

Yeah. And that's what happened last night—I played some stuff I never played before, which was wonderful for me. That's all I ask. For somebody to trip me over the edge, for somebody to take me over the precipice. Make me do something I never heard before. Get me in trouble! Good, I love it! I like danger like that, because it makes me come up with some new stuff, new ideas. I don't want to bore myself! It's like, "Oh man, I've heard that before. You played that last night!" No. I want to avoid that. I want to stay alive, myself. It's the same way in an interview, too, exactly the same, it's *got* to be alive; otherwise it's dead. If it dies, man, we're all in trouble.

Someone I know who played Dixieland music when you did, and who in fact played with you once, told me recently that your playing was pretty far out even when you were playing Dixieland.

Well, I did have progressive tendencies from the start, really; you know, I was in traditional music, but I guess I was geared to go forward, from the beginning. I was always interested in "zero" improvisation, in other words, starting from zero, and finding my own way. And if you go your own way, it's going to be a little bit weird until people get used to it. So if you don't know what you're doing, and if you're going your own way, it's going to be far out [laughs].

Do you still play the clarinet at all?

No, I don't. I use the piano as a laboratory, but no, no, it's a temptation to me always . . . I saw a little clarinet a few weeks ago in a pawnshop—it was just beautiful. But I resist those temptations, because I don't want to take away from the main event. The soprano is so demanding, and so fulfilling. There's so many possibilities, and I'm still finding out what can be done with it, and what should not be done with it. So it's enough for me. Between that and the writing, that's plenty. I don't want to get sidetracked. I would love to play baritone, I would love to play clarinet, but it's a whole world in itself.

Do you find yourself going into higher registers as years go by, or going into a different area?

Doing different things in those areas. I find myself more able to particularize, because I have the experience now, and I can *hear* better than I used to. And I can imagine better, because I've heard a lot more, so sure, there's a lot of new possibilities. It's ongoing, man, it's ever unfolding. And that's it, that's the life, man. The fact that there's more that you don't know about yet.

Could you talk a little bit more about practicing?

It's research. Part of it is like muscle-building, and technical readiness building. But part of it is research, and that's the part that's interesting.

When you redo an old tune, is that research too?

Yeah. It demands to be done. These things insist on being done. They're there, and you see them again at a certain point, you say, "Well, now I know what to do with that better." There's something that doesn't change about it, the melody doesn't change. But the embodiment changes, the realization, the structure may change. The rhythm may change its guise, but it doesn't change its nature. What you do is you get down to the real nature more. It becomes itself, you see? The music becomes itself. That's the story. That's what takes time.

I want it to succeed more than before. I want it to fly better. It's like you strip things down, and you remove unessential parts, and you give it a new paint job, you make it slightly different; you clip it here . . . and then you send it back out again and you see if it flies better than it did twenty years ago.

But also it helps you become a better player.

It does. All these things do. That's how I got to here, is from all those experiences. Any kind of musical experience can do that for you: if somebody says, "do this," or "go in this door and play me a little solo," or "go and write this," or "accompany this person"—every one of those things, you come out of it learning something. Something you didn't know before, something you didn't hear before. So it's a collection of hundreds, thousands of experiences like that that give you a certain richness, flexibility.

My impression is that you pretty much get free rein to do what you want on the RCA records.

Oh, no! Oh, no . . . are you kidding? A big company like that? Well, it's always a struggle when you're working with a record company. It's a collaboration, but it's also a struggle. You want to do what you want to do, and they want to do what they want you to do, and you have to satisfy them and satisfy yourself and satisfy everybody. So it's a kind of a negotiation that goes down; you give a little, and you take a little. So far it's worked out great. But certain things they don't want me to do. You couldn't say that I just do what I want to do. But in the end, I do exactly what I want to do! [laughs].

Is RCA the only major American record company that you think you would want to work with?

Oh, they're the only ones that asked me! That's all. So far it's been great. I hope to do another one for them, too. But they didn't want to hear about a big band, for example. That's not what they wanted. So I did that for Hat Hut.

What would their reason be for not wanting the big band record?

Won't sell. Usually they say, "It won't sell," or they say, "It won't get airplay." It's the same kind of thing. Listen, these guys are experienced producers. You can't argue with them. They do know, and they're *right*. It's not that they're wrong. But, it's a struggle to do what you want to do, so you have to negotiate.

I was talking recently to a jazz musician who feels that he gets so much freedom recording for a Japanese label now that he wouldn't want to record for a big American company even if he were offered a contract, because he's tired of the restraints.

Well, I like restraints. I like to see what I can come up with that will cool them out, and still be something I want to do. It's a challenge to me. I like that. It's always been that way. In the old days, it was even harder; now,

I can pretty much do what I want. Some years ago, companies would propose ridiculous things for me to do. Columbia wanted me to record Vivaldi with strings. I would play the Vivaldi on the saxophone, and they have strings and a rhythm section, and it would sell like mad, right? So I didn't go for that one [laughs]. It's important to say no sometimes, very important.

Your record *The Straight Horn of Steve Lacy*, from 1962, with your pianoless quartet, seems pretty jarring even now. It must have seemed much more jarring then.

We couldn't get one job with that group. I saw [the baritone saxophonist] Charles Davis last night, and we were talking about that record. It's thirty years since we did that, and it sounds very fresh now. At that time, it really puzzled some critics and club owners. It was just considered too unusual. And that was it. You know, before this group that we have now, I had many, many other groups, and they all broke up, never lasted. But then finally you get the right combination, and it stays. But you have to go through those heartbreaking . . . and they're really heartbreaking [experiences]. Because they're good. But we couldn't find jobs! And if you don't have work, you don't have a group.

Regarding the Voice: Steve Lacy and Irene Aebi

interview by Jason Weiss

The following interview was conducted live in front of an audience, on 27 October 1993, as part of "The Archaic Smile" series of talks, organized by Marshall Reese and Steve Clay at Clay's gallery in New York, Granary Books. The year before, Lacy received a five-year "genius" award from the MacArthur Foundation. Framing the interview that night, he and Irene Aebi performed three songs as a duo: to begin, "Art," based on a late poem by Herman Melville; in the middle, "To Hal," based on Jack Spicer's poem; and to close the evening, a new piece finished that day, setting to music the death announcement of a friend, Lawrence Lacina. The interview was eventually published in the literary journal *Hambone* (1998) and reprinted the following year as the liner notes for *The Joan Miró Foundation Concert*, a duo record made by Lacy and Aebi.

Many people think of your music, Steve, as coming out of the tradition of Monk and certain other jazz masters, and they seem to miss the essential quality of voice that is very central to your sound. Not just in the way you play, but in the fact that you've been working regularly with Irene for nearly thirty years. How do you think Irene has made a difference in your work? How has she helped the music grow?

Lacy: In a way, she promulgated the songs, she invited the songs. All my life I've been interested in song and dance, words and music. However, without a great singer to work with, I don't think I would have written all those things. I would have had to find someone else, and I don't think I would have. So, it was a question of "please" and "okay." In other words, life itself. The word is vital.

Irene, you come from a very different place than Steve. You're Swiss. You were classically trained originally. How did entering the jazz world affect your approach to singing? Did improvisation pose any particular obstacles?

Aebi: No, the improvisation I liked very much, though I don't improvise with the voice. But I liked that I sing, and then there is improvisation, and then that makes me sing different. And my background, well, I was Swiss, the Swiss yodel and they have pretty strong voices, because we have valleys in between people, so we have this projection. And in jazz you have to know how to project. Though it took me a long time to project, because the songs weren't that easy and [the group was] very loud.

The first extended work that you engaged in was a piece called *The Way*, a six-song cycle based on Witter Bynner's translation of Lao Tzu. Steve, you wrote the first song in 1967, but it wasn't until 1979 that the quintet recorded the full version. On the record you noted that you first got turned on to the work in 1959, which therefore makes twenty years you were reading six poems. Can you describe the gestation of the work, and how the circumstances of performance affected the result?

L: Well, first it starts with words, and then you mull them over. And it could take a number of years of mulling before it turns into music. The cycle is called *Tao*, and the first piece I wrote was "The Way," in '67. It took about eight years of mulling before I found the pitches that go with those words. And of course Irene had to be there, it was written for her. Then after I found the pitches for the words, it took me years to find the foundation for the bass part. It was rewritten and rewritten many, many times, before it was in place, before the underpinnings were there. And I'm still working on it, actually. But the other five pieces were written in the late '60s, and then the whole cycle was in place. But it took quite a few years after that before we dared to do it with the words. The first version we did was on a record called *Wordless*, because there were no words. We did them instrumentally and sketched them out, in solo form, in different ways, and finally by 1979 we were performing them, the quintet, and we recorded it. Then after that, we let the whole thing rest for years, and a few years ago I did a solo version of it [on *Remains*, recorded in 1991], as it is now. And probably in the late '90s we'll take it up again in another version, with the words again. So it's an ongoing thing, it's a lifelong struggle really.

Irene, how long was the process for you till you felt you had gained possession of the songs?

A: Well, I had a lot of technical problems with Steve's music. You said I was classically trained—I went to the conservatory when I was studying violin, but I took my first voice lesson when I was forty. Gunther Schuller had recommended this voice teacher in Zurich, and she was horrified when my mother made the rendezvous saying, "My daughter's a jazz singer." She said, "Oh, my God!" So, it turns out that she's helped me quite a lot, and I've been working with her since then. She helped me so I wouldn't strain my voice, because Steve's material is very hard. You need to be something between an opera singer and a *chanson* singer, but he has such an extensive range. And if you're too classical it wouldn't fit either. So I think I was the right person. But it took me a long time. And now I can say each time I learn, it's getting easier.

The most ambitious project you've undertaken together is the work with Robert Creeley's poems. *Futurities* was based on twenty poems by Creeley. It was written as a ballet which Douglas Dunn and Elsa Wolliaston performed together. The sextet was augmented to a nonet—eight musicians and voice—and it was a full evening's performance. The set was designed by Kenneth Noland, one of his big chevrons with fluorescent paint that changed color with the light. First of all, how did Creeley's short, crisp poems take on such a big dimension?

L: Usually we work with small poems, and when you set them to music they become longer in time. And then if you repeat them, that's even longer in time. And then, if you do some improvisation and come back to them, that's quite a lot of time. So that's why we work with short poems. Now, some of those things were just a few lines. One of them is like a haiku, "The Eye." And the longest one there is "The Rhythm." So if you put twenty of those together with improvisation and all that, it runs about two hours. And that's perfect, it's an evening's entertainment with a break in it—ten songs, a break, and ten songs. It was designed like that for an evening's dance theater. Creeley was the man who wrote about love and marriage, and all the foibles of love, and the idea was to take a set of his poems and make like a jazz wedding. It worked pretty well, we played it all over Europe, and my dream is to bring it to the States.

Creeley is a poet who is very attuned to jazz, and certainly to music. How did his particular ear, his sense of phrasing and rhythm, affect the music that resulted?

L: The stuff was clear as a bell, to begin with. Especially the ones I chose were so simple, for the ear and the eye, and to deal with them, they were cut so succinctly, that it was relatively easy to set them to music. Because you could see them. He's one of the clearest poets I ever worked with. They were so expertly cut, like surgically, just pared down to the bone, no dross.

At what point did you meet Creeley?

L: I met him shortly before I started to write those things. I knew his work a little bit before then. But we met in Paris, Pierre Joris brought us together, because there was a radio program to do and Pierre knew he liked jazz and he knew I was dealing with poets. So he brought us together, and we did a program where he read and I improvised behind him. Then I was very struck with the poem "The Rhythm," and that was the beginning of the whole work. Then he sent me a book, and I started picking out things and the work was under way. It had a life of its own. That was in the early '80s. They were written in '82, '83.

Irene, did reading the work or meeting Creeley affect you in a particular way?

A: He walked in the house and we started to talk about some other poets I knew back when I was twenty-one in San Francisco, and he told me I knew the right guys. Jack Spicer, Robert Duncan. So that was nice, right away we got along.

With regard to meeting the poets whose work you're singing, what about your encounter with Samuel Beckett, for example? Was that the only time you met him?

A: Yeah, I just stared at his shoes. We were sitting on the floor watching some performance—a ridiculous performance outside of Paris. He likes to go to those kinds of performances that nobody goes to. We were sitting on the floor, in a loft, and I looked at his shoes. I just thought, Wow, I'm sitting next to Samuel Beckett, look at his shoes. You know, he didn't talk much. And then Steve gave him a bunch of records. And we made those three songs, three love songs. I would have never thought Beckett wrote love songs. So we called them existentialist love songs. Because the last song is, "I would like my love to die . . . *je voudrais que mon amour meure / qu'il pleuve sur le cimetière. . .*" But they're wonderful. Anyway, it was made into a ballet.

L: It was about 1979 that we met Beckett and that I set those three pieces into this cycle [*Sands*], with his blessing. He was extremely generous, he'd give you the shirt off his back.

Let's talk about Brion. Brion Gysin was the closest thing that you had to a regular lyricist. The first song was "Dreams," from about '75. As you've described it, Steve, the melody came to you in a dream.

L: It was written in '69, to Italian words by a playwright named Falzoni. I dreamed up this music based on his lyrics, called "Sogni." The melody was nice, but the words, nothing ever happened with the song. It was just lying there for years, and I thought, well, Brion Gysin invented the Dreamachine and he knows a lot about dreams, maybe he could give me some lyrics for this thing. So I gave him the melody and I said, "Please, can you dream up some words for me?" A few days later, he came and gave me these lyrics, and they were startling, like a dream. In fact, the first phrase is "Like a dream."

It's one of his permutation poems. The lines "Like a dream" and "so you seem," and then they just keep turning around.

L: And it fit like a dream, it was amazing. Then we recorded that in '75. Irene sang it in double voices, in major seconds. That was our first collaboration with Brion. Then he showed me all these other things he had, lyrics that had been sitting around, some of them since 1949. And they were fantastic! "Nowhere Street," and all these pieces that were for a musical that never got off the ground. Also, the cut-ups of William Burroughs's stuff that he had, from *Naked Lunch.* They were just begging for a composer, and there I was. So, we started to work together, and we realized almost twenty different pieces together.

Were there any particular ways that your collaboration affected your sense of reading?

L: First of all, it was Brion's own way of reading them. Brion was a great performer. He said he was born for a microphone, and I believe it. He had a way of reading his own stuff that was fantastic, it was really like a jazz musician. And every time he read it, it was different. He would play with it, it was really improvised, he was winging it. I've always been interested in pinning down speech sounds, speech rhythms, and getting the music exactly from the way people say it. Because if you say, "Hello!"—there's two pitches already, *BA-bom*, that's already a piece of music if you can write that down. So the distinction between words and music, for me, is very . . . next door, really. And my job is to get from one to the other, like a transmuting. So with Brion it was a pleasure, because it was already music, it was already jazz. And we both were good friends with Brion, we both loved him to death, and we both listened to him and the way he dealt these things. He showed us how it should go. But at the same time, they weren't written for him to sing—they were written for Irene to sing. So they had to be able to be sung by her, but they had to be true to the spirit and the nature of his way of delivering them. So that was fun.

Irene, you heard his delivery of the things you were going to sing. How did that affect you?

A: It didn't influence me too much. Sometimes he came on too heavy, he'd get carried away, like in "Nowhere Street." So I'd do it a little bit colder. And then in "Somebody Special" he told me that I have to be the voice of a little boy. He had a problem with ladies, he said that women were biological errors. He didn't say that to the end of his life, but you could feel it. So I tried to sing it like a little boy, and at that time I was young, it was fine. But a lot of songs I haven't done yet, and they're not all up to me to do, because some of them are very masculine. Like "Blue Baboon."

And the pieces from *Naked Lunch*.

A: Well, that was fun.

L: We did that with two voices, though.

A: Yeah, it had a male counter-voice.

That was also a ballet, *Stuff*.

L: Well, that was some heavy stuff, I didn't want to touch that stuff. It was all about junk. The thing is, I knew all about junk myself, and because I knew about it in the past, I didn't want to sing about it. But after about seven years of saying no, no, no, no, the stuff started to write itself. And I said, Oh my God, this stuff is coming out.

A: But it was beautifully written, and there was a point where we had to sing about needles and blood, it was wonderfully voiced and very hard to sing. Except we were singing very classically, and Steve said, "Well, you sound like two nurses in a hospital, you don't sound like junkies." It was cute, I liked it that way, *justement*. It's always nice to change things.

L: That's another work we'd like to bring to the States some time, *Stuff*. It's like dance theater, but it's all about junk. It's sort of a violent ballet. And it's all cut-ups of Brion, from Burroughs, from *Naked Lunch*.

Irene, you were telling me previously that once you have a song that Steve has written and you're going to start working on it, from that point you take it and go to your singing coach, and you work it out very precisely with the coach. And then, after all that, you come back to Steve. So he's not involved.

A: No. Sometimes he wonders, Ah, wow!

L: Yeah, the coach knows more about it than I do, really. And so does she.

A: It's out of his hands.

L: Once it's written, it's about realization by the person who's going to realize it.

So she ends up surprising you sometimes.

L: Oh, yeah.

A: Well, when we take a song, we just analyze it like any piece of music. Like we say, where is the high point, what we're going to do, accents. What we're not going to do, what would be heavy-handed. We also learn how to take dishonesty out of the song. So that takes a long time, especially if the text is good. All we want is really to get that right. And we don't work too much on emotions. Emotions are there in the voice anyway, and I think we don't have to work on emotions but on having good taste, in our choice of how to do the phrasing.

Your latest big project, *Vespers*, is a song cycle based on seven poems by the Bulgarian poet and recent vice-president Blaga Dimitrova. It sets a new tone in your work, reflected in the fact that the piece really seems to work better in churches and cathedrals. What was it you found in her poems that carried the music into that realm?

L: Well, they're little mystical texts, about life and death, and faith and hope and prayer, and communication. They're very small-scale, but they're very deep. They're very simple, but they're very profound. It's not the kind of thing you could sing in a nightclub.

A: But I did. And it was a disaster. The *New York Times* critic was there, it was a Tuesday night, the first set. It was part of the deal, we got money from—

L: It was a funding requirement.

A: And we couldn't find a church in New York that fast. We had this gig at the Sweet Basil, so they said, "Well, let's do it there." We had to do it five times, in order to qualify for that grant. So the jazz critics were there, and there were some Japanese people eating spaghetti, and the octet was jammed up on this little stage. We'd been recording the whole day, and I thought, Well, I sound pretty good, I've been singing for two days in the record studio. And then we gave out the words. But the jazz critic said he found the lyrics dreadful and the singing as well, and that I had an attitude. Well, maybe that came because I'm a Protestant and I really enjoyed singing them in the churches, because they're mystical songs. There is a beautiful poem at the end of *Vespers* that I like the most, that goes "Thank you, day, for being gone," and then, "Thank you for the blues, thank you for the pain," and at the end it says, "And above all the things I thank you for not forcing me to thank you on my knees." That's a wonderful thing to sing in a church. It's beautiful. And the churches are nice in America. They're large, and they have a beautiful echo. You don't need microphones. And everybody behaves.

Was there something about the material that dictated using a bigger group?

L: I don't know, I thought it needed a certain resonance. These things have a life of their own really, I try to stay out of it as much as possible. My job is to do what's supposed to be done. But it's the work itself that tells me what has to be done, it's not a conscious thing on my part. *Me* is inconsequential. It's the work itself that tells me what it needs. I had the idea from listening to the work, and looking into it, also to do it in churches and all, that it needed some more resonance. And finally, it had to do with the availability of certain musicians, and we zeroed in on French horn and tenor saxophone.

Some of the texts that you have chosen over the years are so delicate, or powerful, or so concentrated, that it seems only an intimate setting can do them justice. The first of these, I think, was *Tips*.

L: Yeah, *Tips* is based on Georges Braque's notebooks, and *Tips* is advice to artists, things that were very good advice to myself as an artist. And in the course of saying them to myself over and over again, they started to become music. So we made a kind of little piece out of it. But as you say, it's not something you do in a nightclub.

A: In schools.

L: In schools. It's like a didactic work, really. So we set it for just voice and two saxophones.

More recently, in the late 1980s, there's *Rushes*. Ten poems by Russian dissident poets: Mandelstam, Tsvetayeva, and Akhmatova. The composer Frederic Rzewski worked with the two of you on that, as a pianist. And now the three of you have just begun to work on the Judith Malina poems [released in 1995 as *Packet*].

A: I had the idea, I really liked those poems of hers, from a little book called *Poems of a Wandering Jewess*. I carried that around for a long time until my feminist moment began. There's a long poem called "The Melancholy Life of a Woman," and Steve made wonderful music to it. But we have a lot to do yet.

L: See, but these kinds of things, you have to find somewhere to do them. And where you going to do a thing like that?

A: We were just in Chicago, at this conference with the MacArthur people, and there were lots of scientists and interesting research people. I said, well, we should do this piece, "Particles," based on Richard Feynman, which is about molecules and atoms and the universe. So the scientists were very pleased, they loved it, they were smiling.

L: And you could never do that in a jazz club, that's for sure.

Do you think of "Particles" as specifically a duo piece?

L: I don't know. The duo is a new venture for us. It's only in the last year or so that we've been doing duos.

A: It took us twenty-seven years.

L: It took us a long time to boil it down. And now it works very well. It's the kind of thing you can do in all kinds of places. So it's opening up a lot of doors for us. Also, it allows us to do the kind of material that we don't know how else to realize it for the moment. But all the stuff we do, it can be done in trio, quartet, sextet, it can be done with an organ, with strings, it depends on the situation.

Another recent project along that line is *Thirteen Regards*, which are thirteen Tsvetayeva poems in French.

L: Yeah, that we're going to do for the French radio next month. That's going to be done with harpsichord, voice, and saxophone.

A: There again, they're very fine, very feminine songs. I read her autobiography, and I really tried to find out how she feels. And that's very important too, to read about those people, what kind of life they had. In that sense, if you don't know them in person, you can read about them and what they've been through. Tsvetayeva had an awfully hard life, and she was incredibly brave. She had two children, she never had money, her husband was always sick, and she was in love with Pasternak, and Rilke. And she wrote these wonderful letters in the middle of the night, when she had the only free moment to write. So, this made me sing very different when I read about these people. I really feel like I can read them in their voice. It's not me singing that, taking their words away and making them to my own emotion. They don't need anything, they just need to be sung.

In works like that, does the tradition of art songs seem to enter in more than jazz tradition?

L: Well, yeah, I've been accused of writing art songs for so long that I began to believe it, really. We started to call it art songs, why not? And that's what they are, but they're sort of jazz art songs, in the sense that there is improvisation attached to them and that what I do is jazz-based. I've been told that I have this field sewed up to myself. And it's true that there are not too many people working in those terms. But what Irene was just saying is very important, that you try not to betray the spirit of the poet, as if they were alive. So that you get their blessing, whether they're dead or alive.

Often with the songs, one of you has turned the other on to a poet.

L: Oh, she turned me on to many. For example, Jack Spicer. And the Judith Malina. And she asks for things that I would normally not have touched.

A: Yeah, once I went to Canada and met this old lady, Mary Frazee. She's a painter and she's almost blind, and she was really angry because she's going blind, but she was a wild, incredible person, and anyway we really liked each other. I told her things about my life and then she made those songs to me. I told her I was traveling with this bunch of guys, and they're machos, and we go on the road. So she made me this song called "A Complicated Scene." And so I came back with these poems, some were funny, and then there were poems like "If Wishes Were Horses," and there were love poems. Steve said, "Oh, no, that's too Irish." We had just read these Beckett songs . . .

L: For me, they were so soft and almost squishy. I couldn't handle it. It's too corny. And then the thing started working in my mind without me realizing, and after a while they started writing themselves. And finally they came out, nine of them. We called them *Puppies*, because they were soft and cuddly. And it turned out great. The whole thing's been recorded [Art Song Trio, *Puppies*, 1997]—with harpsichord, clarinet, and voice, I'm not on it—but the record company's been sitting on them for many months now.

A *Petite Fleur* for S.B.

interview by Philippe Carles

Since the beginning, Lacy always gave credit to Sidney Bechet for inspiring him to pick up the soprano saxophone. In April 1989 he wrote in the liner notes to the reissue of the complete Bechet sessions for RCA: "Sidney Bechet is 'The Love of My Life,' for the sound, the swing, the sense of the lyric form, and, especially, the burning passion of his style." Referring to the concert at Central Plaza mentioned below, Lacy writes, "He took my breath (and everyone else's) away, with his thrilling, New Orleans style arrangements of standards and classics. When he paused for dramatic effect, it was overwhelming! One could hear the people gasp, and the glasses chatter."

Lacy performed Bechet's tune "Petite Fleur" as well as Ellington's "The Mooche" on *Hot House*, the 1990 duo record with Mal Waldron for RCA. The following comments on Bechet appeared, as a monologue, in *Jazz Magazine* (February 1994).

The first time I heard Sidney Bechet, I was fifteen years old: it was "The Mooche." I knew the tune by Duke Ellington. I flipped—the combination of the band, him, the piece . . . He was on soprano. I started collecting the records then . . . It was a 78 on RCA, the other side was "Wild Man Blues."

I never met him but I saw him twice, when he came back to New York on tour (he was already living in Paris). There were two concerts at the Central Plaza, with Vic Dickenson on trombone, Cliff Jackson on piano, I don't remember the drummer anymore. Maybe Art Trappier . . . At the time, I had already started the clarinet and I was still playing a bit of piano. It was from hearing Sidney that I decided to get myself a soprano. The same year, I had the soprano . . .

He makes me think of Edith Piaf, because of the vibrato, the resonance, the intensity, and that French sound . . . If I chose to live in France, like him, it's not an accident, he influenced me, it was inevitable, I was programmed to come here, it was written . . . Although I didn't come because of that . . .

When I made the record with Mal Waldron where I play "Petite Fleur," I had Sidney in mind, obviously. That was an homage, a challenge. It was so famous, I heard it a thousand times in Paris. The first time I came, in 1965, I heard "Petite Fleur" . . . I had all of Bechet's records, especially the RCA, the Feetwarmers from 1923, the Blue Note, all the 78s. Today I still have them on cassettes.

When I heard the recordings from his French period, I was horrified, I didn't like it at all. What bothers me is the material, the pieces, and the accompaniment. It's as if they were split in two, him on one side and his disciples on the other. His music seemed diluted. The records he made in 1941 were magnificent, all the musicians were superb, there was Sid Catlett, his equals. Here [in France]—I wouldn't want to be cruel—there were worshipers, fans, disciples, but creators, no . . . He was always superb.

Sculpture and Jazz

interview by Alain Kirili

Lacy collaborated with artists from other disciplines since early in his career. Occasionally he performed with painters or sculptors and their work (most of his many records featured painters that he liked on the cover). One such event was with Japanese artist Yukio Imamura doing live action painting, along with Lacy and the dancer Shiro Daimon, in the third of three evenings at the Musée d'Art Moderne in Paris that Lacy dedicated to the late Brion Gysin at the end of 1986. Starting in the early 1990s he worked sometimes with the French sculptor Alain Kirili, at galleries as well as at Kirili's loft in lower Manhattan. Lacy described their collaboration in an interview with *Le Monde* (3 March 1994): "In his studio he sculpts while I play, or else I play at his openings, like in New York recently before his pieces. I walk around among the sculpture. It's like a personal choreography. Suddenly—we call it a 'baptism'—it creates effects on the senses, people look at the work with a different eye. They listen to the music differently as well."

Over the years Kirili has invited a number of adventurous musicians to perform with and among his sculptures, including Cecil Taylor. The following interview, in Paris on New Year's Eve of 1994, appeared in his book *Sculpture et Jazz* (Paris: Stock, 1996).

Steve, last night and the last time I saw you at the concert with Shiro Daimon, you told me of your concerns about the current situation in jazz. Could you speak more about that?

I have the impression that there is an ossification of the music whereas I love it when it's really lively and unpredictable. I sense that most of the good musicians in America, the masters, are all in the universities. They're no longer free to compose creative musical works. On the other hand, maybe something good will come out of this situation, new music that's freer, that's come out of this moment of imprisonment and partitioning. The music is like the Indians on the reservations. Even me, I've brought out a book with all my findings: that too is a sign. But it's also because I'm sixty years old now. What I hear, in general, it's always the same thing. But, for me, jazz is invention.

Do you lay claim to the word "jazz?"

Yes, yes. I've always liked that word. I belong to that designation. That's it.

What would be your definition of it?

For me, jazz is a mixture, a mingling, it's a music for dancing, for singing, for listening to. It's an invention. It's very complicated and I'm not going to explain it now, but it's a collective spontaneous combustion. It was an era, a moment, a situation, a mix of people and instruments, of African, American, European, South American origins. Truly a mix.

About this word "jazz," you who give the impression of departing from it sometimes, it's nice to hear you say it's a word you still like, that retains a certain force, because I think all the same it's one of the most beautiful words of the twentieth century.

Yes, yes, yes, I agree, really. And I like the word's mysterious origin. No one can say exactly why this word exists, there are a lot of theories but it remains mysterious, and maybe that's the best.

I'm always moved to see how, at a given moment, an artist chooses a medium. I started with painting and then suddenly I became a sculptor. You tried photography . . . And then finally, your marriage was with the soprano. Can you tell me why, subjectively, that instrument, the soprano?

It was a call. I heard Sidney Bechet, who was playing a piece by Duke Ellington. The combination of Bechet, Ellington, and that instrument produced an amazing effect on me, an irresistible call. It was as if I discovered my own voice. It was a certain *life force*, a *sound* rising up, a sublime shock. I fell in love with that material, with that instrument, with Bechet as well.

Bechet was the first jazz musician I met as a child. He came to our house and played in the kitchen. I was quite young.

He was a magician. What's more, there's a book about his life called *The Wizard of Jazz.*

These questions are always very difficult to answer. Why, at a given moment, do I like iron, aluminum? You speak about the material of the soprano. What stimulated you, seduced you, what made you choose that tonality, that sound of the soprano which, often, many musicians use only as a second horn? You've devoted your life to it, you've enlarged the repertoire.

In the choice of material, the choice of instrument, the choice of a tool, there are several aspects. First of all, there is the material itself, it's made of brass which vibrates by way of a plastic mouthpiece and which allows a reed made from cane to vibrate in turn. It's the voice of the cane itself. With the wind, one can hear the whistling in the cane, it's the voice in the material itself. We needed Sidney Bechet to rediscover that.

With the soprano, there is a timbre, a tonality.

Another aspect of my choice is the melodic register. It corresponds exactly to the right hand on the piano.

Something exceptional about you is that you respond to appeals coming from domains other than your music. That's very rare, there are so many people, artists, creators who are monolithic.

Yes, who are stuck in their domain. I hate that. I've always liked painting, theater, songs, dance, cinema, the sciences . . . So if I play jazz, it's in order to make use of all that.

I attended your beautiful show with Shiro Daimon at the auditorium of Les Halles this month. I noticed that his choreography stimulated your music.

Absolutely, I've been working with Shiro for eighteen years, sometimes two or three times a year, and it's always very enriching and surprising. He never disappoints me. He's an actor and in Japan being an actor means he can dance, sing, act, and also direct. He comes out of kabuki and Noh theater, and he's going toward jazz and freedom. He's a unique artist. In Japan, artists like him who break with tradition, who mix genres, are not encouraged.

The fact that he deconstructs and produces a sort of collage between kabuki and Noh would certainly make him seem an iconoclast . . . I'd also like you to tell me about the Five Spot in New York. What memory do you have of the place?

I lived two minutes away. I was part of Cecil Taylor's quartet and we played there for two weeks in 1956 and 1957. For us, it was very important. When we started there was sawdust on the floor and at the end of our engagement, when they saw that jazz really worked, they got rid of the beer bottles and took away the sawdust. It became a classier place. There was room for about sixty people at most . . .

I've seen the photo of the club on the album of *Eric Dolphy at the Five Spot*. Do you remember meeting artists there?

The painters started coming even before our engagement, and above all when Monk was there. There was de Kooning, Franz Kline, Herman Cherry, David Smith, and [Jackson] Pollock. All the painters went to the Cedar Bar. To the Club as well, where they gathered once a week to discuss painting with a lot of passion. Franz Kline loved jazz, de Kooning as well. For Monk, they were there every night.

Who introduced you to Monk?

I kept after him myself. It was in '58 when I recorded the album *Reflections* based on his music, with Mal Waldron and Elvin Jones. That was the first record of reflection on Monk's music. Before, he was the only one to play his own music.

Did he listen to it? What did he think?

He appreciated it a lot and he started to play "Ask Me Now" again until the end of his life. He hadn't played that since the '40s. I used to keep after him a lot because I was crazy about his music. I asked him tons of questions. But in fact, it was Nica the baroness [Pannonica de Koenigswarter] who persuaded him to come hear me when I was playing at the Five Spot with Jimmy Giuffre. Jimmy Guiffre took my trio and called it his quartet. At the time, he didn't know what to do and found my trio interesting but it didn't work out very well. He fired me after two weeks but during those two weeks, John Coltrane came and that's where he took notice of the soprano's tonality. After that, he started to play one. So it was during those two weeks that Monk, persuaded by Nica the baroness, came to hear me. In June, I was hired by Monk to play in another club. The Jazz Gallery was run by the same owners, the Termini brothers. That club held two hundred and fifty seats, it was on St. Marks Place. It was very nice, with an excellent acoustic. I played there for sixteen weeks with Monk. It's incredible that the place no longer exists. There were loads of people every night. Monk would arrive very late, toward midnight. Everyone was waiting but when he arrived it was superb, no one said a thing. We played till three or four in the morning.

I'd like to come back for a moment to John Coltrane. So you introduced him to the soprano . . .

He wasn't familiar with the soprano and when he learned that it was the same key as the tenor, it was a call for him. A few weeks later, I heard him play by telephone from Chicago. Don Cherry called me from Chicago and said, "Listen to this," and I heard Coltrane playing soprano.

One day you told me a splendid story about visiting Monk at home. You attended the rehearsal where he was watching his hands play in the mirror on the ceiling . . .

In his apartment, he had a mirror on the ceiling. He did a lot of research on the sound, the sonorities, the harmony. Really he was an inventor, a mathematician, a great musician. He found all his pieces, all his sonorities by watching himself in the mirror. It offers ideas and creates a sort of distortion, it turns things around. It disconcerts and he loved being disconcerted.

Creation comes from the handicaps one creates for oneself, it's a sort of confrontation. The wonderful film *Straight No Chaser* shows it well. Monk holds a handkerchief in his hand, a glass of whisky, he's wearing a big ring, a hat, an overcoat, and he's playing! It's probably what he'd call the best conditions for creating!

He loved mistakes. He was capable of making mistakes deliberately after someone who had messed up in the middle of his pieces. He played with the mistakes of others as well as his own. He loved that. There's a fairly well known anecdote where Monk attends a studio session with a big singer. She's marvelous and everything comes out fine, so Monk whispers in her ear: "Make a mistake." Perhaps it was Abbey Lincoln . . .

The story of Sonny Rollins and his rehearsal studio under the Williamsburg Bridge is an important one. You were there.

That was fantastic, a miracle, a revelation for me. Something very important in my conception of sound because there, under the bridge, we were inundated with sounds. There was the traffic of cars, planes, sometimes a helicopter, boats, horns, and all of that very loud. So it was no easy thing, in that noisy environment, to make our own sound heard. I was horrified. My sound was so small. Sonny Rollins was big, formidable and as loud as the horns from the boats. At the start I was tiny, I was crushed, so sad, frustrated, and then we played some interesting things, we played things by Monk, "Ask Me Now," we discussed harmonies, scales, shop talk. It was fantastic, but to play, to have a sound in that environment, was impossible. So I was very unnerved. Then the second time, it seemed to be clearer, more distinct, and the third time I began to really make a sound. I heard myself better at the same time that the sound emerged more. So the third time it began to not be so bad, and when I went home it was a veritable revelation. At home, it was easy to play, the sound was bigger, more evident. It was as if I had been working with weights.

It's in difficult conditions that one surpasses oneself. Sonny Rollins's idea was excellent.

You have to play against obstacles. You have to set up obstacles in order to call forth the strength. I was a bit intimidated because Sonny Rollins was a giant but really he was so nice with me, he helped me a lot. I tried to play like him, that was impossible but, by trying, I found my way.

One Shouldn't Make Too Much Noise, There's Enough Already

interview by Franck Médioni

The end of 1994 saw the publication of Lacy's book *Findings: My Experience with the Soprano Saxophone* (CMAP/Outre Mesure), which included not only his reflections on playing the instrument but also numerous exercises, études, compositions, and musical analyses. To celebrate the book, *Jazz Magazine* (February 1995) made him its cover story and offered brief testimonies to Lacy from twenty-three European and American saxophonists (Lol Coxhill, Michel Doneda, Jimmy Giuffre, François Jeanneau, André Jaume, Lee Konitz, Dave Liebman, Joe Lovano, Evan Parker, Michel Portal, Steve Potts, Sonny Rollins, Louis Sclavis, Archie Shepp, et al.), as well as the following interview.

25

When you started playing, there were almost no soprano saxophonists . . .

In effect, no one was playing it in 1952. I found my way all alone, therefore. A lot of musicians helped me along. Playing with them, I was really able to experience the many potentialities of the soprano, what music to play on that instrument. Its register is quite vast, as big as for the right hand of the piano. There are a lot of territories to explore: the moon on high, the earth below. The tonality is very feminine—I've studied the voices of women singers a lot. Louis Armstrong also played very high, with a lot of excitement, like in the operas of Puccini.

How do you perceive today the free movement in which you participated?

Necessary, salutary, and unavoidable. The music was starting to die and only a certain radicalism could keep it alive, to look after its spirit and sense of invention. Hard bop was all stuck in a corner, rigid. We had to make that revolution to maintain the freedom. But the important thing is also knowing what to do after, which is what we're doing now.

Stripping things down is part of your aesthetic concerns . . .

One shouldn't make too much noise. There's enough already. The less of it there is, the better.

Could one say that part of your music is articulated between construction and deconstruction?

Of course. I work on a piece by constructing it and deconstructing it. Of the initial phrase, there's nothing left at the end. But there's always the construction of the structure. Monk used to say, "Dig it." You have to excavate, evaluate, go all the way in order to understand a musical idea.

You don't play many phrases . . .

Too many still, sometimes. We have to be suspicious of the means at our disposal. The better one becomes, the worse one can play. It's crazy . . .

That's the opposite of what should happen . . .

Yes, but that's how it is.

What place does the blues have in your music?

Fundamental. It's the foundation of jazz. I started with the blues. I played with Kansas City musicians like Jimmy Rushing or Buck Clayton, great blues players. I was young, eighteen, but I understood what it was. New Orleans style was another form of the blues. Cecil Taylor and Monk were masters of the blues. Even in life, the blues is unavoidable.

Do you work at your instrument a lot?

I try to practice every day. Scales, working on harmonics, arpeggios, sound, rudiments . . . Sometimes I work on certain pieces.

How did you conceive your book?

It deals with everything I'm doing, everything I tell people who come to see me, who ask me for advice about the saxophone. I tell them all the same thing. This book speaks about my way of working, with certain exercises, and relates my experience with the soprano.

Who is it intended for?

Saxophonists, especially soprano, but perhaps also certain pianists or flute players.

Does it include specific modes of improvisation?

Yes. There are a few pieces that allow one to imagine and work with improvisation. But above all it's the technical aspect of the instrument that is treated. It's neither a guide nor a manual for improvisation.

You regularly teach master classes. Do you think you have a responsibility to teach?

Of course, it's always a pleasure—I learn a lot as well.

You've worked extensively with literature, using texts by Mandelstam, Lao Tzu, Cendrars, Beckett, William Burroughs, Brion Gysin . . .

One has to innovate. The presence of the voice in the music allows a certain suppleness, it's more human. It's another point of departure, therefore the arrival is different. We treat literature musically. We're not the only ones to do that. In France, André Hodeir already did it.

You also work with choreographers, painters, sculptors. Is your purpose the union, the unity of all the arts?

All the arts come out of the same thing essentially. There's space, there's time, and sound, colors, objects, bodies. There is a unity between all the arts. It seems logical to me to mix them. Maybe it's due to the influence of Duke Ellington, who worked a lot with song, dance, theater, in every domain. The unity was the music, it was everywhere, the whole thing was imbued with it. Before he was a composer, Ellington was a painter, besides. I'm a situationist in the sense that the music evolves as a function of different situations. Whether it's dance, theater, or painting, it's the situation that determines the music. I'm also a materialist, it's the piece, the sound, the material that interest me.

Your definition of jazz?

A search that is collective, friendly, fraternal, but also war. It's a dissident music by nature, origin and vocation. "We want to play like that, never mind the others, we want to play our own way." It's a partisan music. We're partisans of the music.

Your discography is one of the largest in the whole history of jazz. How do you explain this bulimia of recordings?

We had to mark each phase in the evolution of our music. It's like a photograph. Comparing allows us to forge ahead. I still have a drawer full of things that have not been realized . . .

Did you ever think of creating your own label?

How frightening! I'm not a businessman at all.

In what ways are you critical of your discography?

There are way too many recordings. Out of something like two hundred records, there must be twelve or thirteen that I regret. I also regret having made good records for gangsters. On some, I wasn't in good form. For others, I said yes when I should have said no. Others are poorly recorded, or poorly mastered—the speed is wrong, too slow. That drives me crazy. There are two like that. Aside from these failures, I'm content. I like nearly all of them. I'm very pleased with *Vespers*, and with nearly all of the records on Hat Art. I also like *Evidence*, recorded in 1961 with Don Cherry; *Gil Evans plus Ten* was fabulous. I'm happy with almost all the sextet's records.

Do you feel you've been recognized for what you're worth?

Too much and maybe not the right way. Some things are too much appreciated, others not enough. But that takes time, and I wouldn't want to complain.

Living Lacy

interview by Gérard Rouy

This short interview appeared in *Jazz Magazine* (March 1995) on the occasion of Lacy's newest project for himself, Aebi, and the pianist Frederic Rzewski, *Packet*, which reunited him with old friends. He traces the development of the work and the histories involved, starting with a series of concerts.

It's a *packet* of songs that comes from a *packet* of poems written by Judith Malina of the Living Theatre, which I've combined with one song by Julian Beck. We're going to perform that for two nights in Lille, in Treviso, Italy, we'll record it in Paris for the New Albion label, and present it for two nights with Judith at the American Center in Paris. So that makes a *packet* of concerts. At the American Center, we'll also make a *packet* of music, we'll play a piece by Frederic Rzewski, *De Profundis*, based on a text by Oscar Wilde, an incredible piece where he recites and plays piano at the same time, a sort of one-man show with sighs, whistling, sounds, flaps. Rzewski is one of the greatest composers and pianists in the world, he's a genius. He too was associated with the Living Theatre and knew Julian Beck and Judith Malina well. What's more, the Oscar Wilde piece is dedicated to a member of the Living Theatre who died years ago. So there's a connection between all these things. At the American Center I'll even play a bit of Thelonious Monk, because all that began during the bebop era in the 1950s in New York.

I was very involved with the Living, we were together in Italy in the '60s, in '68. I was also supposed to do the music for the play *The Connection*, for the European version, but that didn't work out, I was afraid. I was afraid of the drug, and that's precisely the subject of the play; I'm not afraid anymore. At the American Center, Judith Malina will be there with her partner Hanon Reznikov. That's all that remains of the Living Theatre. They work a lot, they find groups everywhere, they stage things in the street, it's always street theater. They're based in New York but travel all over Europe.

So Irene Aebi will say the texts and sing the songs . . .

It's a cycle of songs, the subjects are quite varied: the life and death of women, getting old. They're rather theatrical songs, concerning women. Julian Beck's song is about theater. Some things are ironic, tragic, there are blues, waltzes, all sorts of forms, it all makes up an ensemble.

Scratching the Seventies

interview by Étienne Brunet

Some twenty years later, the five albums Lacy made for Pierre Barouh's Saravah label in Paris were reissued by the label in 1997 as a three-CD set, *Scratching the Seventies / Dreams*. Those albums were: *Roba* (1969), *Lapis* (1971), *Scraps* (1974), *Dreams* (1975), and *The Owl* (1977); the first was recorded in Rome, the rest in Paris. At a time when his sextet had been dissolved and he was performing almost entirely in trios and duos, and as a soloist, it was fitting that these recordings—which displayed so much of his musical research from an earlier period, and his first flowering as a composer—should be made available again. The saxophonist Étienne Brunet, active in the French improvised music scene for two decades and a co-producer of the reissue, interviewed Lacy in Paris on 5 August 1996 for the liner notes, and thus was able to get him to discuss at some length both the times when the music was made and each of the many works that went into these recordings.

Was Europe a voluntary exile for you?

The first time I came for a gig, a change of scene, for pleasure, for my own interest. Then I met Irene Aebi. We left for a long trip to Buenos Aires. We returned to New York in '67 and it was worse than ever. I was there with Irene and we did two or three concerts in the whole year! On the other hand, we experimented with the use of voice in our music for the first time. We formed a band with Karl Berger, Enrico Rava, Kent Carter, and Paul Motian. We came back to Europe for a concert in Hamburg. After that, nothing more. Everyone went their own way. Irene and I spent two years in Rome and we returned to Paris in 1970 to scratch around, to find good musicians and work. There were a lot of good musicians. They were all available. A number of them lived in the same hotel that we did, the Hôtel de Buci. There was Sunny Murray, the guys from the Art Ensemble, Ronnie Beer, people from northern Europe, French, Africans, Americans, it was a beautiful mix.

In and around all that we found Beb Guerin, François Tusques, [Henri] Texier, [Jacques] Thollot, Aldo Romano. Everybody was in the same soup and no one was rich. There was not a lot of work but there was a good spirit. I liked it a lot, we had a great time. Everyone was broke but we had fun. It was interesting, a very nice sort of fermentation, very free, without complexes and without money, without hope, without despair but with joy. There was a real love for the music and a willingness to experiment.

The musicians at that time were inclined toward total improvisation?

Yes, exactly. Of course, I arrived with all of what I'd been up to, with my compositions. I wanted to play them with the musicians here. I was looking for musicians who were able to decipher my music, to play it. But I couldn't ask that of them right away. You have to stimulate others before asking them for a favor. You've got to turn them on before they turn you on. You have to find a common ground, a lingua franca. That common thing was to play free. Everyone could improvise! I also had some simple pieces with little abstract drawings, *post-free* pieces with some directions sketched out. We could also play Monk's tunes. There were no problems playing! There was a lot of total improvisation. From the point of view of an ensemble, the guys from the Art Ensemble of Chicago were masters of improvisation. At the time they were a quartet. Don Moye was my drummer. But they had a lot more work than me, so they took my drummer and I couldn't say a thing. What could I have said? Besides, we were good friends. I was also good friends with Braxton. In '70, with Bénédicte Pesle, who helped us a lot, at the Théâtre de l'Épée de Bois we organized a sort of marathon of dance, art, and music that lasted a day or a weekend, I can't recall. The public came en masse. It was a complete success but once expenses were paid, there was no money left for the musicians in my band (Irene, Jerome Cooper, Ambrose Jackson, and Kent Carter). Anthony Braxton played solo at the marathon too, which impressed me a lot.

Was there a sort of musical philosophy that went with the hopes of the time: change the world and make people better through the music?

Yes, there's always been a certain idealism in jazz. If that idealism disappears, I'll disappear as well. When the music becomes cynical, it's death. Our politics were to survive by playing an uncontaminated music. We had a real desire to find a collective originality. Each of us had come from another country, with another history, other manners, other habits, other tastes for playing together. In that period the American Center was very important. We felt free there. Everyone used it as a rehearsal space, a place to meet and perform. We did some things that worked and others that didn't. At the American Center I directed a workshop that lasted a year and a half: the Free Jazz Workshop. It was my idea. It was very interesting. Anyone could come and do whatever they wanted for three hours, once a week, for ten francs! It was terrific, there were instrumentalists, painters, dancers, and children. It was really *free*, delirious. But it was serious too, after several weeks it sounded really good! This Free Jazz Workshop was part of our concept of *Roba*, developed in Rome in '68 with *art pauvre*. It was a concept of material, freedom of the material. The possibility of taking any material at all and using it any way you want. No constraints. Not easy, though. Since the '60s, I had that idea of the material. To play, to juggle with the sound material, with the *Roba*. It's an Italian word that means thing, material, condition. *Roba* means a lot of things.

The album *Lapis* was recorded in 1971. What's the significance of the title?

That's my first solo work. The idea came to me after hearing Braxton play solo at the Épée de Bois. I wanted to record in a studio first before playing alone in public.

Lapis is a very old word. Lapis lazuli is a stone. A sort of writing in the stone. A trace, a notch, a mark in the stone. I allowed myself all the freedom in the world and then some. I was very influenced by the ideas of Marcel Duchamp: to be able to put absolutely anything into a work of art. I really enjoyed making that record.

At the time that was a very new method, to record using overdubs!

I had already heard a record by Brion Gysin called *Electronic Poetry*. A record that used overdubs, very experimental. I was struck by the many possibilities of re-recording. So I prepared the material for my record and I had fun using all sorts of objects: knitting needles, ashtrays, keys, finger snapping, loose change, and also silence. Daniel [Vallancien], the sound engineer, was very sympathetic. He helped me a lot and we had a real collaboration. I liked that record a lot and I was very proud of it.

It's a very avant-garde record. In "Cryptosphere" why did you use a recording by Ruby Braff? I like that idea a lot. It's very surprising!

That idea embodies the years when we were scratching. Literally I scratched the saxophone through my hair. It's a sound I used. The idea of "Cryptosphere" is the music that's hidden. It's the music under the rug. There is a normal music at the center of the piece and another music, hidden in the corners, on the ground and behind the furniture. It's the idea of a hidden sphere. That piece is dedicated to Frederic Rzewski. He's the one who explained this concept to me. I was very impressed! So, I asked the sound engineer to choose a record of *normal* jazz by chance and he brought me the one by Ruby Braff! Perfect! We played the record and I experimented with unusual sounds. I used the saxophone in an original manner. I scratched the reed through my hair. It's an image, a cryptospheric painting. On that record I play a programmatic music, a descriptive music with the traffic and car noises in "Highway" or with the rain and the wind in "Precipitation Suite." I wanted to make a music between writing and painting.

Can we go piece by piece through your third album for Saravah, *Scraps*?

I haven't listened to those recordings in years. *Scraps* is a bit more colorful but just as experimental as *Lapis*. "Ladies" is a portrait of Billie Holiday: she was magnificent! But I think it wasn't elegant enough for her as a tribute. "Obituary" is a death announcement that we received. Gordon Mac Intyre was a good friend of Irene's and mine. We had known him in Rome and he died in India. It was a shock to me reading that announcement and I set it to music as is! It's a nice homage and rather free. "Scraps" is a sort of description of Lenny Bruce. I had seen him in New York and he really inspired me. Comedians are great improvisers and they proceed the same way that we do. They write a lot of material, and then they plunge into the unknown. Each reply contains a certain percentage of improvisation and of something new. We proceed likewise: in music there's always something new that appears. "Name" is part of the Tao cycle, it's an instrumental version. "Torments" is based on a text by the painter [Gaston] Chaissac. It's a song without words dedicated to Erik Satie. I used his harmonies. I like Satie more and more.

Is your music always written in reference to an artist?

Almost always. There's literature, painting, theater, and dance in all the music we play. Even if it seems to be solo saxophone, it's always based on something else which is based on something else, and so on! There's always baggage behind this music. "Pearl Street" evokes a nostalgic memory of a street in New York in the 1950s. That piece is dedicated to Arnold Schoenberg. At the time I knew how to write a melody and a bass line. The music was clear at the top and a little at the bottom. But at the center I wasn't yet in a position to write real harmonic or rhythmic structures. I was a budding composer . . . We combined written elements and improvised. I didn't really know what to put for chords. I had written bass and piano parts that were too complex. It was too hard to decipher. In spite of all that, Michael [Smith] and Kent [Carter] played those parts that were so difficult!

"The Wire" is an homage to Albert Ayler. The metronome beats out the last minutes of his life. "The Wire" signifies the end, the wire that marks the boundary and announces his death. The two sopranos and the two cellos play in the high register. This piece is the last in a cycle called *Shots*. I've written a lot of music connected to a human being's death, or in memory of someone or to save a person from death. It's one of my most important themes. In this record all the pieces are an homage to the dead! *Scraps* is a sort of elegiac record.

For the cover of this recording you used a child's drawing. The shortcut from childhood to death is disturbing. What do you think about it twenty years later?

At the time it seemed more alive to me than that! For me, the rapport between a record's cover and the music is fundamental. Each time we listen to a record, we touch its cover and we see its image. I liked that child's drawing and found it very fresh, very innocent and inventive, in the spirit of our music. That album is called *Scraps*, which means fragments, little things that are found. The other meaning of the word is scuffle, at the time it was really a scuffle to survive. I was broke and life was not always evident!

The album *Dreams*, which came out in 1975, was the beginning of a fruitful collaboration with the great and joyful Brion Gysin. Was it a turning point in your work?

I had met him two years before. We became inseparable friends. He was a painter, photographer, poet, performer, inventor. He had done an electronic poem using a pistol shot recopied many times on magnetic tape. It really swings. Everything that Brion touched was brought to perfection. He was a great artist, incredibly creative. He had imagined a dream machine and naturally I asked him for lyrics to "Dreams." We played that piece often. "Dreams" is recorded in multitrack, I even play a piano part that's barely perceptible, like a little bell in the distance. For me, that piece is my best work from the '70s. Everything we've played since then unfolds from that musical dream. It was finally clear! Before, we kept stubbornly searching, now we had found the right direction! It's the start of the *poly-free*, the freedom to choose a constraint, to do something written and improvised simultaneously: the *Free not Free* in a way. In three minutes we have a good melody supported by a harmony and a rhythmic structure that were ideal, a color and a story. "Dreams" is the first of my compositions where I was totally satisfied. I've enjoyed listening to that record many times. Irene's work is magnificent, I asked her to do some crazy things and she carried it off with great courage and a sublime artistic spirit. Her contribution is fundamental in my work.

The first piece on the record is "The Uh Uh Uh."

That's dedicated to Jimi Hendrix, it's the only rock tune that I've ever played! I adored Jimi Hendrix. A few years later we did a better version of that piece.

"The Oil" has to do with psychoanalysis, with all the dealings between people, the misunderstandings and innuendoes that I've encountered in Zurich. It's at once a description of the city and an homage to Sigmund Freud. That's a complex city! The rhythm of the piece beats like the heart of Zurich with a heavy, mechanical component. That component picks up from psychiatry, as in all great cities!

"The Wane" is the last part of the suite called *The Woe*. It's about the end of the Vietnam war. "The Wane" is a sort of beguine. It's the only part of that melodrama of war that we still play. It's a meditation on that postwar echo with the shadow of a phrase by Alban Berg.

"Crops" is an homage to Harry Partch, who inspired me a lot. I still study his work. That composition is also inspired by a stay in the Ardèche where I saw lots of agriculture. I was struck by the symmetry and the alignment of the harvests. The piece is a bit rustic. I've garnered Harry Partch's concepts and I wanted to thank him with that piece.

Fifth and last album on Saravah: *The Owl*, with the unforgettable song "Somebody Special."

"Somebody Special" is a sort of children's song that says: I would like somebody to take care of me, but somebody special! The composition is based on five notes and nothing more. The introduction offers that possibility of limitation. It's my secret. If I've invented something, it's right there. Something formal, a way of writing a form, with a manner of proceeding harmonically and making divisions . . . Oh, Duke Ellington was probably the first to play with structures of this type! And Jelly Roll Morton too. You write a little thing for two measures, then another melody for four measures, you improvise on the bridge, you write another element and you return to the introduction. That formal and structural invention is particular to jazz. It does not necessarily exist in "standards."

At each new period since New Orleans jazz, musicians have used more and more changes on a chord, up to the twelve chromatic notes in bebop and free jazz. The collaboration with Brion, the avant-gardist and contemporary, led you to a rigorous modality comparable to that of north Indian classical music: to improvise permutations based on five notes, to the exclusion of all the others. Is it the return to a new simplicity?

Brion was the absolute master of permutations! In Arabic music one also finds infinite variations. But that comes too from Johann Sebastian Bach, and from jazz. I adore limits, as did Brion. Paul Klee, Igor Stravinsky, and Thelonious Monk also loved constraints and voluntary limits. I explain in my book *Findings* how to use two notes: there are only two notes left in the universe, what to do? Working with these two notes seems boring, but with tenacity one discovers an incredible universe where only the imagination and fatigue limit the infinite. Many cultures in the world happily use but five notes. Their instruments can't play more than that.

Does this conception of music date back to your meeting Brion?

No, I was working in that direction well before. My collaboration with Brion reinforced that path. For example, I had written the words to a piece, "Note," where I used the same process, a very limited choice of words: Note, Take, Mind, Friend, Stop. It was like a poetic telegram, and I had thought a lot about that very limited choice of words which functioned musically on their own.

[Getting back to *The Owl*, the record on Saravah:] "Blinks" is a piece in homage to Edward Kid Ory, the great New Orleans trombonist. He played with Louis Armstrong and had his own group. His favorite musical phrase was: *pop, popo-pop, popo-pop, popo-pop* . . . I took up his phrase and constructed a piece that goes up and down harmonically in a loop. It functions very well structurally. We've played it *billions* of times!

"The Owl" is based on a poem by Apollinaire, from *Bestiaire*: "*Mon pauvre coeur est un hibou / Qu'on cloue, qu'on décloue, qu'on recloue* (My poor heart is an owl / That they pin down, they unpin, they pin back down)." It's an homage to Anton Webern. The melody rises up through space, like in his work. It's the first version of a composition that we've played many, many times. I've written and rewritten that piece. I've changed and restructured the rhythm and harmony often, but the melody hasn't changed. On this record we have the first sung version. At the time the rhythm was in 4/4, a bit free; now we play "The Owl" in 4/4 and 5/4. Things become clearer with time. We rework, redefine the harmony, we change the bass lines, we study the composition so that it evolves in a more harmonic sense, more mathematical, more simple.

"Touchstones" is an amulet, a magic stone to touch, a gri-gri for setting one's mind at ease and remembering. "Touchstones" is a small suite of three stories, three magic formulas. "Spell" is a derisive story by Salvador Dalí about a fly salad. It was published in *Paris Match*: "*Prendre cent mouches par personne, laisser macérer dix-sept minutes* (Take a hundred flies per person, let them soak for seventeen minutes) . . ." It's a surrealist salad. The music is dedicated to Chopin. "Wish," after [Francis] Picabia, on the other hand, is truly an existential song: life oppresses me but I don't want to escape, I want to stay, I'm nailed to the center of life. It's dedicated to Boris Vian. It's a real cry from the heart, Irene is astounding. The text of "Lesson" comes from a box of dietetic biscuits by Dr. Ohsawa. He was the inventor of macrobiotic cuisine. He sold his biscuits with a nice poem written on the box. The music is an homage to Tchaikovsky. I liked him a lot and was very influenced by him. I had a real debt to him and I wanted to pay it back.

We always have that strange line drawn between the homage and the leading idea of the composition, that line refers often to personalities who are diametrically opposed.

It's fairly subtle, sometimes I don't understand the reason for it right away. One always has to ask oneself what is the spirit that directs us, that dictates ideas to us . . . It's a sort of collaboration between myself and a person who is probably deceased, an artist, an architect, actor, a musician, etc.

If we didn't have enough room on this reissue, would you allow me to leave out the last piece on the last Saravah record, "Notre Vie?"

No, because it's the beginning of our work with the so-called *chanson française*. I dared to use that sacred tongue which is not my own with texts of very high quality: "Notre Vie" by Paul Éluard, Dalí, Picabia, etc. That's an important and frustrating aspect of all our efforts, because we've had no reaction at all from anyone. Total silence! Not good, nor bad, nothing!

To end, can you speak to me about your friendship with Steve Potts, your faithful companion for the past quarter-century?

Steve Potts is one of my best collaborators, one of the most important in my life. He's my right hand and my heart. He's a great friend and a great musician. His stimulation leads our music to a perfect and miraculous chemistry.

Steve Lacy and Brion Gysin, at the Rencontres Internationales d'Art Contemporain, La Rochelle, France, June 1980. Photo: Michel Cormier.

Sextet, in Salzburg, November 1983. Left to right Steve Potts (as), Oliver Johnson (d), Steve Lacy (ss), Jean-Jacques Avenel (b), Bobby Few (p), Irene Aebi (c). Photo: Helmut Frühauf.

Cecil Taylor and Steve Lacy, Vitrolles jazz festival, France, July 1984. Photo: Guy Le Querrec.

Steve Lacy and Steve Potts, Willisau, Switzerland, 1985. Photo: Manfred Rinderspacher.

Lacy at home, rue du Temple, Paris, May 1986.
Photo: Henry Glendover.

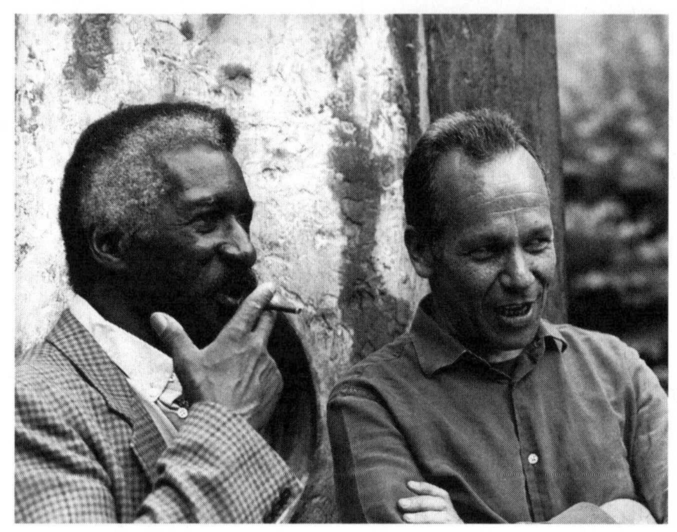

Mal Waldron and Steve Lacy,
Portland, Oregon, June 1987. Photo: Monique Goldstein.

Alain Kirili and Steve Lacy, in Alain Kirili's studio, New York City, 1992.
Photo: © Ariane Lopez-Huici 1992.

Shiro Daimon and Steve Lacy, "Here There Air," Théâtre des Amandiers, Nanterre, France, 1994. Photo: Jean Gros-Abadie.

Gunther Schuller and Steve Lacy at Harvard University, 1994.
Photo: © Paula Lerner 1994.

(opposite) Lacy at home,
rue des Pavillons, Paris, 1997.
Photo: Vincent Lainé.

Steve Lacy, Paris, 1997. Photo: © Lee Friedlander 2005.

Irene Aebi and Steve Lacy performing *The Cry*, Tampere Jazz Happening, Finland, November 1998. Photo: Maarit Kytöharju.

Steve Lacy septet performing *The Cry*, American première, Washington, June 1998. Left to right Petia Kaufman (harpsichord), Irene Aebi (voc), Steve Lacy (ss), Jean-Jacques Avenel (b), Tina Wrase (ss), Cathrin Pfeifer (acc), Daniel "Topo" Gioia (perc). Photo: Michael Wilderman/Jazz Visions.

Trio, Buffalo, N.Y., April 1999. Left to right Jean-Jacques Avenel (b), Steve Lacy (ss), John Betsch (d). Photo: © Susan O'Connor.

Quintet performing *The Beat Suite*, New York City, August 2003. Left to right Steve Lacy (ss), Jean-Jacques Avenel (b), George Lewis (tb), John Betsch (d) (not in picture: Irene Aebi). Photo: Gilles Laheurte.

Monksiland quintet, New York City, March 2004. Left to right Steve Lacy (ss), Roswell Rudd (tb), Jean-Jacques Avenel (b), Dave Douglas (tp), John Betsch (d). Photo: Gilles Laheurte.

Forget Paris

interview by John Corbett

Lacy and Aebi first left Paris for a year's residency in Berlin, where this interview took place in October 1996, published in *Down Beat* (February 1997). That year Lacy was developing his jazz opera *The Cry*, based on twelve poems by the Bangladeshi poet Taslima Nasrin, whose candid writings about the plight of women, as well as their desires, earned her a death warrant from Islamic fundamentalists at home and thus subsequently exile. Bold and stirring in its narrative line, with a sound influenced by its cultural sources, *The Cry* featured a sparkling septet that included harpsichord and accordion, in which women played the major role; on stage, the performers' vests (designed by Pia Myrvold) displayed excerpts of the texts, as if to protect them against the inherent dangers. The work was given its première in Berlin in January 1997, and was due to be presented after that in Paris at the Banlieues Blues festival, but the festival balked when Nasrin, now a sort of celebrity, decided she no longer wanted to perform the Bengali recitations of her text as she had at the première. Recalling the resourcefulness of his early years, Lacy produced the work himself for three sold-out nights in April at the longtime standby of improvised music in Paris, the Théâtre Dunois. The same group recorded *The Cry* the following year and performed it in the United States.

Road Trip: January 1996

[Soprano saxophonist Steve Lacy picks up shop and hits the trail, leaving Paris, the cosmo metropolis that he and his wife and main collaborator, singer and string player Irene Aebi, have called home for the last quarter-century. Their temporary new residence: Berlin. Under a fellowship from the DAAD, the German government's arts foundation, Lacy will live and work in the reunified capital city. But this is only the latest in an ongoing string of road trips that stretch back like a freeway to the early part of Lacy's career.]

chapter one: the road

An imperative to go where the music tells you to go. "I live on the road," muses Lacy, reclining with an espresso in his airy Berlin apartment. "I spend an awful lot of time in airports, on airplanes. And we're not even certain where the next turn will take us. I'm still on the road, man. Paris is finished for the moment. We've used up Paris. It's not a very good moment in Paris right now—they're blowing it! Maybe we'll go back when it swings the other way." Beyond the year-long residency, Lacy says he and Aebi will stay awhile in Berlin, a city that has quickly proven, as he puts it, "very fruitful." Indeed, already he's been the focus of FMP's five-day Workshop Freie Musik, performing with five pianists (Misha Mengelberg, Marilyn Crispell, Ulrich Gumpert, Fred van Hove, and Vladimir Miller), a festival documented on the live CD *Five Facings*. And over this particular late-October weekend, he shares the spotlight (albeit in separate performances) with pianist Cecil Taylor at the Total Music Meeting, as one of "Two Portraits." (Lacy later jokes: "Let's call it 'Two Sketches.' We did what we could.")

"I've always gone where the music takes me," Lacy explains. "It isn't that I want to go here or there, it's that that's where the music is. The music has taken me all over the world. And that's also in terms of living, because I have to live where Irene and I can operate—where I can play and she can sing and I can write and we can have a group and realize things. Berlin has been a refreshing change and opened up everything for me." With change of scenery comes a change of scene, and Lacy has disbanded his longest-lasting band, the Steve Lacy Sextet, paring it down to a more economical trio with bassist Jean-Jacques Avenel and drummer John Betsch. It's been a period of great development and turmoil, honors and knocks: In 1992 Lacy received the prestigious (and lucrative) MacArthur Fellowship, while in the same year, after five records, he was unceremoniously dropped from RCA/Novus, his first liaison as a leader with a major record label. In 1994 his book *Findings: My Experience with the Soprano Saxophone* was published, a crowning achievement in his purposeful and exhaustive self-documentation.

Through triumph and pain, Lacy's main activities continue to center around composing for Aebi's voice. "We're working on an opera all this year, but we're already performing bits of it here and there," he reports. In fact, Lacy's been metamorphosing words into music since 1967, when he adapted Lao Tzu's *The Way*. Ever road warriors, he and Aebi will take off the next morning—the day after his portion of the Two Portraits fest is done—to present the opera-in-progress at a French festival. Strange coincidences abound: Bangladeshi poet Taslima Nasrin, whose work Lacy had already been setting to music, turned out to be the couple's upstairs neighbor when they arrived in Berlin. Now Lacy's turning her text into the opera's libretto. "It's not a coincidence at all; it's one of those written-in-the-stars things. This is what we came to do here—though we didn't know that. It's an adventure also, and it's a dangerous adventure, so we're playing it cool." It's an adventure, of course, because opera isn't exactly en mode in the jazz world these days. "I swore I'd never do it. I swore, oh man, I never want to do that!" exclaims Lacy. "We had enough trouble with musical theater pieces and dance pieces."

Road Trip: 1970

[Based in Rome, Lacy and his Swiss-born wife are frustrated playing with enthusiastic, but amateur, Italian musicians. Lacy can't find anyone whose reading skills are strong enough to perform the music he's writing. And furthermore, there are no good drummers around. "I played this festival in '69 outside of Paris, and there were all the cats from Chicago. There was Roscoe Mitchell, Anthony Braxton, Leo Smith. There were good drummers and Bobby Few the piano player. And I said: Wow, these guys live in Paris, that's where I want to go." Go where the music tells you to go.]

chapter two: mixed media

The Two Portraits pairing suggests a crossing. "Cecil and I have crossed paths for many, many years," the sixty-two-year-old recalls. "Going back to 1953 when he plucked me out of the traditional music and threw me into the avant-garde ocean." Lacy performed and recorded with Taylor for six years. "He's a very important figure in my life; he showed me the way to find my own music. I discovered Monk through Cecil, he turned me on to dance like Cunningham and Balanchine; he clued me in on politics, films, a certain amount of literature and theater, and humanity, people." At the last minute, the whimsical and unpredictable Taylor chooses not to capitalize on a potential (and widely anticipated) mid-fest duet with Lacy, so the soprano saxophonist's sparkling solo set, full of Monk and Lacy's own compositions, leaves the crux uncrossed. "Cecil likes to leave people hanging," grins Lacy afterward, unfazed.

In the four decades since joining "Cecil's gang" (his term), Lacy has immersed himself in collaborations with a wide array of different art forms. This polymorphousness is evidenced at Two Portraits, where Lacy plays with dancer/performer Shiro Daimon and actors Hanon Reznikov and Judith Malina. "I was inspired by Duke Ellington, who was a total arts man. His stuff involved the visual—he was a painter himself—and poetry and dance and music and theater and everything. And on the other hand, Harry Partch. Gil Evans took me to see Partch's show *The Bewitched* in '57 or '58 in New York. It was musical theater with song and dance and speech, and things were falling out of the ceiling and floor, like a happening. But it was completely controlled, it wasn't accidental or chance. A total theater piece, I saw it two nights in a row. Even before that I was taken to see Broadway shows—that's one of the things my family did for me that I'm really grateful for. Plus I've always been interested in painting. Since I was a kid I was interested in art, in fact I used to try to make a little bit myself.

"To me it seems the most natural thing in the world is not to combine but to employ the various media together. Why not? Like Duchamp said, you can put anything you want in a work of art. That was a very important statement and he proved it in his own work. I've always been eager to collaborate with dancers, painters, poets, actors, cinema, whatever. It makes the music move. Music has to be what it normally would not be. It requires something new of the music, and I like that urgency, that need to change, to adapt, to invent." Lacy says he can learn more from a painter, actor, comedian, or clown than from another musician. "Sports figures, too. You can get inspired watching some athletes, get ideas about rhythm, line, timing, dynamics. It's all there. We're in the same boat, we're here to entertain each other . . . until the ship goes down!"

Road Trip: 1966

[A musical turning point comes in the midst of a misadventure in Argentina, with trumpeter Enrico Rava, bassist Johnny Dyani, drummer Louis Moholo, and Irene along for the ride: "Tangled up in the tango! I learned what the tango was, down there, and it ain't funny. But since then tango has been a very deep part of the music I do—there must be hundreds of little tango-type movements in the music I write. It was a disaster. That was the wrong group at the wrong time in the wrong place playing the wrong kind of music, the wrong money and the wrong hotel. And yet it was very important. The music was incredible, but the politics . . . We arrived, and there were tanks in the streets; they were prohibiting the Beatles. It was a fascist jungle, and also there were old Nazis running around. And we arrived with our little free-jazz routine, and the posters advertised: 'Revolution In Jazz!' You can imagine the reaction. We were on one-way tickets, and playing off the door of the theater. It's a recipe for disaster. The rest is history. Nine months we languished down there. We played all we could, and we performed, and eventually we found a small public that appreciated what we were doing. Before the very end we recorded *The Forest and the Zoo.* I made that happen because I thought the music was too important to lose. It was what we'd call the 'hermetic free.' The point of no return. Where the music had the maximum calories in it. There was nothing to say, no words necessary. Just: 'play.' After that, the music went elsewhere."]

chapter three: various freedoms

In the era after the harrowing visit to South America, Lacy's music took a very different turn, right into the period he calls "the scratchy '70s." "After about a year or so of playing completely free," he says, "the music started to sound the same every night. And then it was no longer free. That's when we had to start making another revolution." In retrospect, he categorizes the work after "hermetic free" into two sequential types: "post-free"—which began to put fences up in the music, to "groom" the total improvisation—and eventually "poly-free." "The C major scale came right back. I thought I'd never see it again. But when it came back it was wide open with possibilities. We started adding melodies, written things, modes, rhythms. Sometimes it was free, and sometimes it was free not to be free. Limits are very important. Once you know you're only going to do something for one minute, there's a certain freedom in that. You don't have to worry about the second minute."

Lacy's musical route took him deep into composition and back into performing Thelonious Monk's pieces. As for his own approach, he sums: "You go through the complex to get to the simple. We have an old piece called 'Bone.' We try to get it down to the bone. You want to end up with something that's easy . . . easy to love!" A prolific composer with a writing style as distinctive as his personal soprano sound, Lacy has carefully honed his perspective on working material. "The jazz I like is a mixture of prepared and unprepared," he details. "The unprepared is also prepared, and the prepared is also unprepared. There are four edges. Improvisation is a tool, not an end in itself. It's a way of finding music that can't be found by composing. And composing is a way of finding music that you can't improvise. Maybe certain geniuses can improvise perfect structures, but in general to really make a language structure you need time to work on it, time to think about it and prepare it. And then you can play it in a minute! It's prepared. And you can play it in an unprepared manner. You can play it differently each time, in an improvised manner. This is what Monk is about: a prepared structure that can be played in an improvised manner and can be elaborated upon improvisationally. It promulgates improvisation; the tune is not complete without improvisation. And a lot of what I write is made to be improvised. It's up to you to fill them out." Lacy ponders a minute, then adds: "Monk told me: the inside of a tune is what makes the outside sound good. That's a very succinct definition of form, but it's true!"

Road Trip: October 1961

> [After Ornette Coleman's record *Free Jazz* was out and successful, there were demands for him to produce live concerts by his double quartet. Eric Dolphy wasn't available, so Ornette called Lacy, who was working days at a record store: "We had rehearsals in New York—Don Cherry, Bobby Bradford, Art Davis, Charlie Haden, Ed Blackwell. It was wonderful, the music was very exciting, I was looking forward to the concert, really. We got on the plane, went to a cinema in Cincinnati. On the cinema was written: 'Free Jazz—Ornette Coleman Double Quartet.' Around the cinema was a long line of people waiting to buy tickets for it. And guess what? They didn't want to pay. It was a crisis, man. 'Hey, it's free-jazz, we're not gonna pay.' So they wouldn't pay and we wouldn't play. The concert did not take place, we got back on the airplane, went back to New York, and that was the end of *Free Jazz* in America." And the birth of an archetypal ruse. "Now it's a joke, but it wasn't then. Everybody was hungry, broke. The chance to play some interesting music and get paid for it! To go all the way out there and find a lack of comprehension like that, it was hard."]

chapter four: the horn

In the end, there's the horn. The inimitable soprano sound that Gil Evans wrote lead parts for on his first record, *Gil Evans plus Ten*. Back then, there was no one but Lacy—even John Coltrane was a decade behind Lacy in coming to the straight horn. Now, of course, sopranos are as ubiquitous as, say, Monk tunes. "What do you want your instrument to do and what does your instrument want to do? Those two things are the basis of a style, really. Your own desires and the instrument's exigencies. The soprano, if you take Evan Parker's playing and Lol Coxhill's and Coltrane's and my own, you can see that it can be played in a million different ways. The truth is that it hasn't been played in a million different ways, it's only been played in two or three ways. Sometimes I'm disappointed that somebody doesn't imagine something else to do with that. Maybe they'll come along.

"The main disappointment is that hardly anybody has developed the bottom of this instrument. I must be the only one that's really opened up the bottom." In fact, through tireless work he's extended his lowest note possibility down to a low G through combination of lipping and foot-muting. "I'm waiting for somebody else to really have founded something downstairs. That's perhaps the most interesting part of the horn, the most beautiful part, its most pleasant part." But Lacy points out the excruciating work that goes into such discoveries: "These things are possible if you really want them, but you've got to pay dearly and you've got to sound terrible, so pathetic and hopeless and hapless for a long time until it turns the corner and starts to sound better. To go through those pains, not everybody wants to do that. But the difficulty of playing a thing like that gives it expressive power automatically. It has tension because it's not easily won. It is per se dramatic because . . . maybe you won't be able to do it!" Lacy chuckles with the distinctive laugh of personal experience.

Head Trip: Sometime in the Late 1950s

[Zen was in the air, everyone was reading John Cage and thinking about sound and silence. In New York City, young Lacy had an adventure without leaving his flat: "I was practicing long notes to develop my tone. I started playing two notes. I was working on the smallest interval, the minor second. In those days I was pretty crazy, really, I could do things for long, long periods of time. So I started rocking back and forth on this minor second, between a B and a C, and decided to stay on those two notes for a long time. I played them for maybe an hour. Of course it went through the various stages of boredom, frustration, puzzlement, and it started to get interesting because my perceptions started changing. So I stayed on those two notes, that little interval, for a long, long time, I don't know how many hours, until I started to hallucinate, to the point where that little interval had become enormous. And I had become very small. There I was, this little being in a huge room, and the room was a minor second. And it was uncanny, extraordinary, and I almost flipped because it was real, it was surreal, it was unreal, but it was for real. I found that I could hear so many things within that little interval, it had completely changed its aspects. When I came out of that room and went back to the rest of the horn, everything had changed, there was no relationship that was as previous to that experience of having gone into that little interval. My mind was blown, my ear was blown. That's a very important experience to dig into something to the point where you get beyond. Like Georges Braque said: impregnation, obsession, hallucination. Dig in, obsess, then it's a hallucination, and that's where something is revealed. And you can apply it to anything, break down a wall a day."]

epilogue: where to?

As long as he's lived in Europe, Lacy still doesn't like being known as an expatriate. "I've been out here for thirty years," he says, gazing out the window into the gray drizzle of Berlin. "But I don't want to be an ex-anything. If you're ex-, you're gone, really. You're not there anymore!," he snickers, revealing the New York twang that's stuck with him through thick and thin. Where will the next twist in life's turnpike take him? "I feel a pull from America, and there's a time coming soon when I'll have to go back. I must, for a while, to see what's involved. It's just a question of timing, but it's coming up. I think there's something I'd like to accomplish: I hear a lot of stuff coming out of New York and it sort of rubs me the wrong way. I may be fooling myself, but I thought maybe I could go back there and do something about it." Home from the road or just another pit stop, maybe the peripatetic jazzman will alight on these shores, set them straight like his horn.

In the Old Days

interview by Lee Friedlander and Maria Friedlander

29

Returning to Paris after Berlin, Lacy ended up staying just five more years in his adopted home. In the summer of 1997 he and Aebi moved from their long-time flat on the rue du Temple in the central Marais district to a house with abundant garden on the rue des Pavillons, near the outer edge of Paris in the 20th arrondissement. Thus he was already poised for his exit from the city; as it was, most of his work was far away, so at least he was closer to the freeway and the airport.

During a fall tour of the United States with his trio, on 9 November in New York he sat down with his old friend and fellow MacArthur recipient, the photographer Lee Friedlander, along with Maria Friedlander, to discuss his early years mostly, the 1950s and '60s. Though most of the themes are by now familiar in this book, Lacy here adds many new details, anecdotes, and reflections. This was due, no doubt, to a special sympathy between the two friends: Lee Friedlander had known the music scene for as long as Lacy had; indeed, he was the house photographer for Atlantic Records from the 1950s to the 1970s. The following was one of only two interviews (the other was with the rhythm-and-blues singer Ruth Brown) included in Friedlander's marvelous book of photos, *American Musicians* (1998).

Maria Friedlander: I heard that you grew up in New York City, in Hell's Kitchen.

No, I grew up on 81st Street and West End Ave. Thelonious Monk lived in Hell's Kitchen. It was more Heaven's Kitchen where I came from, a secure bastion of middle-class morality.

Lee Friedlander: So it's the late '40s, early '50s, you're growing up on the Upper West Side. How did you get to hear jazz? Where did you go?

There were the two beer halls on Second Avenue down by Third Street—Stuyvesant Casino and Central Plaza. They both had the same policy—two bucks each and six dollars for a pitcher of beer, a whole pitcher of beer. At first, I used to go there and photograph the musicians because I was into photography in my teens. I had a Speed Graphic and a darkroom and the whole shabazz. So I was more or less a professional photographer at fifteen years old, selling portraits, selling images of the bands and musicians playing at these concerts. I got into the things for free.

LF: I remember what it was like then. Back then you could go and listen. You didn't have to go to a concert hall.

That was very important because it was a matter of a dollar or two. There was no money for anybody but there was enough money for the musicians to live decently. The people weren't raggedy or anything. They made enough money to live well and they had a ball. They really were having a good time. And it was about pure joy. It was a pleasure to play and to hang out and to be in the same profession. A lot of that doesn't exist anymore. There was a rivalry and a competition but there was a friendly spirit, too, a solidarity. You couldn't fool anybody. If you came along and played something, people knew exactly where you were coming from and what you could do and if you could play or not. These guys would check you out and check each other out. It doesn't exist anymore.

LF: How did you start playing?

By the time I was fifteen, I was trying to play at the piano a little bit, improvising at the piano, trying to play Fats Waller transcriptions and listen to Art Tatum and getting really discouraged with the piano.

LF: Because of Art Tatum?

Because of Art Tatum. I saw Art Tatum when I was thirteen, twice. That was really the end of the piano for me. Even the Fats Waller transcriptions—my hands weren't big enough to reach those tenths. I just don't have the right touch for the piano. So I had found a cousin's clarinet in the closet and I started fooling around with that. Then at the age of sixteen I took up the soprano. Later when I went to this school they wouldn't accept me as a soprano student so I chose alto. I bought an alto but I was the worst alto player you ever heard in your life. I mean really a wretched alto. I just had no feeling for it at all. And then later on, I tried tenor for a while. I was no good on tenor either. There were so many great tenor players around and I loved Lester Young but it was impossible. So the tenor was not for me. And the clarinet I gave up because it was too hard. The soprano had so many problems that I just wanted to concentrate on that.

Later, when I was working with Max Kaminsky and his band, I told him one day, "Look, I'm gonna stop playing the clarinet. I just want to play the soprano." He said, "You're crazy. You won't get any work on it." And he was right—he fired me. Nobody else called me to play because soprano sax didn't exist. The instrument just didn't exist. I was welcomed as an additional thing. I was added on by the promoter, but it wasn't a fundamental horn. I didn't fit in anywhere until Gil Evans used me. That was the beginning and, of course, when Trane took it up in 1960, that was the beginning of the history of the modern soprano saxophone as far as most people are concerned.

But back then when I was sixteen, I was still going to these concerts at Stuyvesant Casino and Central Plaza and selling the photos and fooling around with the saxophone. Then I approached Cecil Scott, who was one of the players there, and asked him if he would take me on as a student because I was playing the thing upside down. So he took me on and he showed me the ropes and he really was a wonderful teacher. I studied with him for a couple of years. He not only taught me how to play a little bit but he took me under his wing and enabled me to sit in with all these great musicians—Red Allen, Pee Wee Russell, Jimmy Archey, and the guys from Chicago—Jimmy McPartland and George Wettling, Joe Sullivan, all these guys.

Then the promoter started hiring me as an additional horn. He called me "the Bechet of today." Which wasn't true at all. I think he paid me ten dollars the first time, then it was twenty. Then, as I got a little better, I started working with some of these guys like Max Kaminsky and Red Allen and Jimmy McPartland. I became sort of a regular at these concerts at Stuyvesant Casino. I got to play with the Kansas City crowd—Buck Clayton, Dicky Wells, Walter Page, Jimmy Rushing. I did that for a few years until I felt comfortable enough. Then I started gigging around.

Back then, there were schools of jazz musicians from different locations: the Washington school, the Philadelphia school. Later on the Detroit people came in. But at this time in classical jazz, the three most prominent schools were New Orleans, Chicago, and Kansas City. The Kansas City people were much more progressive, but in those so-called Dixieland concerts they were playing the same repertoire—"Royal Garden Blues," "Tin Roof Blues," and "Muskrat Ramble." That's what we were playing. I learned all those tunes and can still play them after forty years. But that was a wonderful schooling I had. I was really lucky. When I think back on it now, I can hardly believe it really happened.

LF: You didn't mention any of the Ellington guys. Did you ever play with any of them?

Yeah, Sonny Greer. I played with him quite a few times. He was funny. He was really funny. But he was also a great performer.

LF: That must have been really wonderful to hear the Ellington band at that time.

Anytime Duke played anywhere, I was there.

LF: Or Basie probably too.

Basie, too, but more Ellington. I was into Basie on the records when Buck Clayton was with him and Lester Young. I had all those records. That was the early '50s.

Then I went to a music school in Boston for one term and I hated it. It was the predecessor to Berklee. They had this system, a mathematical system for music, these big red books, heavy, that we had to carry around. It was ridiculous. They'd teach you this harmony by numbers. I hated it, really. But at night in Boston I went to hear the first modern jazz I ever heard with Miles Davis. He had Milt Jackson on piano, Phil Urso on tenor, Percy Heath on bass, and Kenny Clarke on drums.

LF: So it was almost the MJQ [Modern Jazz Quartet].

MF: Pre-MJQ.

This was about '52 or '53. Back then the MJQ was the Milt Jackson Quartet. I heard them play many times at Birdland. In fact I was there the night that John Lewis got up to the microphone and said, "Henceforth, the Milt Jackson Quartet will be known as the Modern Jazz Quartet." Everybody cracked up in Birdland. " 'Henceforth'—Who is this cat? What the hell is he talking about?" It was a big joke. But it turned out not to be a joke at all. I don't know whether he said that every night, but the night I was there he did. He probably announced that a few times.

LF: He probably talked Pee Wee Marquette into announcing it that way, too.

Pee Wee Marquette was evil. When I worked there with Gil Evans's band, he wanted a tip from me. You know he got tips from everybody. And at that time I was stupid. I didn't give him a tip so he mispronounced my name all the time. Steve Tracy, Steve Macy, everything but Lacy because I didn't tip.

LF: That's legendary. He did that to everybody.

MF: So after Boston, you came back to New York.

For the rest of the '50s I never really ventured out of New York. But I used to do what they call society gigs. I worked with Jimmy McPartland and Rex Stewart a few times. I was playing with these classical players until Cecil Taylor plucked me out of all that. He had just come out of the New England Conservatory. He reached New York and he found me playing in Jimmy Ryan's. Cecil came up to me and said, "How come a young man like you is playing this old music?" It really startled me because I never thought of myself as either a young man or this as old music. He shook me up. He said, "Come to my house. We'll have a rehearsal." I went down to this ratty place on Sheriff Street. Lower East Side. Rotten street. We used to carry the drums up seven flights of stairs. We'd play there and the neighbors would bang on the walls. The walls were paper thin. Cecil would play and play and play. We'd be playing for hours and the people would be banging on the walls and he'd continue playing. Once I fell asleep and I woke up and he was still playing. He'd play for sixteen hours straight.

Dennis Charles, Buell Neidlinger, and I were the group and we used to rehearse at his house quite a lot. We had very few jobs. Once in a blue moon we had a job in a little club in Brooklyn or something. We played some dance jobs too. The first job I worked with Cecil was at Columbia University. We played in a trio—Calo Scott on cello, Cecil, and myself.

LF: Who was on cello?

Calo Scott. He died a long time ago. A very good cellist. He was a great cellist and he used to pluck the cello like a bass. He sounded like Jimmy Blanton really. It was amazing. He died young. This was the first guy I ever heard playing the cello like that. It was for dancing.

LF: It must have been a strange band for dancing.

This was about '54, '55. I was with him for six years and we played quite a few other dance jobs. Once we played a whole summer in the Catskills for dancing. Not with that group but with another formation. That's a whole story in itself, that summer in the Catskills. We had a job for the whole summer, a contract, in a hotel in the Catskills and the band at that time was a mixed group. It was half black and half white. When we got up to the Catskills and the owner saw us, he said, "Out. No, no. I won't have a mixed band in my resort." We had a contract and everything. We took the train, went up there, and this guy fired us immediately. He didn't even say sorry. That was really a blow. That was the whole summer's work and this was the beginning of July. We were waiting on the platform for the train to come in and take us back to New York and some guy came up and said, "Hey, are you a band? There's a new resort here. They're looking for a band." So we went and checked it out and stayed there the whole summer. It was a place called Shangri-La. It was an interracial resort in the Catskills and we had a ball.

MF: Were there a lot of blacks playing at the hotels?

No, only at Shangri-La, which folded soon after. It was a disaster. It wasn't full. But jazz for dancing back then was normal. People used to dance to all kinds of jazz. We played mambos and rumbas and foxtrots and blues. We learned how to play for dancing. It was very important because if the dancers stopped dancing, you got fired. Very simple really: if they kept dancing, you kept your job. We found out what to do and what not to do. Because you couldn't get any concert jobs at that time, so we had dance jobs. But if you listen now to what Cecil was playing back then, it's so accessible. It's so swinging. It sounded like a mixture of Erroll Garner, Bud Powell, and Bartók.

LF: And after you left Cecil?

Gil Evans called me up one day in 1957. He said, "My name is Gil Evans." I'd never heard of him. He said, "I'm doing a record and I'm interested in using you on my record. I'd like to come over and look at some material." It turned out that he had heard me five years earlier on Arthur Godfrey's talent scout show where I had my own Dixieland band. And five years later he found me. I don't know how—I wasn't in the phone book. But he made inquiries around and he found me. From that moment on I worked with him until he died.

He used me playing lead with Lee Konitz, just two saxophones. He was the first one to imagine using the soprano saxophone as a lead instrument like that. He had me playing lead in that first record, *Gil Evans plus Ten*, made for Prestige. He didn't know how bad my reading was. At the time, I could hardly read at all. He had all these great musicians in the band and they had to keep doing things over and over because of me. I was messing up the part and I was really embarrassed about it so I learned how to read fast, as fast as I could. That's how I started studying paper. That was my coming out, being featured on that record.

I also got a contract to do my own records as a result. Gil launched me into the scene. Gil was a painter. The orchestrations were such that if I just played my part and was cool, the result was just ecstasy, just glorious, beautiful. It would give you chills. Anyway, by that time I was into Monk's music a lot—studying it, playing with Gil, still playing with Cecil, and also playing with my own groups a little bit. Cecil turned me on to a lot of things, to Stravinsky and Bartók and all that.

LF: Jimmy Giuffre was into all that too.

There was a parallel between Giuffre and me. When Giuffre got to New York, he had heard all the new jazz. He took over the trio I had with Buell and Dennis Charles and made it into the Jimmy Giuffre Quartet. This is 1960. We were playing Monk tunes then. But it didn't work out between Jimmy and me at all. It was awful, so he fired me after two weeks. He was a beautiful guy, a lovely guy, but we were incompatible musically. Also, in those days I wasn't flexible. I was very doctrinaire about Monk. He was a very easygoing guy. It was California versus New York. It didn't work out.

That was also the same year that Miles sent for me. Miles was working at Birdland and he told me to come by and bring my horn because he had heard that record with Gil. I sat in with Miles and he liked it. He told me to come back the next day. I was scared to death. It was so fast and I couldn't deal with it really—the lifestyle, Birdland. So I came back the next night but I didn't bring my horn. When he asked me where my horn was, I said, "I left it at the house." Later I found out that he had wanted me in the band to replace Bobby Jaspar, but I didn't know that at the time. I didn't realize that if he was satisfied, I should have been satisfied. A couple of months later I was with Monk, so you can't do everything.

LF: Talk about beginning with Monk.

Back when I was with Cecil Taylor, right away one of the tunes we played was "Bemsha Swing" by Monk. That was my first introduction to Monk's music. Then, in 1955, Cecil took me by the hand and said, "Come on, we're gonna go hear Monk." And we went to a little club downtown. And there was Monk. There were only musicians in this place. There was nobody else in there but it was crowded with musicians. That was my first introduction to Monk live and I flipped. It was so beautiful. So swinging and so sweet and so humorous also. It was just enthralling. I really flipped for Monk when I heard him like that. At that point I started to buy records and try to learn his tunes. Because the compositions intrigued me so much and it seemed like they fit my instrument perfectly. I like to say they fit my instrument to a tee. They used to call Monk "T."

I learned all of Charlie Parker's tunes, too, or a lot of them, but they didn't fit the instrument. The alto goes too low. It's not soprano saxophone music. But Monk's tunes were ideal and difficult, and interesting, intriguing, and satisfying. I started and I've never stopped looking into his music. The first record I made, I didn't know what I was doing. I had a little material prepared, a calypso piece, a tune of Monk's which I had wrong . . .

LF: What do you mean, wrong?

Well, I played it and there were mistakes in it, I found out later. But Monk told me, "Yeah, yeah, you got it right," because he loved mistakes. Anyway, I had a few tunes prepared and we did maybe a half an hour of music. Then we ran out of material and the record wasn't finished. I didn't know what to do. I didn't have that much material prepared. It was my first date. I had Wynton Kelly on piano and Dennis Charles and Buell Neidlinger, but I wasn't well prepared, so when the producer said, "Play a blues," I played the blues really sad, and then I played "When the Saints Go Marching In." It was disheartening. But the record came out and it was pretty good, without the weak fill-ins.

For the second record, two years later, I resolved to be prepared. I had this idea of doing only Monk tunes. I had Mal Waldron on piano and Elvin Jones on drums. It was supposed to be Wilbur Ware on bass, but Wilbur didn't show up for the rehearsal, so I panicked. I called Buell and asked him to do the date. Wilbur later asked me, "Man, what happened to the record date?" And I said, "Well, you didn't come to rehearsal." His response was: "I don't have to rehearse, I know those things." That could have been a wonderful record, even better than it was.

But as it happened, it came out okay. Monk heard it and liked it. He had to like it that somebody was doing a record of all of his music. We played some hard tunes too, some really difficult ones. I knew him a little by that time. I used to go up to him and say, "Hey Monk, you remember me?" After a while he said, "Man, come on now, how many people like you do you think I know? How many soprano saxophone players do you think there are?"

He gave me a lot of encouragement, but he never checked out anything I did until he came to see me with Giuffre. A few months after that, in 1960, he hired me for his quintet at the Jazz Gallery, for sixteen weeks, doubling at the Apollo and jazz festivals also. That was really a crash course, postgraduate.

LF: I remember you talking about Monk's compositions and how he always stayed with a melody.

Monk was a great composer and a great musician. Every detail was a gem. He had diamonds and jewels at his disposal. He could make sounds that were just like jewels. Just precious, fantastic, high-quality gemstones. The melodies were and are very succinct and sublime. They're perfect melodies and they're perfect structures. They're also descriptions of things in New York, activities he had experienced. There is one that evolved from New York games: stickball and stoop ball. There are a lot about traffic, the Hudson River, people in his family, portraits of his cousins and nieces. I really learned about music being about something from him.

LF: I was at a session that Monk did with Blakey's crew. He came in with a briefcase full of music and he wouldn't give it out to anybody.

No, Monk didn't believe in paper. When I was playing with him with Charlie Rouse, he would never show his paper. However, he would be patient. He would play it over and over again at the piano. We could watch his fingers. We could take notes ourselves, but he wouldn't show us the paper because he didn't believe in it. He believed that it caused misunderstanding. He was right, of course. He believed in note by note.

I have a manuscript of his, a photocopy that Roswell sent me of "Trinkle Tinkle." It was written out perfectly, like a mathematician. Monk told me he was great at mathematics when he was a kid and you could see there that he really knew all about space and time and mathematics and numbers.

MF: But he didn't want you to see it.

Not to see it on paper. He wanted us to dig it.

MF: That must have taken a while then.

Oh, yeah, it was very frustrating, confusing, but rewarding and revealing. This was an African thing, though. If African drummers want to teach a young disciple, they beat out the rhythm on their bodies. They go "pum" on the body of the kid. That's how you learn the rhythms, like that.

Monk's lines fitted my horn very well and I could really dig into them. As Monk said, "You've got to dig it to dig it, you dig it?" They were really challenging and fascinating. Every one of them was wonderful and nobody was playing them. I couldn't believe it. I said, "Why doesn't anybody play this? This stuff is great." Monk himself didn't even play these tunes anymore, stuff that he had recorded in the late '40s. This was the middle '50s and "Skippy" and those tunes were gone. They were on record but nobody had taken them up.

LF: Did Monk talk much to you?

He was very communicative with me. To some other people he would clam up. If a policeman asked him, "What are you doing here?" he wouldn't even answer because it was such a stupid question. It got him into deep trouble, including being locked in a madhouse with a strait-jacket. There were several incidents like that when he just clammed up and they locked him up. He couldn't go for this ridiculous stuff. He was tough. He had guts. But Monk was very nice with me. He was so funny, and so generous and kind.

But he got undone later on. He got really undone. Basically it was a loss of appetite. You could call it that or apathy. I call it a loss of appetite. He had a great appetite but he also had a great appetite for all kinds of stimulants. He'd mix them all up. He'd mix up all different things, LSD and beer and amphetamines and marijuana and vitamins and lithium and impossible combinations of things. After a while he got unstrung. That's my reading of it.

LF: How long did you play with Monk?

I played with him in the big bands several times, before and after the quintet, but I played with the quintet sixteen weeks in 1960. All summer, four months. I was with Charlie Rouse, John Ore, and Roy Haynes. It was Monk's quartet. He added me on. People gave him a lot of flack about that. They said, "What are you doing taking this white cat on soprano?" But he did what he wanted to do. He didn't listen to anybody else. He had a lot of imagination and courage to do that. The group was functioning perfectly well but he took me on, maybe because he saw I needed that. I was so much into his music that I needed the actual experience of playing with him to find out what was really happening.

LF: He probably liked the addition, too.

He was intrigued by the instrument, by the sound. When I played in the group, he wouldn't let us play any harmony. He had us play unisons and octaves only because he said that that's the hardest thing to do. "You can always add harmony parts," he said. "That's easy. But to play unisons and octaves, that's the hardest thing in the world." And he was right. It took us weeks to get a good sound. And finally when Rouse and I got our lines hooked up like that it was a beautiful sound. Monk would add the harmonies at the piano. It wasn't recorded. There was a tape of three pieces from a Philadelphia festival circulating with collectors, but that's the only record of that group that I know of.

LF: What about the band you had playing Monk in the early '60s, with Roswell Rudd? That was not an easy period for the music.

At that time you couldn't do what you wanted to do. I had the habit by then of going and bugging record companies and producers, trying to get a record date for myself. It was really discouraging because you'd get up there and talk to these idiots and they'd come up with these stupid ideas. One time I went to Columbia and one guy said, "I have an idea. I'd like you to play Vivaldi with the rhythm section." At that time there was this album of Jacques Loussier playing Bach. It was popular, so the producer had an idea that I could do Vivaldi. I walked out of there. I didn't go for it. Or if you tried to do something they'd hand you back the tape and say, "Okay, kid." I did another date for Atlantic with Don Cherry. We did a half a record and never got to do the rest because it was considered too radical. We were radical in a way, comparatively, because what was in in those days was Detroit hard bop—that was what was acceptable. What we were doing was radical and out.

MF: Rock 'n' roll.

Yeah, that came in. As the music got more and more radical, the rock 'n' roll came in more and more. People just couldn't dance to the jazz anymore. They couldn't sing it, they couldn't dance it, and we went underground. We all went underground. The other people came in and took over: the rock 'n' roll and the pop groups and all that. That was the underground period when Roswell Rudd and I formed that so-called repertory quartet. We couldn't get any work at all, so we invented our own work. There were nights when we didn't make a dime, when nobody showed up. There were nights when we made a dollar or two or five dollars. We wanted to learn that music. We had the idea that if you play this music every night for a certain amount of time, after a while you'd get very free with it. And that's what we wanted to find out. We wanted to find out what kind of freedom that would produce, what would come out of that experience. It was a materialistic investigation. And with Roswell I could correct my own errors. He corrected my errors and I corrected his. The two of us together could hear much more than one. Again, there was no paper. We were only going by the records of Monk's music. We listened to them over and over and Roswell would make arrangements. It was like school days. That's why we called the record *School Days.*

MF: It was like giving yourselves a seminar.

But the important thing was that it was every night, not just Sundays. Each time we played it, we got further and further. It was like an unfolding process. And that's what we wanted. We knew that that was the answer. At first when we were playing this music, it was very stiff. Very rigid, very exactly note for note. But if you execute something over and over again, then you don't have to execute it anymore, then you can take off from it. That's what we wanted and that's what we got. We insisted on that and we got it. We made a sacrifice by having to work days and be poor but it was true, though. We weren't wrong. But at that time nobody else could see it.

A couple of people tried to record us. They didn't understand what we were doing really. I remember one record date, Creed Taylor was the producer. We started to record some of these Monk tunes. He kept stopping the tape. He said there was a clam in there. He was talking about Roswell. Roswell said, "Man, it took me years to get that clam in there." But after a while he stopped the tape so many times. Then he said, "Look, here." And he gave us the tape and the date was canceled. We had done a couple of tunes and we left with the tape under our arm. And of course, the tape got lost. This happened a couple of times. It happened with Columbia, with Verve, where they couldn't understand what we were doing.

So then I had a chance to go to Europe. In Europe there were musicians, record companies, radio stations. Everything that I couldn't find in New York was in Europe. I stayed for a year in Europe. I went to Paris, looked around, played in Italy with Don Cherry, Mal Waldron. It was very interesting. It was a chance to come above ground.

I formed a group there and by then we were really interested in this freedom. I was trying very hard. I was practicing a lot and I was also working with Carla Bley's quintet. There was a lot of freedom with that group. Freedom was in the air, the political changes going on all over the world. And we were trying to break through. I had studied chord changes and structures and tunes and stuff like that so much from the '50s. Fifteen years of trying to come to grips with material and form and content and all these considerations of tempo and chord changes, especially chord changes, harmonics. We were fed up at that time. It seemed like it was locked, blocked, like it wasn't going anywhere. So we were trying to break through and finally we did, in '65, '66. Italy was where it happened for me. I had formed a band with Enrico Rava on trumpet, Johnny Dyani on bass, and Louis Moholo on drums. We were playing in a place in Turin called the Swing Club. We were playing completely free and it was really revolutionary. I had never heard anything like that in my life.

MF: Was it accepted well?

No, people were just eating spaghetti. It was a restaurant in the front and a *cave* in the back. We would play in the *cave*. People were just drinking and eating. Today the Italian public is the best in the world, the best listeners, the best-trained listeners, the best ears. They've had all this operatic tradition. For me, I've gotten the most perfect response in Italy. But in those days, in the '60s, when we were playing this free stuff and all that, they were indifferent. But we were so excited about what we were doing; nobody had ever played like this before. That's when we made the scandal in San Remo. It was the San Remo Jazz Festival and first Ornette was there with his trio, with David Izenzon on bass. They had good success. People liked that. And then we got up and played. They started booing and whistling, "Basta, basta." They blew us off the stage. It was a scandal. That was '66. When you look back on it, there wasn't really that much difference between what they were doing and what we were doing.

LF: I want to know what happened from there.

We went to Buenos Aires with this group. By that time I had met Irene [Aebi] in '66 in May. And in the summer of '66, we went down to Buenos Aires on a contract with a theater to play off the door with one-way tickets. Enrico and his wife, Graciela, arranged that job because she was

Argentine. We got stuck there for nine months. We were playing at rich people's houses and at clubs, tango clubs. Wherever we could get a gig we would play, but we were starving down there. People would offer to buy Johnny and Louis a drink but they wouldn't give them anything to eat. It was really misery down there.

But I learned to love the tango. I heard a lot of the tango down there, the real masters of it, and the history on records. We played opposite Piazzolla. He hated what we were doing. We opened for him in a club called Gotan, tango spelled backwards, Gotan Club. Steve Lacy Quartet and Piazzolla. We played our stuff and the next day in the newspaper we read that he said, "I have to go home and listen to Vivaldi all night long to calm my nerves." He said, "They play with knives in their teeth." There was also a lot of personal jealousy and problems with Johnny and Louis and girlfriends. You know, the tango is all about betrayal. Somebody slashed the drums, things like that. They had an original work of art painted on there by Bob Thompson and somebody slashed them. Whoever it was thought that the drummer was messing with his wife. In reality, it was the bass player.

Anyway, before we imploded, I managed to produce a record out of that, *The Forest and the Zoo*. The music was so well-cooked because we had been playing together for a couple of years. I got this auditorium to record us and we did it in public. At that time it was LPs. The idea was that they were twenty minutes a side, so we played twenty minutes and stopped. We turned the tape over and we played twenty minutes and then we stopped again. And that was the concert. And that was the record. People clapped but it wasn't really understood.

Irene and I came back to New York in '66 or '67 and it was worse than ever. However, we started working on vocal pieces and we had a quintet with Enrico Rava, Paul Motian, and Kent Carter. We went back to Europe with that quintet. We had one or two jobs on the German radio and somewhere else in Holland with that group and then there was no more work. We got stranded in Europe in '68. So everybody came back to New York and Irene and I went to Rome. We met in Rome and at least in Rome we could sort of lay low and deal with being out of work.

We stayed there for '68 and '69. I started working with Musica Elettronica Viva. It's a group I still play with from time to time. Frederic Rzewski is a genius. [Richard] Teitelbaum was playing the Moog synthesizer at that time. We had already started working with Teitelbaum in New York. We were doing protest music about the Vietnam War at that time. Everybody was saying, "Johnson, baby killer" and all that. So we were in WBAI and Irene was hurling these Lao Tzu texts about politics and weapons and things like that. It was like political music. The name of the piece we were doing was "Chinese Food." Texts chosen from Lao Tzu which illustrated the absurdity of war and weapons and things like that.

That was the beginning of a lot of things we did later on. When we got to Rome, Teitelbaum was there and I started playing with that group too. I learned a lot from them. I've been very involved in working with non-jazz musicians, people coming out of the conservatories. Rzewski to me is the best composer I know and also the best pianist. He's a great improviser but he has nothing to do with jazz, except that he likes jazz. He worked with Stockhausen, all of Chopin, Beethoven, but he's not a jazz musician. Fruitful combinations. The exterior collaborations are very fruitful if you get the right people.

MF: Who's in your trio now?

John Betsch and Jean-Jacques Avenel. They're the same people who have been playing with me for years. I've been working with JJ for twenty-five years, and John about eight or nine years. It's important. The long-time association is what does it really.

LF: Because you don't have to start from scratch all the time.

And you don't have to be so polite in playing either. You can take more risks, have more fun, and you can play more complex material that you all know. I'm an outsider in a way. For example, I've been living in Paris for twenty-five years now but I'm an outsider. The other work for me was stardom and I'm not cut out to be a star. It's not my thing. I don't glitter. I'll never glitter. You have to follow your own nature.

MF: It brings a price and it stops your energies to think that's what you are.

LF: Stardom is not about the work. It's about something else. It's a secondary thing. For people that are interested in working, that's all we want to do.

Today, you can become a flash in the pan. You can become what's called a rising star, a young lion, a young Turk, any of these things. All those slots are available because the giants are no longer there to survey. And that's my theory about the power grab, the midgets coming in. When the giants die, the midgets come in and grab the power out of the vacuum. That's my impression about what's going on in New York now, mostly. The '50s really were the golden age of jazz because all the giants were alive. Now they're almost all dead. Now the midgets have taken over. But back then, the giants were in power. I was lucky enough to grow up and to be at the right time, at the right place, doing the right thing. I got to play with all those great people, from New Orleans, from Kansas City, and from Chicago.

The Kansas City people were so beautiful. They were so generous. They were so sympathetic. They were so droll and they had so much taste and humor and knowledge that I was inspired for the rest of my life, being associated with them. I mean, I love the way they play, but when I got to play with them it was even better. I'll never forget any of them. Every one of them had their own sound, their own style, their own manner, their own everything. It was something else, man. Every one of those, even guys who are forgotten now, I remember their sound. I remember Joe Thomas, the trumpet player. I remember Harold Baker, all those trumpet players. I can recall even now in my ear how they sounded, each one of them. I played with Henry Goodwin, who was a growl trumpet player. I played with Jimmy Archey, the trombone player, and the De Paris brothers and Pops Foster and Zutty Singleton.

LF: What you say about the history of music, especially jazz, about the greats all being alive then was the same with photography. In 1950, 85 percent of the history of photography were living people. And the same thing with jazz, Louis Armstrong and Bechet and all those guys.

But, you see, the standards were high then and because these people were alive, you couldn't get away with murder. You couldn't. And if you could play, you were welcome, because the standards were established by the masters and they were right there to survey it. If there was a new bass player in New York, all the bass players would be there to check him out. You couldn't fool anybody in those days. Nowadays you can fool everybody, or almost. Back then, every one of them was a master, an original; each was an inventor of his own style.

30 The Glorious Thirty

interview by Franck Bergerot and Alex Dutilh

The year this interview appeared, in the French journal *Jazzman* (64, 2000), marked a full three decades that Lacy had lived in Paris. Clearly, as he states here, the evidence was mounting that it might be time at last to move on. Nonetheless, throughout his final years in Paris he remained busy as ever on various projects. In the first half of 1998, for example, he recorded his jazz opera *The Cry* in Geneva, and a month later at home he recorded a new solo album, *Sands*, for the Tzadik label (most pieces appearing for the first time, including the only recording of his three songs based on Samuel Beckett's poems). The following year he and Roswell Rudd formed a quartet, resulting in the album *Monk's Dream* for another big label, Verve/Universal; that band, a natural merging of Lacy's working trio and his old collaboration with Rudd from nearly forty years earlier, toured intermittently for the next two years. Around the same time Lacy developed a sequence of solo performances based on Duke Ellington's music, using extended techniques to distill the Ellington band's versions into the sweep of a single horn. He played these pieces throughout Europe and the United States, and recorded them at a concert near Tokyo in the fall of 2000, which can be heard on the album *10 of Dukes + 6 Originals*. The album, produced by Vincent Lainé (who had more or less become Lacy's right-hand man in France and maintained his website) and other erstwhile Lacy supporters, was eventually released on a new label, Senators Records, which was intended as a resource for some of Lacy's future projects.

You don't perform solo anymore. Yet you're one of the pioneers of the genre.

I give concerts, especially solo, throughout the entire world except in France. Apart from the Sunset or the Duc des Lombards, which call me now and then, I really don't count on Paris anymore for working.

When you settled in Paris, what attracted you to Europe?

Work. I had to live, to scramble. With Irene, we invented all sorts of new formulas. I started doing solos in 1972. At that time, there was a mix of rivalry and solidarity with the international community that lived at the Hôtel de Buci, but also with the French musicians. We were all searching, we shared the same conditions of existence. Then the situation deteriorated. I hope it'll work itself out . . . But we have to keep fighting. Including with the taxman, they've been harassing me the past two years for money I earned abroad and with which I paid my musicians, my travel expenses, in difficult conditions. I haven't kept track of all that, it's not always possible, when one handles one's own business . . . Maybe we'll have to leave France. Yet, I'm too fond of living here!

Your exchanges with the arts, dance, poetry, were they simply due to an economic situation?

It was stimulating to be poor . . . and young. But it was possible as well because we were in Paris, with that artistic tradition. Yet we met with a lot of resistance, especially when we worked on Beckett, Éluard, Picabia, René Char . . . They're suspicious of an American who does things in French. When we were with BMG [RCA], the people there didn't want Irene to sing songs . . . Ten years ago, we created *Treize regards*, a cycle of songs in French for voice, harpsichord, and saxophone, on texts by Tsvetayeva, the great Russian poet. It's chamber music, French *chanson*, art song, jazz . . . Nobody wanted that mix, not for a record, nor to do in concert.

Among the formations that you have worked in, what is your favorite?

For a long time the sextet was the real core of my activities. We had reached a miraculous balance around 1985–1986 with the album *The Condor*. But it was difficult to keep the group alive. That's why I continued to play in quartet, trio, solo . . . And then like everything that lasts, the sextet declined and I preferred to stop. Even so, that lasted almost twenty-three years! Today, the real core is my trio with bassist Jean-Jacques Avenel and drummer John Betsch. Without a rhythm section, in jazz, you don't exist. I need a good bassist and a good drummer, and in that respect I'm rather spoiled.

You are faithful to your musicians. Isn't there a danger to always keep the same core?

I've got forty years of faithfulness with Mal Waldron behind me. Twenty-five years with Jean-Jacques Avenel, twelve years with John Betsch. Both have progressed a lot, in swing, in suppleness. In twelve years, they've acquired a great complicity. Faithfulness is a necessary luxury for me. My compositions are difficult. It takes years to learn to play with the same musicians, to play a repertoire. There are pieces that I've been playing for thirty years like "Bone," "The Breath" . . . The things that last are the best. Even a great painting gets better with time. For people, it's the same. Miles Davis loved to surround himself with young musicians. I prefer to work with mature people.

You've just come back from Japan, where you play often. Do you feel a special attraction toward that country?

Japanese painting, theater, literature, and music have always interested me. When I went there for the first time in 1975, I was ready. In particular, I met the drummer Masahiko Togashi and played with him. I also took a lesson with the shakuhachi player Watazumi Doso. His teaching bore upon the nature of music. On the unity between the voice, the ear, the sound, the breath. Ten years later, when I saw him again, I had made a lot of progress!

On your last trip there, did you see Togashi again?

We even played together. He's sixty years old now. He still lives in a wheelchair. It's a miracle he's alive. He plays like no one else. A few weeks ago, in Anvers, I met up again with Takehisa Kosugi who plays electronics, for two nights with the Merce Cunningham Dance Company. Without a rehearsal. For an hour and a half, we improvised on a choreography written for fifteen dancers in costumes. It was terrific!

In October, you accompanied Todd Browning's silent films at the Musée d'Orsay.

When they gave me the video, I was leaving for Japan and I wasn't able to view it until the night before the projection. The film *The Blackbird* was more dramatic, more structured, more stimulating. For the films on the next day, it was more difficult. It worked better during the rehearsal in the morning, perhaps because, as in the studio, when you improvise, it's often the first take that is the best. But these situations are always very interesting. They make the music evolve, they oblige you to find new solutions.

How do you compose?

I have five hundred compositions at the SACEM [the French copyright office for music] and most are written based on texts, even if I play them on soprano. I call that *lit-jazz. Lit* for literature, but also for lit up, the past participle of the verb *to light.* The titles are always important for me. I think I have my own style, even in the choice of the titles, which are rather short, incisive. I don't want to fill up the space too much. Enough of the blah blah blah. What interests me is the grammar, dictionaries.

How did you write the arrangement for "Koko" on *Monk's Dream*, your quartet record with Roswell Rudd on Verve?

I checked certain things on the score, but Roswell Rudd knows all of Ellington's parts, he has a fantastic ear. We simply worked on the arrangements side by side, experimenting.

You've recorded for a large number of record labels up till now. Will there be any more dates for Verve?

I'd like to do a second album with the same group. But, today, you have to constantly propose a new concept, a new guest. I'm preparing another quartet with George Lewis. Certain festivals are interested. George played a lot with the sextet, when Steve Potts wasn't available. As far as recording, it's better not to count too much on the majors. These days, I have my website, which was put together by Vincent Lainé. I have friends all over the world who are ready to produce certain things on the internet. The internet offers new hope for escaping the passivity of the record companies. Maybe at last I'll be able to record *Treize regards* and distribute it on the internet!

You've always played just soprano. Do you regret that at all?

No, that's enough for me. Each day that I work, I find something unexpected. While touring, I'm not able to practice, I only get to warm up and play. But at home, the research continues.

31 Farewell Paris

interview by Gérard Rouy

Just before moving back to America with Irene Aebi to teach in Boston, Lacy took stock of his long sojourn in Europe and looked toward the future, in this last interview in Paris, published by *Down Beat* (October 2002).

For Steve Lacy and his wife, singer Irene Aebi, their last year in Paris did not start very well. In March, two days after Oliver Johnson's death (Johnson had been Lacy's drummer for sixteen years during the '70s and '80s), Aebi was mugged while walking in their neighborhood. The next day, as he was returning from Italy, Lacy was knocked over by a car in a hit-and-run incident. With his legs injured—but not seriously—the soprano saxophonist had to spend a couple of weeks at home in bed.

This was not the way that they envisioned remembering Paris after thirty-three years living there. And it will not be, as life became much better—and very busy—with the onset of summer. The couple prepared to move to Boston, where Lacy has started a new career teaching at the New England Conservatory.

"This summer we're going to Boston looking at houses and getting things ready to be moved," Lacy said in June, well before he began to serve on the school's saxophone faculty. "It's a big move. We have so many books that we could organize a book party, books and records. You can't believe how many CDs young people give me. I have mountains of them."

And in the midst of moving, Lacy did not stop working. In June, the Sunside Club in Paris offered Lacy a series of eight concerts. "They gave me *carte blanche*. I could do whatever I wanted, within limits," he says. "I did a duo with Mal Waldron, a trio with [the bassist] Jean-Jacques Avenel and [the drummer] John Betsch, a quartet with Mal Waldron—something I always wanted to do—and a duo with harpist Suzanna Klintcharova."

In the audience sat a couple of old friends, a few musicians and many young fans. Lacy felt at ease as a master of ceremonies. His tone had never been so clear and round, with swift phrasing and a pitch as precise as a needlepoint lacemaker. During his duo with Waldron at the Sunside, the dance director at the Paris Opera led the investiture of Lacy for his nomination as a Commandeur de l'Ordre des Arts et des Lettres, one of France's highest awards for artists.

In Belgium in July, Lacy performed eight duos in ten days, with Aebi, violinist Michail Bezverhny, pianist Fred Van Hove, bassist Joëlle Léandre [later released as the record *One More Time*], dancer Shiro Daimon, and pianist Frederic Rzewski. Add to that several solo gigs, and a performance with the Musica Elettronica Viva sextet in Ferrara, Italy, and Lacy's summer was musically complete.

Obviously, by moving out of Paris Lacy is leaving behind, but not forgetting, a solid musical foundation. But strangely enough, one of Lacy and Aebi's biggest regrets in the move will be leaving the lovely house they've been renting for five years, in the middle of which can be found a gorgeous private garden in bloom—quite an unusual housing situation in the heart of Paris. "When we arrived," says Lacy, who will have a new album, *The Beat Suite,* with Aebi singing Beat poetry, trombonist George Lewis, Betsch, and Avenel, out this fall, "there was a yard, then it was a garden, now it's a little park. After we leave it will become a forest, then if nobody takes care of it, it'll turn into a jungle."

After these thirty-three years living in Paris, you're taking quite a big step now.

Thirty-three measures. A big step, from expatriation to repatriation after so many years, but there's an end to everything and there's a time to leave, a time to go back home, a time to change. Music is part of those times and those changes, and it's important to be at the right place at the right time, playing the right thing.

So was Europe a good choice? Was it the right place for you?

Europe was happening for me, with France and Italy—especially Italy, beautiful Italy—being my most faithful markets. The more I played down there, the more they wanted me to play. Italy is really beautiful, the Italian ear is trained operatically, lyrically. Plus there's the influence of other cultures, in the painting and the architecture. They have a very cultured ear, and they are able to appreciate what we do maybe more than other people. They love what Irene does. They love her voice.

In speaking about the members of your group, you have said that what you value most are the long-term relationships. Did you learn that from Duke Ellington?

Of course, but you could learn that also from sport, the teams that play together for a long time know each other. They can have more fun, do more sophisticated work. It's a nucleus of people who know each other and can work together. I am not so keen to play with strangers. I like to play with the same people I play with because they know me. When

I play with Mal Waldron, he makes me sound good because he knows me, and also because he is a wonderful accompanist. We've been playing together since the '50s. When I play with a stranger who has never heard me before, or maybe just heard one record, he misunderstands what I play, and he thinks I'm lost. Then he gets lost, then the thing turns into a big mess.

In Europe, you have had numerous long-term collaborations with other musicians and artists.

Yeah, for example with poet Brion Gysin from 1973 to when he died in '86. I still worked with Gil Evans sometimes during those years. I did a few tours with him. When he was in Paris, if I was there he called me up and I joined the band. Then I recorded with him just before he died, his last record. And also the dance thing is very important for us, the various collaborations with dancer Elsa Wolliaston, mime Shiro Daimon, and especially dancer Merce Cunningham. Certain concerts stand out in my memory too, like when I played with percussionist Masahiko Togashi. Nobody knew him in Paris and they flipped, he played so wonderfully.

Little by little you became tired of the French attitude and silence toward your projects. And that directly links to your repatriation plans.

I thought that locally, in Paris itself, there was very little happening, and that I had heard it all. And then the phone stopped ringing, and when the phone stops ringing, it's time to move. That happened some years back. I should have moved then maybe. We were invited to Berlin for the DAAD in 1996—that was good to get out of Paris for a year. So we went there, had good conditions, and we made the opera *The Cry* with Bengali poet Taslima Nasrin. But when I came back to Paris, they asked me to audition for the Orchestre National de Jazz, and I got rejected because I was American, simple as that. I was shocked. At that point I should have left, but I didn't want to leave because we wanted to do *The Cry*. So we stayed, and luckily we found this house and it's been a fruitful five years.

Then Banlieues Bleues, the big festival around Paris, refused to invite *The Cry*.

We had a big political fight about that. We really went to war and lost a lot of our money on it. But we wanted to present an artistic victory, so we kept the work alive even though they wanted to kill it. That was important to experience because jazz is political. Nobody asks you to do what you do. We do it because we burn, we want to do it, we have to do it, and so we fight to do it. And that is a political fight, also with other musicians, with the producers, owners, critics and fans. I learned that when I was with Cecil Taylor for six years in the '50s. I saw what he had to go through to do what he wanted to do. And Thelonious Monk, same story. I saw that; I participated in it.

Are you still a proselyte of Monk's music?

Absolutely. A book recently came out with seventy Thelonious Monk compositions (*Thelonious Monk Fake Book*, Hal Leonard), with the music transcribed correctly for the first time by Steve Cardenas and edited by Don Sickler. Some I don't even know, and they are written out with all the little things. It took years for that book to come out. Up to its release they were all wrong, with errors and a lot of inaccuracies. Now there's a defendable book of Monk's music that anybody can study, play, and learn. It's a milestone.

Everybody's playing Monk now, so it's no longer my job to promote him. But on the other hand, I started first, so I'm further along than they are. So what? I still do a few Monk tunes, but I mostly play my own stuff. And we've been doing some Satie-Lacy concerts, a very interesting experience. I learned to play Satie's "Gnossiennes" on the saxophone. It works very well.

That's nice when things like this come from the outside, ideas that I would not have thought of. It's like my name, which was given to me by Rex Stewart. I would never have dreamed of that myself, my name was Lackritz and he said, "I can't spell that, I just call you Lacy." Later on I heard he was glad he did that; I was glad too. Somebody sent me a paper that he wrote, "Ten things I'm glad I did, ten things I'm sorry I did," and among the first ten, number two was change my name. In my story it all came from Ellington really, the whole love of jazz, the whole musical thing, and it's still true that number one for me is Ellington. Back in the early days I also got to play with Sonny Greer and some other ex-Ellingtonians like Louis Metcalf, and later Sam Woodyard in Paris.

Do you already have any projects set up in America, besides teaching, after the big move?

Yeah. For example, another teacher at the New England Conservatory is Danilo Perez. We've already worked together successfully, and we plan to do some things together. And I already fixed a thing with an Asian-American orchestra from San Francisco, half Asian instruments and half American instruments. I have a lot of people I know with whom I would like to do things, like Joe Lovano and Geri Allen, and there are also maybe people who would like to do things with me.

Then I hope to be able to do some of the things that weren't possible here, like *The Cry* and *Futurities*, the thing we did in the '80s with dance and theater, and *Vespers*. There are lots of things that have never been done, like a set of ten Zen pieces, Buddhist songs.

What kind of a challenge is it for you to go back home?

In America it's a new ball game, a new adventure. Things will be possible that I can't even imagine right now, but I'm going to really miss Jean-Jacques and John Betsch. It took years to develop a rhythm section like that. After so many years we had a very strong and unique rapport. I'll be able to do that once in a while, but not regularly. So we're losing certain things and certain people.

There's a lot of recreational stuff going on in the States, as well as activity in the jazz industry. All the giants died and other people took over. Some of it is very good, and some of it I hope to go against. I hope to come back and combat certain things over there, certain tendencies. I heard Ellington live, studied it for years and years, and played it, and when I hear people re-creating it now, I'm not impressed. People who hear the re-creations, and who never heard the real thing, they think it's wonderful. It's the same story with some of Monk. I hope to put down something interesting there that's not there now. Something else, as Ornette Coleman said on one of his first records.

32

Invisible Jukebox

interview by Christoph Cox

Soon after he began teaching at the New England Conservatory of Music, Lacy sat down at his new home in Brookline, Massachusetts, to submit to the test administered on behalf of *The Wire* (November 2002), for its monthly column in which a series of records are played and the guest musician is asked to identify and comment on them, with no prior knowledge of what has been chosen.

Sidney Bechet: "Ballin' the Jack" (1951), from
The Fabulous Sidney Bechet (Blue Note)

That's a beautiful record. It's Sidney Bechet, of course. He sounds wonderful, thrilling. I've heard this record before. I probably had it. I had a pretty complete collection from the '30s and '40s and some from the '50s. Is that Tommy Ladnier?

It's Sidney De Paris on trumpet.

Oh yeah. I played with him when I was a kid. He was wonderful. They all played so great, all those guys. Each one of them had their own way of playing . . . Jimmy Archey, Pops Foster. Bechet sounds fantastic here.

Do you see a connection between your Dixieland years and the Free Jazz you took up later?

It's all one to me, really. It's all one. It's just different techniques and different repertoire and a different way of dealing with musical situations. But it's a way of life, fundamentally, and it covers all those different things. You know, I've played with all different kinds of people, all different kinds of styles, gone through many different things, and the older I get, the more, like, just *one* it all becomes.

The soprano was an unusual choice. But you've stuck with it.

Yeah, nobody was playing it back then at all. I bought it in a store on 48th Street. They only had one, and it was way in the back, full of dust. Nobody had asked for one in years. There was nothing written for it, it was just in limbo. That was part of the reason I stayed with it. I saw the possibilities; the field was wide open. So I was able to play with all these wonderful musicians just because I played an instrument that nobody else played. It didn't take anybody else's job away from them.

Thelonious Monk, "Off Minor" (1957), from *Monk's Music* (Riverside)

Well, yeah. No question about this. It's from *Brilliant Corners*, it's "Off Minor." No, from *Monk's Music*, with Coleman Hawkins and Coltrane.

A critic once said that though your career has spanned the history of jazz, you somehow skipped bebop. (He thought that Monk, too, was beyond bop.)

Well, Monk was the brains of the bebop revolution. He supplied the structure and a lot of the language of the whole bebop thing. Even the look: he had the beret, the dark glasses, the goatee. Monk was the *king* of bebop, really. And I didn't skip over anything. I learned all of Charlie Parker's tunes and Benny Golson's tunes, Sonny Rollins's tunes. You know, in the '50s, there were these jam sessions at various musicians' houses—Bob Dorough's house, Gil Evans's house—and in order to participate in those sessions, you had to know the latest tunes, the latest bebop tunes: "Airegin," "Doxy," "Oleo," "Stablemates." So that was part of my education. I went through all that pure bop stuff. No, that's a myth that I skipped over bebop. My course was zigzag and helter-skelter. But you see, in New York in the '50s, everything was going on. The giants were there. You know, you call it Dixieland, but that's a meaningless word. I played with the people from New Orleans. I played with the people from Chicago, from St. Louis, from Kansas City. And a lot of them played the same repertoire, but in very different ways, different styles, different schools. So I call it "traditional jazz." But "Dixieland"? No.

Monk did play quite differently than a lot of bebop pianists.

Space, yeah, he's into space. He *knew* more than a lot of the other musicians. He was a better composer, the most important composer. He did his research at the piano, so as to get new sounds out of it. He had the ideas, really, and the other musicians used to visit him to get the ideas—myself included, of course. That was headquarters. Monk directed the show.

I suspect that some of Monk's "research" rubbed off on you.

Yeah, I've been on a quest myself for more than fifty years now, and I'm still looking for new sounds and trying out new things and learning a lot. It's interesting teaching now because I'm learning a lot from teaching, getting a lot of ideas from the students, just from hearing what they're doing.

Cecil Taylor, "Roses" (1990), from
Double Holy House (FMP)

[Chuckles and smiles] Is that Cecil? [laughs and listens some more]. Crazy [laughs again]. What is it?

It's from an FMP disc recorded a few years after Taylor's great poetry record *Chinampas*. There's a clear connection between Monk and the early Cecil Taylor records that you played on.

That whole thing to me is like the Ellington school, really—Monk and Cecil and Miles and myself. We all are part of that Ellington school. That was the link between all those musics. But Cecil was so far ahead of everybody that the few of us that appreciated what he did just marveled at him. Most people did not appreciate it at all. He was considered a terrorist, a musical terrorist. The club owners would lock up their pianos, the drummers would walk off the stage, and the critics would scribble furiously. Just a few people liked it. Recently I heard that Jack Kerouac was there when we played at the Five Spot and that he liked it. He thought Cecil was a very good bebop pianist. See? [smiles]. In retrospect, that seems the most balanced judgment of all. It took about twenty or thirty years before the tide turned and Cecil went from the Hall of Shame to the Hall of Fame. When I played with him, we didn't have very many concerts, but we worked a lot for dancing. We played mambos, rumbas, foxtrots, blues. And people danced. That's how we survived.

So were you putting your career at risk playing with Cecil?

I was doing other things simultaneously. From '57 on, I started working with Gil Evans; and I also had my own little trios and some more traditional things, with vibes and guitar and bass—almost like a Benny Goodman type of a thing. I had several groups like that at the same time. Plus I was working with other people who would call me. I remember I even worked with strippers once, you know?

You continued to follow Cecil's path of taking the music further "out."

Well, in and out, in and out, out and in, out and in . . . *on and on*, more likely, really! In order to go on, sometimes you have to go out. And in order to go on, sometimes you've got to come in. You've got to follow the music.

Anton Webern, "Six Bagatelles" (1911–13), from Arditti String Quartet, *Viennese School Vol. III* (Auvidis Montaigne)

Well, that's Webern. I adore Webern, I always have, since the '50s. Everybody listened to Webern. We all went that way and me too, wow, like a ton of bricks, man! I played all the songs for soprano [voice] on the soprano saxophone. I transcribed them all. The beauty, the specificity of it all, and the sound, and the density, and the brevity, and the brilliance of the form, and the use of space and . . . there are just too many great characteristics. It's just wonderful music, really. And for me as a future songwriter, it was extremely important to see how those songs were made, what he did with language. When I worked with Gil Evans, I was the poorest reader in the band. So I was very embarrassed and I wanted to learn to read as quickly as possible. And the music of Webern was the most difficult music I could find that I loved. I spent weeks on one or two measures. It was so difficult—those floating rhythms, and the space, and the dynamics, and those slow tempos, wow! But I finally got them and I learned how to read that way.

Did your own composition ever go in a twelve-tone direction?

I have one piece that is dodecaphonic, a piece called "Cloudy," which I wrote about thirty years ago and I'm still working on. It's a set of eleven tone rows. So, you know, I've used those techniques. But I've used them for isolated pieces. I've used chance techniques, twelve-tone, a whole lot of different techniques. Improvisation is a technique too. It's important for me to cover the spectrum, the gamut of possibilities, to use all the tools that are available to us. I haven't monkeyed with the computer yet, but I probably will at some point.

[Listens some more] Killer, wonderful music. Amazing. He was shot by an American soldier in 1945. He went out to smoke a cigarette after dark, after the curfew, and an American soldier just popped him off, just like that.

Musica Elettronica Viva, "Spacecraft" (1967), from various artists, *Ohm: the Early Gurus of Electronic Music* (Ellipsis Arts)

Is that Musica Elettronica Viva?

Sure is. Sounds noisy even by today's standards.

This was before I was with them [laughs]. That was a beautiful period in Rome, the late '60s. It really was "la dolce vita." Things were really relaxed. There were a lot of beautiful things going on. People were generous, and there was no paranoia. It was a really sweet time. I wound up living in MEV's studio for a long time, at Via Peretti. I'm still closely associated with Rzewski. I just played with him August 1 in Antwerp. And I played in MEV this past June in Ferrara, with Garrett List, George Lewis, Rzewski, [Richard] Teitelbaum, Alvin [Curran] and myself. I love all those guys. Working with them was a very, very important experience. I learned so much from Rzewski, from Teitelbaum, from all of them. Too many things to enumerate. Rzewski plays my music fantastically well. He can play rings around anybody. I wasn't there for this, so I can't say anything about it [laughs]. If I had been there, it would have been a little different [laughs].

Was it this wild when you joined them?

It was pretty wild. It was a wild and experimental period. There was a lot of research going on. We were playing a lot outdoors, playing with traffic sounds and playing objects. We were also doing a lot of political things and a thing they called "Zuppa," "soup," where amateurs were encouraged to come in the studio and pick up horns that they never played before and make sounds. Our job was to make music out of those sounds. It was like a Prometheus type of experiment that lasted for quite a while. There were many experiments and wonderful associations. I also met some of the great composers through them—[Morton] Feldman, [Giacinto] Scelsi, Giuseppe Chiari, and other wonderful people.

What made you leave this scene?

MEV was wonderful, but it was an improvisational group. It wasn't built to perform my compositions. I was writing things for Irene to sing, and that was no place for her to sing in either. So we had to find our own thing, really. MEV was wonderful and all that. But it was a certain thing, and I was going somewhere else.

Evan Parker, "Conic Section 3" (1993), from
Conic Sections (Ah Um)

[After a few seconds] That must be Evan Parker, right? Can *be* none other than Evan! I haven't heard this one. Beautiful.

You two have played and recorded together . . .

That's right. We've done many things together. Duos, trios, big bands, Globe Unity Orchestra, Kenny Wheeler's big band, Company, lots of things.

But the two of you have rather different approaches to the instrument.

Very different. One obvious difference is that he's into continual breathing and I'm not. I don't even want to be. For me it's very important to stop. For him it's important *not* to stop [laughs]. That's one big difference. Very important for me is the space between. That's something I learned from Monk. He told me, "It's very important what you *don't* play." And he told me, "Don't play everything. Let things go by." I'm also into structure; and I'm fundamentally a writer. Themes are very important to me, whereas Evan makes up the theme on the spot. It's a different way of working. After I'm gone, the structures will still be around, if they're any good, whereas the playing will be gone.

Of course, part of what I do is this kind of free playing. Since the mid-'60s, I've done free playing with Derek Bailey, Evan Parker, Misha Mengelberg. I even do that with students. But I also work with pieces, with structures, with themes. Those are both valuable techniques, but they're not the same, though you can combine them, conjoin them. To have a good variety of approaches and of stories is important to me. Each piece is a story. Each piece is about something. Once I saw a film about Cambodian musicians and one of the performers said, "Well, the normal Cambodian musician knows one thousand pieces. That's normal," he said [laughs].

Center of the World, "Winter Echoes" (1973),
from *Last Polka in Nancy?* (Fractal)

Sounds like some of the stuff we used to do with Alan Silva.

Good guess. Alan Silva is in there. But it's the pianist that I thought might tip you off. It's Bobby Few with the Center of the World Quartet.

I *thought* that was Frank [Wright], but I wasn't sure. Well, that's part of my Paris experience. One of the reasons I moved to Paris was that I heard this group at a festival in Amougie in '69. I said, "Wow, that's the piano player I've been looking for." I was crazy about Bobby right away. He was the first pianist I heard after Cecil that had something to say of his own. Other people had little wrinkles here and there, and some little things that were interesting. But he was a pianist that had his own thing post-Cecil and was not hung up on Cecil. In fact, he wasn't hung up on anything. He was totally original and very well developed. But he was working with Frank and I didn't get him for ten years.

Jack Kerouac with Al Cohn and Zoot Sims (1958), "Poems from the Unpublished 'Book of Blues,' " from *Blues and Haikus* (Rhino)

[Listens intently for a minute] Is it Kerouac? Might be Al Cohn and Zoot Sims with him?

Exactly. You've done a lot of work with poetry, especially with the Beats. But your approach is quite different than this.

What they're doing here is decorating the poetry. They're accompanying it, enhancing it, filling in, improvising. What I do is set the words to music very precisely. They become songs that can be repeated and fleshed out.

What attracts you to the Beat poets?

I was in the same milieu in New York. I met [Allen] Ginsberg back in the '50s, and Kerouac came to hear us play with Cecil Taylor at the Five Spot. So I was accompanying the Beat poets in that way already in the '50s. And, well, I've been into poetry for a long time. Irene also. She knew some of the people from the San Francisco scene before I did, even. So, together we have a nice knowledge of, and friendships with, a lot of these poets, including [Robert] Creeley, Anne Waldman, and, until he died, Ginsberg, [Brion] Gysin, Judith Malina. They were all into jazz, especially bebop. It was the same time, and it was a simultaneous revelation, really. Every one of them was into jazz and also action painting, which was the glue between the two things. [Listens again for a moment] He's got a beautiful voice, a great voice, huh?

Do you like Al Cohn and Zoot Sims's accompaniment?

I like the whole thing. It's great. I used to love them, and I knew them very well too. Zoot was a dear friend . . . of everybody. He was one of the most lovable and funny musicians in the world. He was just a really colorful figure. I admired him very much. And Al Cohn was very nice to me, very generous, very encouraging.

Katsuya Yokohama, "Yamagoe" (1976), from *Zen: Katsuya Yokohama Plays Classical Shakuhachi Masterworks* (Wergo)

Well, it sounds like Watazumi Doso.

Close. It's Katsuya Yokohama.

That's his student, his most famous student. Doso was a great master for me. I took two lessons from him and studied his music a lot. I still have seven or eight LPs of his. They're masterpieces, all of them. He's one of the greatest improvisers I've ever heard in my life, maybe *the* greatest. He had an amazing life, full of colorful stories, like real Zen food. I was lucky enough to meet him, go to his house and have a lesson; and then ten years later I had another lesson. They were very far out lessons, but they were very important to me.

Were you playing shakuhachi?

No, no, just the soprano saxophone. I have a very cheap shakuhachi, like a Woolworth type of thing. I've had it for twenty-five years and I can hardly play it. It's a very difficult instrument. But Doso was an extremely important influence on me, and I retain a great admiration for him. He was the most modern improviser I've ever heard in my life. He surpassed anybody I could think of, including Braxton, or Derek Bailey. Doso, to me, was just . . . whew, outside all of that, really. Of course, he didn't even admit to being a musician. He said, "Music? No, it's just *practice*."

Your playing has a certain affinity with classic Japanese aesthetics.

Yeah, Japanese culture is really large for me: Kabuki, Noh, the literature, the poetry, the costumes, the painting, the woodblock prints, and the food, too. This music is really trying to get to the heart of it, boiling it down. [Yokohama] is good. But Doso was better. Doso was like . . . whew, like Charlie Parker compared to all the other alto players, you know?

Are there other nonwestern musics that have influenced you?

Indian music, very profoundly. In the late '50s, Gil Evans gave me a record. He said, "Here, listen to this." It was a Ravi Shankar record. That was my introduction to Indian music; and I never stopped pursuing it further and further. I went to India [in 1980] with the Globe Unity Orchestra for fifteen days: five days in Delhi, five in Bombay, five in Calcutta. We played with some Indian musicians.

Bhob Rainey, "Sweet Sonk" (2001), from Jon Mueller, Bhob Rainey, and Achim Wollscheid, *Folktales, Vol. 2* (Crouton)

[Listens intently for several minutes] Now there you got me, man.

It's Bhob Rainey, a young Boston-based soprano player.

He uses some of my techniques, I see. But you know, once you find a technique, anybody's welcome to it. It's nice, though—very sensitive, very interesting, nicely sustained.

He's part of a group of improvisers in and around Boston who work with extended techniques and often very quiet, small, delicate sounds.

That's a school of playing, yeah. They're welcome, really. There's enough of the blowhards around. In Rome, when I was living in the Musica Elettronica Viva studio, there were neighbor problems so that we couldn't make noise after ten o'clock at night, or we'd be in trouble. So we put a ceiling on the music. We'd improvise until three o'clock in the morning, but at a very, very, very low level. Nothing louder than this was allowed. And we got away with it for awhile. At least we kept the research going like that. And the neighbors couldn't complain because they couldn't hear it. But it was happening [laughs]. This is like Feldman's music or something like that—beautiful. Is there an audience for this?

Yes, a small but dedicated one.

No kidding. That's good to know. It's like what we used to call the "cryptosphere," you know [laughs]? That's one of my old pieces, "The Cryptosphere" [on *Lapis*]. We put a record on a turntable—a normal jazz record [Ruby Braff's "Was I to Blame?"]—and we recorded things in the cracks: the hidden sphere. It's quite an interesting record, really, on Saravah. Actually, that's where "The Wire" is too, on an old Saravah record [*Scraps*]. I listened to it a few months ago and it was fantastic. I couldn't believe it myself. I said, "Wow, did we do that?" It's an amazing record. I think we had two cellos, two sopranos, and a metronome. It was supposed to be a portrait of Albert Ayler, about a life cut short by the wire—down to the wire. But, I mean, wow, that's a hell of a record. Here it is thirty years later, and it sounds different, sounds different now.

33

Big Kisses from Boston

interview by Franck Médioni

Though Lacy recorded *The Beat Suite* before he left Paris, it did not come out until the next year. The band included his most regular collaborators—Irene Aebi, Jean-Jacques Avenel, John Betsch—as well as the trombonist George Lewis, who had worked with him on many occasions. The following short interview appeared in *Jazz Magazine* (May 2003), preceded by this editorial comment: "Back living in the United States, the saxophonist sends us his 'best regards,' in the form of a record, and brings us up to date on current events: his own, and the other . . ."

My project of a record devoted to the poets of the Beat Generation goes back almost forty years. I knew those poets personally . . . *The Beat Suite* is a small collection of texts by the most important poets of the Beat generation: Jack Kerouac, Allen Ginsberg, William Burroughs, Bob Kaufman, Lew Welch, Gregory Corso, Robert Creeley, Jack Spicer, Anne Waldman, Andrew Schelling, and Kenneth Rexroth. All big fans of bebop, they were very interested in rhythm, melody, harmony, and of course improvisation. And the excitement of the language, since bebop was a new language. They too created a language, a new poetic approach. They were also interested in *action painting*, in Pollock, de Kooning, Kline . . . I chose texts that were "transparent," singable, short enough to be set to music—the one by Robert Creeley we recorded before on *Futurities*, with George Lewis on trombone already . . . George and I have been connected for at least twenty-five years. We've played a lot together, as a duo, in a trio, and quintet. I prefer lasting connections, so that this organic music is played by musicians who know each other well. George is one of the greatest musicians I know, and he gets along well with Irene. That's important because the singing and the instrument, the trombone, must really be together. We're going to do a tour with that band—Jean-Jacques and John are not "orphans," the adventure continues—we're going to play in New York in August, at the Iridium. I hope we'll be able to present this project in Europe.

America

Settling in Boston, I left a lot of friends and musicians. Irene and I were sad to leave France . . . But something was calling me: the New England Conservatory. America was calling me as well. I'd been an expatriate for thirty-five years. A moment comes when you have to go back home . . . In Boston, the school where I teach is fantastic, it's the best I know. The conditions are ideal, flexible enough for me to do tours. And for the first time, I have a bit of security, and a beautiful house that looks out on a park—the air is less polluted than in Paris . . . Students and professors are on a good level. I direct two octets and I also have about twenty students, singers, pianists, bassists, guitarists, trombonists, and a lot of saxophonists whom I give private lessons. They study Thelonious Monk's compositions and my own, and we discuss politics! It's frightening what's going on in the United States, it's the most awful moment that I've known. We're really against all that here. This American government is a catastrophe, a nightmare!

34

The Art of the Song: Steve Lacy and Irene Aebi

interview by Ed Hazell

Though diagnosed with cancer in the summer of 2003, Lacy managed to continue teaching at the New England Conservatory that fall. As the year progressed, experimental medical treatments seemed to have stabilized his condition, and he resumed a limited schedule of performing. In December, he visited London briefly and took part in a recording session led by German musician-arranger Hans Koller that included several Lacy compositions. Later that winter, he performed his piece "Sweet 16" with a large wind orchestra in Boston, and in March his *Beat Suite* quintet was recorded in concert there. Soon after, he and Roswell Rudd played an all-Monk repertoire for a week at the Iridium in New York with their Monksiland band, which included Avenel, Betsch, and the trumpeter Dave Douglas. Before the end of that month Lacy and Aebi were in Spain, playing at a foundation in Majorca, but already Lacy's health had begun to decline again.

This interview with Lacy and Aebi, which appeared in *Signal to Noise* (summer 2004), took place at their home in Brookline, Massachusetts, on 18 January 2004, and focuses on their long collaboration together.

For almost forty years, soprano saxophonist-composer Steve Lacy and vocalist Irene Aebi have pioneered a form of jazz art song nearly unprecedented in the history of improvised music. Perhaps only Ellington got there first, with his literary song setting of the Book of Genesis, but no other jazz composer has made art-song writing such an integral part of their life's work.

Using texts by poets and artists, primarily from the twentieth century, Lacy has composed more than two hundred songs with Aebi's voice specifically in mind. Lacy has organized many of the songs into suites of works by a single author, or by several authors organized around a single theme. Many of the songs, although certainly not all, have been recorded. The most recent is *The Beat Suite* (Sunnyside, 2003), with texts by ten Beat poets. Other suites include *The Tao Suite* on *The Way* (Hat Hut, 1980), with text by Lao-Tzu; *Futurities* (Hat Art, 1985), a multimedia work including dance and text by American poet Robert Creeley; *Packet* (New Albion, 1995), with text by Judith Malina and Julian Beck, co-founders of the Living Theatre; *Vespers* (Soul Note, 1993), with text by

Bulgarian vice-president and poet Blaga Dimitrova; and *The Cry* (Soul Note, 1999), with text by Bangladeshi poet Taslima Nasrin.

From the staggering quantity and the consistently high quality of these songs, it's clear that few relationships between a composer and a performer have been so fruitful, or few talents so well suited for each other as Lacy and Aebi. Yet it's equally true that few talents have been so maligned or misunderstood as Irene Aebi's.

Critical response to Irene Aebi's singing is too often confined to brushing her aside with a phrase. Too often, critics simply say that Aebi is "an acquired taste." She's "the controversial singer." "The critics are divided about her," they say. By diminishing her contribution to the music, however, the real significance of what Lacy and Aebi are actually doing, and how they are doing it, has been obscured. To understand what Lacy and Aebi are up to, you have to forget the dismissive language and listen again with fresh ears. When you do, the radical accomplishment of Lacy's jazz-lit songs and Aebi's unique interpretation of them becomes more evident.

Aebi has made conscious choices to sing the way she does based on both her personal preferences, the nature of her instrument, and the material she performs. If these choices subvert expectations and lead the listener into unfamiliar territory, then it should be seen as the exhilarating risk that it is, a fascinating rethinking of the role of the singer in a jazz group, and a careful consideration of the appropriate ways to approach the performance of modern poetry set to music. In Aebi's unique sound and efforts to define the singer's relationship to the text, Lacy's unprecedented jazz art songs have found the unprecedented interpreter they deserve.

The Voice

One simple fact lies at the root of the critical misapprehension of Aebi's singing—she is not a jazz singer, and she doesn't want to be one. "I never ever considered myself a jazz singer," Aebi says as she and Lacy sit at the dining room table in their modest Brookline home on a clear, cold afternoon. "That was my difficulty."

"When I met Irene," Lacy says, "she only had a few records. One of them was Louis Armstrong singing gospel songs, one by Paul Robeson, some Italian music, and that's all."

"I didn't know about jazz," Aebi says with a laugh.

"She found out soon enough," Lacy says, smiling.

"For me, my preferred singer is Lotte Lenya," Aebi says. "People ask me if I won't sing Kurt Weill. After Lotte Lenya? I think I will not touch that material! Everybody who does Weill after Lotte Lenya ruins it. Nobody can do it as well. The same for my singing standards. They have been done by certain people so fantastically. I don't know, Ella Fitzgerald is a great, great singer, but I'm European." She imitates a jazz singer's vibrato and melodic embellishments. "My nature is not like that," she says of that style of singing. "I hit the notes."

Indeed, when Aebi sings a note, she lands directly on it; there are no scooped notes or embellishments or messing with the melody as written. It's not a very jazzy way to sing, but it possesses its own compelling beauty—bright, precise, and clear. Her voice has a bell-like ring to it in its upper reaches and a more opaque, dusky sound down low. Lacy was attracted to Aebi's voice because it was so foreign to jazz, and he has used her sound as one of the defining characteristics of the work they have forged together. "The way she sounds on 'Lesson,'" says Lacy, referring to a song on *The Owl* (Saravah, 1977), "that's what I heard first from her—that mountain voice, that yodel. That was the sound that turned me on in the first place when we met in '66."

Aebi's phrasing and enunciation are as precise as her intonation, without slurs or elisions. She never bends a phrase to fit the feeling of swing but instead hews to the rhythm of the words and nails them down. For Aebi, the words themselves are paramount. In a way, when she sings she's trying to get out of the way and let the words convey their message and the emotion, instead of interpreting or imposing her own meaning on them. It's at once intensely passionate and analytically removed, selfless and involved. She walks this tightrope every time she sings and she puts her voice at the service of some of the greatest poetry of the past one hundred years. There are no other singers, in any genre of music, that, to my knowledge, have sung as many musical settings of modern poetry. None who have developed a style so suited to the exposition of contemporary music and poetry.

The Band

Aebi and Lacy may not have shared the same love for jazz when they met, but they did share a love for poetry. Before she met Lacy, Aebi had left her native Switzerland and lived in San Francisco, where she hung out with the city's poets, including Jack Spicer, Lew Welch, and Bob Kaufman. Lacy and Aebi met in Rome, but in less than a year they returned to New York, where he began writing songs for her. The first two were "The Way," based on a text by Lao-Tzu, and "The Sun," with words by R. Buckminster Fuller. "They were both written around the same time," Lacy says. "In fact, we went to Europe with a sextet with Enrico Rava, Karl Berger, Paul Motian, Kent Carter, Irene, and myself and we had a suite of songs [*The Examples Suite*]: 'The Way,' and 'The Sun,' and there was a thing called 'The Thing,' and another one, 'The Gap' [these last two were recorded on *The Gap*, 1972]. They were conceptual, graphic pieces. That was a great band, but we only did a few gigs in Europe and then it collapsed. That's when Irene and I went to Rome."

"There was one that used the words of a singing telegram," Aebi remembers.

"That's true," Lacy says. "That one goes back to 1969—'Note,' that's on the record *Moon*. We did 'Chinese Food,' too. It was all improvised, but Irene declaimed. There was synthesizer [composer Richard Teitelbaum], saxophone, and she declaimed the lyrics of Lao-Tzu, having to do with politics and war. It was a protest we did against the Vietnam War in '67."

From Rome, Lacy and Aebi relocated to Paris, where they lived for over thirty years. It was there that "The Way" gradually grew into *The Tao Suite*, a cycle of six song settings of the writings of Lao-Tzu. Lacy recorded an instrumental version of it in 1971 on *Wordless*, with a short-lived quintet featuring trumpeter Ambrose Jackson and drummer Jerome Cooper, but the full realization of it had to wait until 1979, when Lacy's working quintet recorded *The Way* on Hat Hut. Lacy continues to tinker with *The Tao Suite* to this day. At the time of the interview, he was arranging it for a student vocal ensemble at the New England Conservatory of Music, where he has taught since 2002.

Lacy, who's able to maintain stable groups for long periods of time, kept together a regular quintet, with saxophonist Steve Potts, bassist Kent Carter, and drummer Oliver Johnson, for most of the '70s and into the early '80s. Aebi played cello and violin and occasionally sang Lacy's songs. "I came late to singing," Aebi, who is a classically trained violinist, says. "Steve pushed me into singing. I didn't want to be called a singer; it's a dangerous thing to do."

In the beginning, Aebi's reluctance and her sense of the riskiness of what she was doing were sometimes transmitted in her singing. In jazz, a genre of music where effortlessness and confidence are prized, the obvious effort, the high emotional price it cost her to sing, was discomforting. And yet Aebi's emotional honesty and courage, and the revelations of the words and the compositions, made fascinating listening. Clearly something new and exciting was afoot.

Aebi says that even the musicians in Lacy's band resisted her style and often displayed little interest in the songs. "The rest of the band didn't want to hear the words," she says. "Nobody knew the words, nobody in the band had any idea of what I was singing. They just knew the title. It was almost a John Cageian situation, you know. It was scary to be the singer in that band. I had to learn. I didn't grow up in America; I didn't know what to do. So it was a good school, but it was a hard school. You couldn't get away with shit. But if you did something nice, they showed their appreciation. They weren't really gallant to me, I must say. I guess I didn't expect it, either."

It was with this quintet that Lacy and Aebi worked out a way of integrating vocals into the group that is uniquely their own. For in addition to not sounding like a jazz singer, Aebi also doesn't present herself on stage like one, and the way in which she fits into the ensemble is entirely different from the way a traditional jazz singer "fronts" a band. Aebi and Lacy chose to embed her voice within the group rather than place her out front like a jazz singer usually is. Aebi's unique sound pushes out from within the band, with all those elements that are alien to jazz generating an inner friction—a European-American fusion—that's an essential element of Lacy's songs. "I wasn't into being up front and doing all the things that singers do," Aebi says. "I didn't have a nice dress or a nice look, I don't know, or the right attitude. I can't stand it in front; I like it as part of the mix, as part of the group, that's what I like. We tried mixing me up front on a record once, it was horrible. It's just the nature of the thing. And it's not a singer's band, that was never the intent."

Although it was not a singer's band, the group's albums almost always featured at least one song. Aebi's confidence grew as a singer, and in 1982 she began lessons with a Swiss voice teacher recommended by composer-jazz historian Gunther Schuller. "You know I've really worked hard on my voice. Steve's stuff is difficult to sing—there are these sudden big intervals that pop out. It drives you crazy, the big intervals. And oh my god, I'd ask myself, what voice could do that? Especially in the beginning I felt that way."

Band members began taking more interest in the lyrics she was singing. By the early '80s bassist Jean-Jacques Avenel replaced Carter, and pianist Bobby Few joined the group to make it a sextet. John Betsch replaced Oliver Johnson in the late '80s. "She's right that in certain periods, they just weren't interested in what she was talking about," Lacy says. "They just wanted to get on with it. Their attitude was, whatever she sings is fine; I'll play my part. However, when we work with someone like [pianist-composer Frederic] Rzewski or [harpsichordist] Petia [Kaufman], they know the words. They're really into that. And by now, Jean-Jacques, he really wants to know the words. Betsch and [trombonist] George Lewis want to know the words."

The Words

The words are the inspiration for the music, shaping every aspect of the songs, and Lacy's taste in poets is of a piece with the playful intelligence of his composing. Lacy favors the writings of poets and painters in the modernist naysayer tradition, the individualists who reject conformity but embrace a creative tradition. The Dadaists and Surrealists, like Kurt Schwitters, Marcel Duchamp, and André Breton, certainly influenced his choice of "found" poetry in early songs. Their ironic humor, rejection of conventional values, and confrontational style also resonated with Lacy's music. But the American poets of the Beat generation (Lacy's generation too), who loved jazz and infused its rhythms into their use of language, come closest to Lacy's own sensibility. They rejected high-brow language and favored the plainspoken (as did Beckett, another Lacy favorite). It's a mode of expression that is accessible (even democratic), craftsmanlike, and precise. The Beats too displayed a playful irony, an interest in eastern philosophy, and held common cause with modern artists who also interest Lacy. Lacy wrote many of his best songs to poetry by Beat artist Brion Gysin, a writer and painter whose work heavily influenced William S. Burroughs, and like Lacy, was an American expatriate in Paris. Lacy's interest in art in opposition to oppressive cultures extends to dissident poets of the Soviet bloc, as well, including Osip Mandelstam and Anna Akhmatova.

"Well you know, what I learned from Cecil Taylor is about language structure," Lacy says, "and poetry is language structure already. So, to transplant that into a jazz setting and to make a new language structure out of it, is a process. It's like a transmutation, like alchemy. Of course, the rhythms, and the form, and even the number of measures, everything comes out of the words. All the changing time signatures and all that, come right out of the words. I don't change any word ever. I respect the original prosody, how it's on the page, and how it's supposed to sound."

Selecting the poems and determining their proper order in a suite is an important part of the process. "Well, it takes some time. It's a lot of mulling over to do. The *Thirteen Regards,* that took me several years to put together. And once I had them written, it took me almost a year to figure out the order. Also there's a lot of research to be done beforehand, about the best translations to use and the different possibilities of putting them together. And they're cyclical for the most part, so they make a circle, but they're detachable also. And, you know, they were written for Irene."

After *The Tao Suite*, the next major vocal work that Lacy recorded was *Futurities*. One of Lacy's masterpieces, *Futurities* is a setting of twenty poems by Robert Creeley. "The song cycles always grow out of one song," Lacy says. "In the case of Creeley, it was a song called 'The Rhythm.' He came to my house, introduced to me by another poet [Pierre Joris] in Paris, who asked me to do a radio show with Creeley, where he would read and I would play the saxophone. And the poem he was reading was 'The Rhythm.' He sent me more of his stuff and it started to write itself. I wrote twenty songs in less than a year; the orchestration took another year. That was also cyclical: it starts in early morning and goes to the night; that's one cycle. There's another cycle having to do with being young and getting older; it's about the life of a couple. I chose the poems to represent the life of a couple. The dancers were a couple too. And we had this magnificent altarpiece of [Kenneth] Noland's which was made in fluorescent paint so that when the light hits it, it changes from black to green. So for two hours, you watched this amazing painting changing colors."

"But Steve is very mysterious," Irene says of his creative process. "I think there's a direct line to his subconscious. Sometimes it just pours out. I remember once just sitting around and I asked him, what are you doing, and he turned it into a song. It's called 'Wasted' [on *Troubles*], one of the few songs he wrote lyrics to."

When Aebi begins working on a song, she not only works on the music, she learns as much as she can about the poet's life. "We did this suite of Zen poems by Ryokan recently in Holland," Aebi says. "Of course, I always read the stories about the poet, to find out how he lived. Ryokan was charming; he liked a little plum wine; he went begging, playing with the children in the village. All this Japanese imagery that you see in paintings, that's also in the music—it's painting and images and the story of this person, and then his poems, his voice.

"From my point of view, I cannot work differently. I must work very carefully, and then it comes out. I really have to be a good actor too, when I sing those things, because I am singing about somebody else. Akhmatova, Mandelstam, we're talking about prison camps and terrible suffering. Mandelstam died in Siberia. I'm not talking about myself. You cannot fake that. It has to grow."

The Form

After Lacy has a song, he's got to find a way from the song to the improvisation. Tin Pan Alley songs have chord changes that improvisers can use to unite song and solo. Lacy's songs don't follow changes, so he's found another technique to unify performances. "Very, very often, most often, we use a form where the introduction sets up the piece," Lacy explains. "After the song, it returns to the introduction. I got that from Duke Ellington in the first place. Whatever we do, Ellington did it first, or suggested it. Including all the stuff about superior lyrics. One of my inspirations for writing songs was Ellington. Ellington suggested these formal transitions between a four-bar introduction and a thirty-two-bar tune and then a recapitulation and a solo. He put those things together in a superior way.

"For me, it's also based on experience over the years," Lacy continues. "One of my jobs was to turn the soloists on. To have the material turn them on, so they could make sense out of it and they could improvise something that had to do with the material. That's something that I learned playing Monk, really. There's got to be some kind of cohesion. Otherwise, you just take a solo and it makes no sense at all."

The Sound

Just as the melodies come out of the words, so do Lacy's orchestrations. "In *Futurities* there was one song called 'Heaven.' Now, there are harps in heaven, so I wanted a harp. We had our sextet—all these things are based around the group—but I wanted the trombone to fatten it out and I wanted the harp to go to heaven. Then we needed to mesh all that with the bass and piano, so the guitar. There was no doubling in the parts either. The bass played one part, the guitar another, harp, and all that, and that was all meshed together to support the three horns and the voice. That was a choice by ear, taste, appetite.

"For *The Cry*, I wanted to get this Indian sound. First of all, we were working with Petia [Kaufman], that was one of the first choices. Then, with the Bengali rhythms and the Indian mood of the thing, I wanted the accordion, to get a sound like a harmonium. I wanted that Indian flavor, not with a tabla and tambura and like that, but with a Western sound that was like it. Then we were working with this other saxophonist and clarinetist, Tina Wrase. And the accordionist was working with this Brazilian percussionist, so we all came together like that, with Jean-Jacques on bass."

The most recently recorded song cycle, *The Beat Suite*, gets its distinctive sound from the unison playing of Lacy and Aebi. With Lacy's vocally inflected soprano sax and Aebi's hornlike delivery, their sounds mesh beautifully. "Unison is one of the great secrets of music," Lacy says. "Certain unisons are very powerful. Doubling is not so interesting, but unison and octaves . . . When I worked with Monk, Charlie Rouse was the other horn and Monk would only let us play unisons and octaves. He said, that's the hardest stuff in the world to do: if you can do that, you can do anything. And so after a few weeks, we got that going really good. And Monk put in the other notes at the piano. It was beautiful.

"A critic once asked me at a conversation in public, 'Why do you do unison?' I didn't know what to say. Now I know. It's a positive thing that we've developed, and it gives Irene a sense of security and also for listeners too. And sometimes it's even nice with the piano playing the melody also with us in unison."

The Blessing

The personal and artistic connection between Lacy and Aebi is in a sense a template for the way Lacy has put together all aspects of his songs. The bands that perform them are all long-standing collaborators, and most of the poets whose work he's set to music are also friends and acquaintances. "What's really important is the fact that through the years, we've been able to collaborate with all these really great people," Lacy says. "We knew Brion and Burroughs and Taslima, all the Beat poets, and Judith Malina. It goes on. It's beautiful. We knew Beckett and he gave us his blessing. It's very important to get that approval. That's a big part of it, not only the rights to do it, but the blessing.

"We're working with the same bunch of friends that we've been working with for years," Lacy continues, "so the way the music grows is organic, but it's personal, too. It's a gang of friends, people that we know."

PART 2

writings by steve lacy

In the liner notes to many of his records, Steve Lacy often wrote a page or two about the compositions at hand: their inspiration, their nature, the conditions of their creation. Periodically, he also reflected on current projects in his notebooks; sometimes he wrote on other musicians and artists as well, usually in response to a request. In the selection of his writings presented here, most were found among his papers and transcribed; a few are reproduced in his own, clear handwriting. The following comments will help to situate them.

"MEV Notes," unpublished, likely dates from 1968, since it makes reference to Allen Bryant, who left the group about a year later. In 1968 Lacy returned to Rome with Aebi, and that was when he first began to play with Musica Elettronica Viva (MEV). The group was founded in Rome in 1966 as a loose collective of mostly American experimental composers that included Alvin Curran, Frederic Rzewski and Richard Teitelbaum. Though the various members took separate paths a few years later, the group continued to perform together on occasion as MEV, even to this day. Lacy's last appearance with MEV took place in Ferrara, Italy, in June 2002; besides the core trio of Curran, Rzewski, and Teitelbaum, the other performers that night included the trombonists Garrett List and George Lewis, both longtime members of the group.

Curran, who had never seen these notes until recently, finds them "a wonderful description of the MEV music and the wild raw moment in which it was lived." He suggests that the notes may have been Lacy's first impressions "of this anarchic free music which was made with very primitive home-made electronic instruments and amplified found objects." In his essay "Twelve Years of American Music in Rome" (published in the journal *Soundings* 10, 1976), Curran elaborates on the group's activities in that initial period: "For two years the MEV studio became the scene of an intense musical and social (political) struggle, which took place on many levels. The individual and the collective were pitted against one another—any of us who still harbored ideas of being composers had to compose quietly on the side. The exclusion of non-group members from playing gradually became taboo itself. At first, musicians were only admitted to sit in: finally, 'non-musicians,' wives and children were let in.

In a still later stage, the whole public was invited to participate . . . And night after night crowds of people came in to play or to listen to this overwhelming, continuous music, which could have easily been the accompaniment to some tribal ritual—a ritual of initiation and preparation. In fact, it was. And the ritual was simply the social upheaval and related phenomena that was then beginning to manifest itself everywhere, west and east."

"Roba," unpublished, probably dates from the early 1970s, since Lacy wrote it in a flawed, though more than passable, French. He is describing a piece from the late 1960s in Rome that was directly related to the kind of musical research he was doing with MEV. During the course of interviews 9 and 26 in this book he also comments on the piece, which was recorded in June 1969 and issued as his first album for the Saravah label.

"Garden Variety," likewise unpublished, is also from the early 1970s and describes another piece from the same period, which Lacy continued to play a little after moving north to Paris. The occasion for his notes on this piece was a performance of it in Amsterdam, among the first concerts at the Bimhuis (which opened in 1974), in collaboration with several Dutch musicians and others.

"FMP" was probably written in 1979, for the tenth anniversary of the musicians' collective Free Music Production, based in Berlin. Lacy's tribute, apparently unpublished, celebrates FMP's dedication to promoting concerts of improvised music, an enterprise that is still going strong. Hundreds of adventurous musicians from Europe and beyond have appeared in concerts and festivals produced by FMP as well as in its extensive catalogue of recordings.

"What About Monk?" is an appreciation of Lacy's greatest musical mentor, written in 1980 (and unpublished?), less than a year and a half before Monk's death. By then, Monk had long sunk into a silence from which he would not emerge. Lacy, meanwhile, had returned to performing Monk's music after a decade's hiatus.

"He Flew," a tribute to Stravinsky, appeared in French translation in the journal *Le Monde de la musique* (27 October 1980). Lacy's piece "Straws," dedicated to the composer and written when he died in 1971, was recorded on the album of the same name in 1977. Lacy describes that version on the notes to the record: "[It] used a single strand of the melody superimposed on a tape I made of three clarinet players and two saxophonists (myself included) trying out reeds in a room at the Vandoren Reed factory in Paris."

"In the Upper Air," on Albert Ayler, was written at the request of *Jazz Magazine* (September 1996), where it appeared in French translation among commentaries by twenty-four other saxophonists as well as an interview with Albert and Donald Ayler conducted by Valerie Wilmer in 1966.

"Shiro and I" celebrates Lacy's twenty-year collaboration with the Japanese dancer Shiro Daimon, who still lives in France. The text was published in the program booklet (which also included a text by Marcel Marceau) for a two-week festival in Paris, in February 1997, of works conceived and performed by Daimon, including the duo with Lacy "Here There Air."

"Short Takes" was published as liner notes to the record of the same name by the French bassist Joëlle Léandre and the Japanese pianist Haruna Miyake, recorded in 1998 at the Egg Farm (eighty miles north of Tokyo and the site of several notable Lacy albums), which also produced the record. Both musicians are conservatory-trained and have been active in contemporary, classical, and improvised music. Miyake played for the first time with Lacy in a duo in October 2000 ("Four Days at the Egg Farm"; the other three days featured duos and trios with the drummer Masahiko Togashi, as well as the solo concert issued as *10 of Dukes + 6 Originals*). Léandre collaborated with Lacy occasionally over the course of more than two decades in Paris, and commissioned a piece from him ("Vêtement"), which she played in recitals along with works by John Cage and Giacinto Scelsi. Their duo during his series of farewell concerts in Belgium in 2002 was released posthumously as the record *One More Time.*

"Yoshizawa," also from 1998, pays tribute to the late Japanese bassist Motoharu Yoshizawa, with whom Lacy worked during his first visit to Japan in 1975. They made two records together, in June of that year: *Stalks*, in a trio with Togashi, and *The Wire*, in a sextet.

"Made in France" presents on one packed page a summary of Lacy's and Aebi's activities in France from 1970 to 2000, listing major works and other projects, record labels, dancers and poets they worked with, and festivals, clubs, and other venues where they performed.

"Song Sources," undated, written on a small piece of notepaper, offers a quick overview of the many sorts of texts that Lacy drew on to write his music.

“Residency Statement” describes a project that never took place, planned for the late spring of 2004, around the time of Lacy’s death. In it Lacy proposes a three-week workshop for musicians who wish to take part in the development and performance of two late works that were dear to him and which remained mostly unknown in the United States.

MEV Notes

The music is outrageous—inexorable;
absurd (when confronted) combinations of old hat &
new stridency—the long line held till the
pt. of hard edge—Allen's organ & Alvin's tpt like
laser beams, a continual plaint, a sense of roaring /
crying—browbeating / wheedling / flexing / soaring thrust / trust
there is Mahler / Webern / Beethoven / Verdi /
things not left to go slack—mutuality—
Stankiewicz—sound of electricity—clank—swarm—crawl
—swivel—sensation of ominous pushing—a juggernaut
mashed—Cesar's crushed machines—there is
communication—heightened awareness—lift—
terrible intensity—sly rudenesses—snotty—snide—
boyish pranksterism—plenty of American Howard Johnson
style jazz ('30s)—baseball—open air—sunshine—
orange juice—Goodman riffs—nostalgic incorporations
wide open spaces—a radio announcer—something fanatic in the pantry—tendency to wallow in the big
contour—steel workers & the cop on the beat—
a kind of Pawnee banshee wail—industrial hymn
hoot & peep & pop & swat & holler & chirp—/ down home
blue Idaho slant (Charlie Barnet?) something aristocratic—pure (in the worst political '30s sense)—marvelous
cohesion / contagious focus—like
a steam locomotive—evocations of all sorts
of communications—a sweeping parade of optimism—headstrong,
convincing (but unquestioning—for each other's licence)
blues moaning trains with mournful thud—(Midwest)

MEV NOTES

THE MUSIC IS OUTRAGEOUS - INEXORABLES; ABSURD (WHEN CONFRONTED) COMBINATIONS OF OLD HAT & NEW STRIDENCY - THE LONG LINE HELD TILL THE PT. OF HARD EDGE - ALLEN'S ORGAN & ALVIN'S TPT LIKE LASER BEAMS, CONTINUAL PLAINT, SENSE OF ROARING / CRYING - BROWBEATING / WHEEDLING / FLEXING / SOARING THERE IS MAHLER / WEBERN / BEETHOVEN / VERDI / THRUST THINGS NOT LEFT TO GO SLACK - MUTUALITY - STANKIEWICZ - SOUND OF ELECTRICITY - CLANK - SWARM - CRAWL - SWIVEL - SENSATION OF OMINOUS PUSHING - A JUGGERNAUT MASHED - CESAR'S CRUSHED MACHINES - THERE IS COMMUNICATION - HEIGHTENED AWARENESS - LIFT - TERRIBLE INTENSITY - SLY RUDENESSES - SNOTTY - SNIDE - BOYISH PRANKSTERISM - PLENTY OF AMERICAN HOWARD JOHNSON STYLE JAZZ (30's) - BASEBALL - OPEN AIR - SUNSHINE - ORANGE JUICE - GOODMAN RIFFS - NOSTALGIC INCORPORATIONS WIDE OPEN SPACES - A RADIO ANNOUNCER - SOMETHING FANATIC IN THE PANTRY - TENDENCY TO WALLOW IN THE BIG CONTOUR - STEEL WORKERS & THE COP ON THE BEAT - A KIND OF PAWNEE BANSHEE WAIL - INDUSTRIAL HYMN HOOT & PEEP & POP & SWAT & HOLLER & CHIRP - / DOWN HOME BLUE IDAHO SLANT (CHARLIE BARNET?) SOMETHING ARISTOCRATIC - PURE (IN THE WORST POLITICAL 30's SENSE). MARVELOUS COHESION / CONTAGIOUS FOCUS - - LIKE A STEAM LOCOMOTIVE - EVOCATIONS OF ALL SORTS OF COMMUNICATIONS - SWEEPING PARADE OF OPTIMISM - HEADSTRONG, CONVINCING (BUT UNQUESTIONING - FOR EACH OTHER'S LICENCE) BLUES MOANING TRAINS WITH MOURNFUL THUD - (MID WEST)

LEAD IRRATIONAL-MACHINE RHYTHMS

BELLS - SOLITARY BY THE TRACKS - LATE SHADOWS - ~~[illegible]~~ ~~[illegible]~~ ES - COLORS PHENOMENAL - VARIETY OF IRON GREY'S - STEEL BLUES - ICE YELLOW SULPHUR - BROWN TO MAUVE - GREEN ~~[illegible]~~ + SILVER. ~~[illegible]~~ RUSTY TIN (UNEARTHLY - BIRDS - DINOSAURS - CRYSTAL (PICASSOID)) SIGNAL OF AN APPROACH - PATENTLY ARTIFICIAL TEAR - ~~[illegible]~~ NO GIMMICKS EVERYTHING SERVES THE MUSIC - LOWING - RUMBLING - SWARMS OF LOCUSTS - VERY DRY + HOT + SPACIOUS - VIRILE, 30'S FARM WITH WILD HORSES, NEW MACHINERY + WARTIME CLOUDS - MODEL T - TRACTOR + CRICKETS - CORN + MORE DANCE BAND ECHOES - TRANSMUTED + SEEN FROM IMPOSSIBLY DISTANT POINT - RATIONALIZED + QUINTESSENTIALISED - ABSTRACT DRONING ARGUMENT LEFT HANGING - TOM SWIFT ELECTRIC ORGAN - AS IF PRE WORLD WAR II - REALLY COME TO TERMS WITH PITCH - ~~[illegible]~~ TAP DANCE WITH BRASS PYRAMIDS - MOSTLY ALL ABOUT MEN BEING WITH EACH OTHER ~~[illegible]~~ AT SUNDOWN ON A PRAIRIE CREPUSCULAR REFRACTIONS - BURNISHED COPPER, STILL POOLS WITH HIGH TREES + A FEW BIRDS. A RECALL TO THE COLORS W. PATRIOTIC CAUSE - JINGOISM - BACK OF ONE'S OWN NECK MOCKERY - STUNNING COMPLEXITY OF DECORATIONS EXHILARATED ~~[illegible]~~ ON THE MUSIC - LIKE MONORAIL CAR RACING INTOXICATION WITH CULTURAL (CIVIC?) PRIDE (RIGHTFULLY ~~SEIZED~~) IN CLEAN ORCHESTRATIONAL ACCOMPLISHMENT - (CREAM CHEESE) ALLOYED ~~[illegible]~~ ~~[illegible]~~ - MALLEABLE WITHIN THE TERMS OF THE CRAFT

ELAN | LIFT - BURN - SMOKE - HURL - NAIL - SAIL - WADE - RUN - DIP - WEAVE - REACH - SCOUR - CURL - SLAM - ~~[illegible]~~ SPIN - LEVEL - HIGH - LEAN - SOLID - BEEFY - STRAIGHT - WINNING

CORUSCATED - HARMLESS HEARTFELT
PRISMATIC - AMAZING BLOOD PRESSURE
FABLED RUDE MUSCULARITY

SHEELER
ROCKWELL
BURCHFIELD
HOPPER
WYETH

SPECIAL EARS
CALF'S EYES
BUCK SKIN
· LARGER THAN LIFE

[*page 2 of manuscript*:]

lead   irrational — machine rhythms
bells — solitary by the tracks — late shadows — colors
phenomenal — variety of iron greys — steel blues — ice
yellow sulphur — brown to mauve — green & silver —
rusty tin (unearthly — birds — dinosaurs) signal of an
approach — patently artificial tear — crystal (Picassoid) — no gimmicks
everything serves the music — lowing — rumbling —
swarms of locusts — very dry & hot & spacious —
virile, '30s farm with wild horses, new machinery
& wartime clouds — model T — tractor & crickets —
corn & more dance band echoes — transmuted & seen
from impossibly distant point — rationalized & quintessentialised — abstract droning argument left hanging —
Tom Swift electric organ — as if pre-World War II —
really come to terms with pitch — tap dance
with brass pyramids — mostly all about men being with
each other at sundown on a prairie
crepuscular refractions — burnished copper, still
pools with high trees & a few birds — a recall to the
colors w. patriotic cause — jingoism — back of one's
own neck mockery — stunning complexity of decorations
exhilarated on the music — like monorail car racing intoxication
with cultural (civic?) pride (rightfully sensed) in
clean orchestrational accomplishment — cream cheese alloyed —
malleable within the terms of the craft
elan — lift — burn — smoke — hurl — nail — sail — wade —
run — dip — weave — reach — scour — curl — slam — spin —
level — high — lean — solid — beefy — straight — winning
special ears   coruscated   — harmless   heartfelt
calf's eyes   prismatic   — amazing   blood pressure
buck skin   fabled rude muscularity
larger than life

[*sideways across left margin*:]

Wyeth Burchfield Sheeler
Hopper (Rockwell)

Roba

Material, thing (Italian slang). Some friends at our place (Irene and me) in Rome. We lived in an old warehouse space that had a good sound. The same group every day, and we'd play for hours. Some amateurs and a few professionals: the music free of all restrictions. The form only as it happens. Nothing forbidden.

We would change instruments sometimes and play objects that made sounds (walls, windows, tin cans).

There was nothing to say about the music, it was the thing we did, that's all. We wanted to really cook the material among us until it came out nice. Never a question of doing it in public for money. Music like that, completely crazy, most people aren't interested (now a bit more, perhaps). For us that research was a necessary pleasure.

It continued like that for several months, and then it was over. Fortunately we recorded it on tape in an art gallery (formerly a garage). The recording engineer was the American composer Alvin Curran who comes in whistling on the second side. These tracks are extracts drawn from very long takes and for me they represent traces from a beautiful time and valuable friendships.

Garden Variety

Means "harmless," "without danger," like the type of snake found in gardens.

First version was in Rome '68–69, then Paris '70.

This is a piece which brings the outdoors indoors. It uses natural sounds on tape, various musicians & a dancer, as well as certain items found outside & used as decor (branches, leaves, etc.).

Once the elements & players are assembled in the space & the form determined (the length of tape, etc.), the piece finds its own way freely.

In this version the sounds on tape come from Amsterdam (parks, streets & gardens). The musicians are 4 strings & 4 winds plus the dancer & we will use short films as well.

Steve Lacy—sop. sax
Willem Breuker—clarinets
John English—trombone
Peter Bennink—bagpipes

Irene Aebi—violin & cello
Lodewyk De Boer—viola
Derek Bailey—guitar
Maarten Altena—bass

Harry Sheppard—dancer
Films by M. Samson
(& perhaps some additional guest musicians)

This piece is gratefully dedicated to John Cage.

FMP: 10 Years Jubilee

The thing about FMP is the *cumulative* effect of 10 years production of some of the best free music presented in Europe. The resulting public is a very *knowing* one.

FMP were the *only* people to invite me to Germany with my group, & later in solo, then the group again, this year solo & with Company. Each time, there were *several* chances to perform on different evenings & in different programs.

This allowed musicians an opportunity to present varied programs & the listeners a chance to see & hear each music from *several* vantage points & in differing contexts. Always, an *attempt* was made to achieve good *sound* & if possible to record, photograph & otherwise *document* the concerts.

An undertaking like this which *succeeds* & lives & continues to bear fruit can only be commended & encouraged. This kind of program influences the *whole scene*, not just Berlin.

There has always been a *good* spirit of hard work & long preparations, followed by the joy in presentation & the ultimate reflection & reconsideration afterwards.

Each time I've played at the Academie or the Quartier, there has always been an eager & attentive crowd of people. This seems to me to be the *most* any artist can ask for. The rest is up to *them*.

Another important point is the way musicians can listen & play with others that they might *not* have heard otherwise. Many interesting encounters have happened in 10 years. These kind of events make *living* history & cause many changes to occur within & without the musical community.

The last point has something to do with *politics*, & the fact of the *survival* & *acceptance* of *non-commercial* music.

What about Monk?

Now mysteriously retired, after more than 3 decades of activity, Monk was the *searchlight* (beacon) for the bebop revolution. His house and piano were *headquarters* for Bird, Diz, Bud, Klook, and all the others, including later disciples like Randy Weston, Coltrane, even myself.

Born and raised in New York, *all* of Monk's music is about the city and its varied people and situations. The school of *Ellington*: Harlem, Broadway, Lucky Millinder, Cootie Williams, Coleman Hawkins, *countless others*, the influence of *Tatum*, school of Fats Waller, James P. Johnson, way back to early roots, all intact and growing with each experience.

Small groups, big bands, dancers, singers, shows, solos, *information* for a developing talent. Monk has *always* gone his own way, and *always* knew what was going on.

Some characteristics: *mathematics*, acoustic sensibility, the ability to *see* where the music is. Perfect *swing*, *power* and *concentration*. An unparalleled grasp of the "*mise en place*," and *total control* of the *timeseat* in the *rhythm section space*, at home *within* (inside) *the beat*.

Thelonious had the necessary means to *carve space*, using certain plastic discoveries, painstakingly worked out over a long period of time, on the *piano*. This music was elaborated and shaped into certain working structures, so as to have *something to play*, *something to play on*. These pieces were *deliberately* made, so as to "trip-up" advanced players into *extending* their musical capabilities and venturing into *new territories*. Anyone who ever worked with Monk learned a great deal, and improved their musicianship, taste, and imagination.

I saw this happen with John Coltrane, in New York ('58–59), at the Five Spot Club, in quartet with T. M. At first clumsiness, then awakening, pursuit, doubt, courage, perseverance, penetration, revelation, transcendence. The whole process gone through in 6 weeks! For me, it was *unforgettable*.

Later ('60), when I worked with the quintet (Charlie Rouse, Roy Haynes, John Ore), Monk opened up *new worlds* to me, also on a personal, ethical and political plane. He showed me *what not to do*, and left the rest up to me! *Years later*, I began to understand. The main thing he showed me was to *stick to the point*, the point being, to "*lift the bandstand!*"

Steve Lacy
(Paris, 27 Sept. '80)

He Flew

We used to call him "Straws." When I met Cecil Taylor in the 1950s, he was coming out of the conservatory (New England, I think) and he would talk about this guy "Straws": "Straws did this," "Straws did that." I always wondered who was this guy "Straws?" And finally I learned it was a nickname for Stravinsky. "Straws." Then I started listening to all that, and it changed my life, it was truly like a bomb.

Stravinsky was a sort of specialist. If, for example, someone came to see him asking, "Could you write something for amplified IBM typewriter and elephant, with Elizabeth Taylor onstage, and also Walt Disney," he would have listened attentively, then wondered: "Say, can I write that?" And he would have done it. Nothing, not any sort of commission scared him. He loved constraints. As Braque said: "Limited means engender new forms, incite creation, make the style." Stravinsky thought exactly the same thing: "I work within certain limits, the more there are, the more I'm inspired." He was a composer of circumstance. And I think a lot of people don't understand that kind of professionalism. He drove them crazy going right and left, going backwards . . . But he always knew what he was doing. He was a very foxy gentleman.

One of the most common mistakes about Stravinsky is, in my opinion, the incomprehension of his final works. People write absurd diatribes, the most ridiculous things about the period when, according to them, he "embraced the serial system," or something like that. That's ridiculous. Stravinsky never changed. What counted for him was his "method." The fact that he considered music as an ensemble of rhythmic intervals led him logically to that method—I don't believe in the word "system," twelve-tone writing was not a system but a method, that's a much more interesting word. Stravinsky was interested in all sorts of things: mechanical, natural, human, inhuman, sacred, diabolical . . . He could tackle anything. He arrived very late at the serial method but in the music he composed at that point are some of his best works . . . What is more important for an artist than to be able to say to others: "go fuck yourselves, I'm going to do my thing in my own way." Stravinsky understood that very young. I don't know where he learned that but it's fundamental, and he helped me to learn it too. It's a matter of courage, guts, audacity;

it has to do with having confidence in one's "equipment" or with developing it to the point that one can have confidence. He was a very methodical worker. He turned his back on the critics. Sometimes he tossed off letters to answer them, but in general, at the moment they attacked him, he was already far away, elsewhere, they couldn't reach him. That drove them crazy. He was someone who could fly: he flew.

What impressed me about Stravinsky was not only the singing, but also the dance. I think everything he did was dance. In fact, he himself was a dancer. I saw him conducting, at the end of his life, and it truly was a dance. Not in the manner of Bernstein, who resembles something like an Indian warrior. His dance was truly functional, pragmatic. It was in the blood, for real, not for show. I saw him when he was very old, small and fragile. His wife and Craft had to help him mount the podium, they practically had to carry him. But once he was in front of the orchestra, he conducted with one hand on his hip, and it swung, the whole orchestra was swinging. It was unforgettable. And when the applause stopped, they had to help him step down, because he had become like a little insect again, trembling, barely able to remain standing.

I think what made Stravinsky the man of his century is that he arrived at a new appreciation of the raw material of sound. He studied with Rimsky, who championed a certain style of orchestration, and so he had a very good ear for the instruments, especially those he truly loved: clarinet, harp, percussion, brass and some piano. Stravinsky started out from previous centuries, and he came to the 20th century by applying himself to the basic characteristics of sound material itself, without pausing at the habits transmitted by previous generations. He stuck with that until the end of his life, such that in his final works he forged new sonorities that were completely invented, never heard before, equal in their newness at least to everything that had been made in the electronics studios, but produced by natural means. He put two clarinets together, in a series of intervals that were staggered rhythmically and the sound was as new as anything they could have invented in the studios of Boulez. And it was alive, expressed in a human way, interesting to play for the musicians and fascinating for many years. But it was produced with the simplest means, with just the purity of his ear and, well, his famous nose. He used to say that he always trusted in his nose. If you listen to his *Requiem*, at the end there are sounds that are completely new, as if they weren't made by an orchestra.

It took him sixty or seventy years to reach a point where he heard well enough to be able to compose things like that. He worked very slowly, in a very methodical way, he started and never stopped.

In the Upper Air: Albert Ayler

A. A. was an inspiration for all forward-looking jazz players in the '60s (and an irritation for all backwards-looking players), especially saxophonists, but also rhythm sections, and other horn players.

His approach, and the research into the upper partials that he initiated (late '50s), was a fundamental element in the growth of the new ("free") jazz that grew up around the younger musicians trying to break through the limits and conventions of so-called "hard-bop."

Ayler, in effect, pointed the way upwards and out, towards *space*, and down to the *ground*, resulting in a new synthesis: *simplicity* of structure (text), one theme at a time (tonal); and *complexity* of rhythm (texture), *a new color*, multiplicity of tonalities. The resulting freshness and originality had an irresistible thrust, and enabled the rhythm section to break up the time, in a completely free, new way.

The first time I heard this music, I laughed hilariously, it seemed like an impossible joke. Later, after many listenings, I began to see and hear what was going on, and like many others, my playing was greatly stimulated by his influence.

His premature death was a mysterious tragedy.

Steve Lacy
Freiburg, June '96

Shiro and I

20 years gone by in a zen flash, like that! Our *rencontre* was fateful, and immediately fruitful. A duo like that (there are no others) must get "off the ground" the first time, and become better, or remain as good, each time after. That is the way it was, and still is with Daimon-san.

No 2 shows we did were the same, no 2 theatrical situations. Sometimes it was just the 2 of us, other times with members of my group, also a different premise/story, depending always on the fabulous, dramatic imagination of Shiro.

Improvisation and preparation
Imagination and realization
Contemporary and traditional
East-oriented West going towards Western-minded East
Meeting and collaborating in Paris '76 (?)
Continuing in Italy, Germany, Switzerland, England, Belgium
Organically
With risk and surprise
Pleasure and gratefulness.

Kabuki-Woogie
Noh Baby
Here There Air
Fête du Daimon

Shiro Daimon, a complete artist:
music—dance—voice—theater—poetry
transformations: magique sur scene.

Steve Lacy
Berlin, 23 Jan. '97

Short Takes

Joëlle Léandre—bass violin
Haruna Miyake—piano

Improvisation is the *method* for finding and playing the music, which can only be made in that way (on that day).

"Free music" (god-child of jazz) is by nature *spontaneous play*, with no rules, except: keep the music alive, and stop before it dies. Short takes are a good strategy, for making sure that the invention stay fresh and lively (in the '60s, we experimented with free pieces of 2 seconds).

Duos are a *special* challenge, precarious, exposed, vulnerable, and seemingly "limited," except when you have the "right" partner: then it can be *magical, unlimited*, more than just synergy, an *artistic fulfillment*. (affinity/ empathy/ respect/ understanding/ alacrity).

Music like these two ladies make, is a series of discussions immediately producing *realised inventions*, cumulatively finding their own forms. The result is *discourse in a new language*.

Musicians (especially improvising) can turn each other on, or off. Some combinations produce really high-level discovery, with others, there is nothing happening.

We can *always* tell (so can the listeners) when the stuff is good. The music takes *off*, and the clock goes *fast*. Surprise and pleasure take us away from nowhere, and when it is over, there is nothing to say but, "Yeah! Thank you."

Steve Lacy (130898) Paris
Away from nowhere = Out there!
$1 + 1 = \infty$

SHORT TAKES

{ JOËLLE LEANDRE · BASS VIOLIN
{ HARUNA MIYAKE - PIANO

IMPROVISATION IS THE METHOD FOR FINDING AND PLAYING THE MUSIC, WHICH CAN ONLY BE MADE IN THAT WAY (ON THAT DAY).

'FREE MUSIC' (GOD-CHILD OF JAZZ) IS BY NATURE, SPONTANEOUS PLAY, WITH NO RULES, EXCEPT: KEEP THE MUSIC ALIVE, AND STOP BEFORE IT DIES. SHORT TAKES ARE A GOOD STRATEGY, FOR MAKING SURE THAT THE INVENTION STAY FRESH AND LIVELY. (IN THE '60 S, WE EXPERIMENTED WITH FREE PIECES OF 2 SECONDS.)

DUOS ARE A SPECIAL CHALLENGE, PRECARIOUS, EXPOSED, VULNERABLE, AND SEEMINGLY 'LIMITED', EXCEPT WHEN YOU HAVE THE 'RIGHT' PARTNER: THEN IT CAN BE MAGICAL, UNLIMITED, MORE THAN JUST SYNERGY, AN ARTISTIC FULFILLMENT. (AFFINITY/EMPATHY/RESPECT/UNDERSTANDING/ALACRITY);

MUSIC LIKE THESE TWO LADIES MAKE, IS A SERIES OF DISCUSSIONS IMMEDIATELY PRODUCING REALISED INVENTIONS, CUMULATIVELY FINDING THEIR OWN FORMS. THE RESULT IS DISCOURSE IN A NEW LANGUAGE.

MUSICIANS (ESPECIALLY IMPROVISING) CAN TURN EACH OTHER ON, OR OFF. SOME COMBINATIONS PRODUCE REALLY HIGH-LEVEL DISCOVERY, WITH OTHERS, THERE IS NOTHING HAPPENING.

WE CAN ALWAYS TELL (SO CAN THE LISTENERS) WHEN THE STUFF IS GOOD. THE MUSIC TAKES OFF, AND THE CLOCK GOES FAST. SURPRISE AND PLEASURE TAKE US AWAY FROM NOWHERE, AND WHEN IT IS OVER, THERE IS NOTHING TO SAY BUT, "YEAH! THANK YOU."

Steve Lacy (130898) PARIS

AWAY FROM NOWHERE = OUT THERE!

1+1 = ∞

Yoshizawa

The first time I went to Japan, it was 1975. Aquirax Aida, the brilliant "Diaghelev-like" producer, had come to Paris and arranged for me to tour Japan, in the company of percussionist Togashi and bassist Yoshizawa.

This trio was immediately successful. Both musicians understood my music and manner of performance, well enough to generate a coherent series of concerts, and several recordings, which still sound good after more than 20 years.

Yoshizawa was an instinctive, completely "free," musician, who could improvise by himself or with other sympathetic players (like myself), under many different circumstances. He also had a wonderful rapport with Togashi, which made it easy to play with the two of them.

Yoshizawa was also very talented with his hands, and he made very fine *objets d'art* and jewelry, out of wire and metal. I still have one very amusing piece which he gave me, we had a lot of fun together.

I treasure our all too brief association, and we will all be deprived of a unique and inspiring collaborator and friend.

Steve Lacy
Paris, 10 Nov. '98

Made in France

[*column one*:]
Major Works
Garden Variety
Tao • Packet
Precipitation Suite
Tips • The Cry
Brackets
Sands
Artemis
Score • Clangs
Futurities
13 Regards
Anthem
Rushes
Vespers • Birds & Stones
Shots • Hedges
The 4 Edges
Points • Remains
Noh Baby • 5 Colors
Kabuki-Woogie
Roba • Landing
More Than 150 Recordings (LP & CD)
Many of them done in
Paris, for many companies:
BMG/RCA • EMI • Verve • Hat Art
Black Saint • Free Lance • In Situ •
Tzadik • Silkheart • Potlatch • Saravah
Publication: "Findings" • "Prospectus"
Festivals:
La Rochelle • Nîmes
Lille • Strasbourg
Paris (Villette • Banlieue Bleues
Fête Ouvrière
L'Humanité • Estivale • Cluny)
Parthenay • Souillac • Coutances

MAJOR WORKS (1970-2000) STEVE LACY AND IRENE AEBI MADE IN FRANCE

GARDEN VARIETY
TAO · PACKET
PRECIPITATION SUITE
TIPS · THE CRY
BRACKETS
SANDS
ARTEMIS
SCORE · CLANGS
FUTURITIES
13 REGARDS
ANTHEM
RUSHES
VESPERS · BIRDS + STONES
SHOTS · HEDGES
THE 4 EDGES
POINTS · REMAINS
NOH BABY · 5 COLORS
KABUKI-WOOGIE
ROBA · LANDING

SOLO
DUO
TRIO
QUARTET
QUINTET
SEXTET
OCTET
BIG BAND

FREE JAZZ WORKSHOP
AMERICAN CENTER
CENTRE CULTUREL U.S. (RUE DRAGON)

CENTRE CULT. FRANÇAIS
ROMANIA
SICILY
AUSTRALIA
CANADA

COLLABORATIONS
SCULPTORS · PAINTERS
POETS · CLOWNS · ACTORS
MUSIQUE FOR CINEMA
AND TELEFILMS (PARIS)

THE MUSIC OF THELONIOUS MONK!
AND THE MUSIC OF DUKE ELLINGTON
SIDNEY BECHET LEGACY

L'EPEE DE BOIS - AUX HALLES
LA COUR DES MIRACLES · DREHER
CAMPAIGNE PREMIÈRE · FORUM
LE CHAT QUI PÊCHE · JAZZ UNITÉ
RIVERBOP · NEW MORNING ·
LE PALAIS DES GLACES - SUNSET ·
L'ÉCOLE PREMIERE - CHAPPELLE LOMBARDS
L'ÉCOLE D'ARCHITECTURE · JUSSIEU
LA SORBONNE · LE DUC DES LOMBARDS
L'ALLIANCE FRANCAISE · CAFÉ de la DANC
JEUNESSE MUSICALE · LES TREILLES
MUSEUMS: D'ARTE MODERNE (PARIS)
CENTRE POMPIDOU
D'ARTE CONT. BORDEAUX
STRASBOURG · ALBI
D'ARTE ARABE (PARIS)
DE L'ECTRITICITÉ "

MORE THAN 150 RECORDINGS (LP+CD)
MANY OF THEM DONE IN
PARIS, FOR MANY COMPANIES:
BMG/RCA · EMI · VERVE · HAT ART
BLACK SAINT · FREE LANCE · IN SITU ·
TZADIK · SILKHEART · POTLATCH ·
SARAVAH

CENTRES CULTURALES
THEATRES :
CONCERTS
CLUBS · CAVES

D'AMANDIERS · LONGWY
MOUFFETARD · MALAKOFF
DUNOIS · COURBEVOIE
CRETEIL · NANCY
CHÊNE NOIR (AVIGNON)
BORDEAUX · ORLEANS
LILLE (OPERA) · BLOIS
PALAIS GARNIER · TNP
COLMAR · THEATRE de la VILLE (PARIS)
ORTF · ARTE · MEZZO
TOULOUSE TF 2
LYONS · PLEYEL
ARRAS · CHATELET
VILLENEUVE D'ASQ
NORD OUEST PASSAGE (PARIS)
AMERICAN CTR. (BERCY!)
CENTRE · CULT SUISSE
CHATEAU VALLON
MARSEILLE · TOURS

GIL'S CLUB
LA PETITE JOURNALE
PETITE FAUCHER
INSTANTS DECHIRÉ
PALAIS DES ARTS

PUBLICATION: "FINDINGS" · "PROSPECTUS"

FESTIVALS: LA ROCHELLE · NIMES
LILLE · STRASBOURG
PARIS (VILLETTE, BANLIEUE BLEUES
FETE OUVRIÈRE
L'HUMANITÉ · ESTIVALE · CLUNY)
PARTHENAY · SOUILLAC · COUTANCES
NEVERS · TARBES · NICE · NANTES
ROUEN · RENNES · AVIGNON · PAU
BIARRITZ · REIMS ·

DANCERS + CO.
DOUGLAS DUNN · THEATRE de SILENCE · BRICOLO
ELSA WOLLIASTAN · SHIRO DAIMON · PIERRE DROULERS
MERCE CUNNINGHAM · VIOLA FARBER · D. PETIT ·

SCHOOLS
SEMINARS
STAGES
MASTER · CLASSES
VERNISSAGES
FUNERAILLES!
HOSPITALS
PRISONS
ASILES
PARADES · TEP
FÊTES · CNDC · IRCAM · FDTN. CARTIER

MORE THAN 60 FRENCH SONGS
WRITTEN ON LYRICS OF DAUMAL ·
SUPERVIELLE · PICABIA · BECKETT ·
DALI · BRAQUE · ELUARD · GUILLEVIC
APPOLINAIRE · CHAISSAC · ALPHANT
CENDRARS · CHAR · VALERY · JULIET
TSVETAEVA · MANDELSTAM · AKHMATOVA

MEMBER:
SACD
SACEM
MORE THAN 500 COMPOSITIONS.

LA SAINTE CHAPPELLE (PARIS)
TRINITÈRES (METZ)
MULHOUSE · BELLEFORT
ARLES · AIX

Nevers • Tarbes • Nice • Nantes
Rouen • Rennes • Avignon • Pau
Biarritz • Reims

Dancers & Co.

Douglas Dunn • Théâtre de Silence • Bricolo
Elsa Wolliaston • Shiro Daimon • Pierre Droulers
Merce Cunningham • Viola Farber • D. Petit

More than 60 French songs

Written on lyrics of Daumal •
Supervielle • Picabia • Beckett •
Dalí • Braque • Eluard • Guillevic
Apollinaire • Chaissac • Alphant
Cendrars • Char • Valéry • Juliet
Tsvetaeva • Mandelstam • Akhmatova

[*column two*:]

solo
duo
trio
quartet
quintet
sextet
octet
big band

Free Jazz Workshop

American Center
Centre culturel U.S.
(rue du Dragon)

Centre cult. français

Romania
Sicily
Australia
Canada

Collaborations

sculptors • painters
poets • clowns • actors
musique for cinema
and telefilms (Paris)

The Music of Thelonious Monk!

And the Music of Duke Ellington
Sidney Bechet Legacy
Centres culturels
Théâtres
Concerts
Clubs Caves
Gil's Club
Le Petit Journal
Petit Faucher
Instants Déchiré
Palais des Arts
Schools
Seminars
Stages (workshops)
Master classes
Vernissages (art openings)
Funérailles! (funerals)
Hospitals
Prisons
Asiles (asylums)
Parades
Fêtes
Member:
SACD (Société des Auteurs et Compositeurs Dramatiques)
SACEM (Société des Auteurs, Compositeurs et Éditeurs de Musique)
more than
500 compositions

[*column three, a continuation of the many clubs and theaters where they performed; first, in Paris*:]
L'Épée de Bois • Aux Halles
La Cour des Miracles • Dreher
Campagne Première • Forum
Le Chat qui Pêche • Jazz Unité
Riverbop • New Morning
Le Palais des Glaces • Sunset
L'École Première • Chapelle des Lombards
L'École d'Architecture • Jussieu
La Sorbonne • Le Duc des Lombards

L'Alliance Française • Café de la Danse
Jeunesse Musicale • Les Treilles

Museums:
D'Art Moderne (Paris)
Centre Pompidou
D'Art Cont(emporain) Bordeaux
Strasbourg • Albi
D'Art Arabe (Paris)
De l'Électricité (Paris)

[*Centres culturels, theaters, clubs (continued)*:]
D'Amandiers • Longwy
Mouffetard • Malakoff
Dunois • Courbevoie
Créteil • Nancy
Chêne Noir (Avignon)
Bordeaux • Orléans
Lille (Opera) • Blois
Palais Garnier • TNP
Colmar • Théâtre de la Ville (Paris)
ORTF • Arte • Mezzo
Toulouse • TF2
Lyons • Pleyel
Arras • Châtelet
Villeneuve d'Asq
Nordouest Passage (Paris)
American Ctr. (Bercy!)
Centre Cult(urel) Suisse
Châteauvallon
TEP • Marseille • Tours
CNDC • IRCAM • Fdtn. Cartier
La Sainte Chapelle (Paris)
Trinitaires (Metz)
Mulhouse • Bellefort
Arles • Aix

Song Sources

Letter (from a word to a
Postcard paragraph)
Quotation
Saying
Slogan
Poem
Lyric
Bit of prose (sentence or two)
Dialogue
Exercise
Mantra
Prayer
Obituary
Recipe
Credo
Advice Admonition
Warning
Proverb

Residency Statement

May 17–June 6, 2004
(application deadline: February 9, 2004)
Atlantic Center for the Arts (New Smyrna Beach, Florida)

During the three weeks, I would like to direct the study, practice, performance, and recording of two works of mine, which have never been heard in their entirety in America. They are both scored for ten musicians, including Irene Aebi and myself. I am interested in working with nine dynamic, talented, and motivated musicians that play violin, viola, cello, bass, flute, clarinet (doubling on bass clarinet), trombone, piano and percussion in addition to any singers that may be interested in this residency. I will be working, not only collectively with all Associates, but individually, on musical composition, poetic structure, instrumental questions, especially concerning improvisation, both thematic and non-thematic (free), which for some players, especially from classical and contemporary music, remains an arcane art worth discussing and illuminating in practice. I will also direct a vocal workshop for those who are interested, along with Irene Aebi, drawing upon our 35 years practice and hundreds of songs based on poems and texts by painters, philosophers, writers, scientists, and poets, such as Georges Braque, Jack Kerouac, Judith Malina, Herman Melville, Kurt Schwitters, Robert Creeley, Galway Kinnell, Lao-Tzu, J. Craig Venter, George Ohsawa, Buckminster Fuller, & others.

The first of the two works that will be explored during the three weeks is called *Traces*. There are ten pieces in this cycle of Zen-songs, settings of lyrics by Ryokan (1758–1831), the beloved poet-recluse-calligrapher of Japan. Irene Aebi will sing the words, taken from the English translations of John Stevens (*Dewdrops on a Lotus Leaf*, published by Shambhala), accompanied, and with improvisations and musical commentary, by myself on soprano saxophone, along with the viola, cello, bass, flute, clarinet (doubling on bass clarinet), trombone, piano. It was composed in 1998, and orchestrated in 2003 for some performances in Holland and Belgium with The Barton Ensemble. The second work is *Particles,* for the same vocal and instrumental set-up. The text is an autobiographical poem written by Richard P. Feynman, the great and genial physicist, late in his life, and published in his book *What Do You Care What Other People Think?* (Norton). This piece, composed in 1990, will feature collective, rather than solo improvisation.

Application Criteria

I would like to work with eight musicians. The chosen Associates should be able to read and execute well, have experience in improvisation, perhaps some knowledge or feeling for Zen Buddhism, and a taste for science as well. A jazz background is not at all required. Applicants should submit cassette tapes or CDs of their work, along with brief samples of performances of jazz or contemporary pieces; a short improvisation (thematic or non-thematic are both okay); and a paragraph or two on their background stating how and why they are interested in this project.

PART 3

song scores

“Dreams” (1975)

poem by Brion Gysin

“Mind’s Heart” (1982)

poem by Robert Creeley
from *Futurities*

“3 Haiku” (1998)

poems by Ryokan, translated by John Stevens
from *Traces: 10 Zen Songs*

♩=40
DREAMS
WORDS : BRION GYSIN ('74)
MUSIC : STEVE LACY ('69,'75,'93)
1. A DREAM LIKE
LIKE A DREAM
DREAM A LIKE
A LIKE DREAM
2. LIKE A DREAM
LIKE A DREAM
LIKE A DREAM
A LIKE DREAM
SO YOU SEEM
SO SEEM YOU
YOU SEEM SO
YOU SO SEEM.
SO YOU SEEM
SO SEEM YOU
YOU SEEM SO
YOU SO SEEM.

♩=72
MIND'S HEART
(ROBERT CREELEY)
INTRO
2X
SAX
PIANO
RH
LH
1 BAR ALONE
ACC FIG CON-TINUES
A
MIND'S HEART, IT MUST BE THAT SOME
TRUTH LIES LOCKED IN YOU.
B
OR ELSE,
LIES, ALL LIES, AND NO MAN
TAG
TRUE ENOUGH TO KNOW THE DIFFERENCE.
TO HONORE DAUMIER
12 SEPT. 82
WORDS: ROBERT CREELEY
MUSIC: STEVE LACY

3 HAIKU
(RYŌKAN)
#1.
INTRO.
♩=64
THIS WORLD: A FADING
BASS
NO 8VA
(ARCO)
TAG
MOUNTAIN ECHO,
VOID AND UNREAL.—
8VA
#2.
♩=58
WITHIN— A LIGHT SNOW
(PIZZ.)
8VA

THREE THOUSAND
REALMS;
WITHIN THOSE
REALMS
TAG
LIGHT SNOW
FALLS.

#3.

♩=48

AS THE SNOW EN_ GULFS MY HUT AT DUSK — MY HEART,

(ARCO)

TAG

TOO, IS COMPLETELY CONSUMED. —

WORDS : RYŌKAN
TRANS : JOHN STEVENS
MUSIC : STEVE LACY
31 MAY '98

TO ROSWELL RUDD

Selected Discography

Steve Lacy plays on all titles and is the leader except where indicated. The following lists only about a third of his total recorded output. Dates signify the year the record was released.

1954 • Dick Sutton Sextet, *Progressive Dixieland*; Jaguar
1956 • Whitey Mitchell, *Whitey Mitchell Sextette*; ABC-Paramount
Cecil Taylor, *Jazz Advance*; Transition
1957 • Gil Evans, *Gil Evans plus Ten*; Prestige
1958 • The Gigi Gryce–Donald Byrd Jazz Laboratory and the Cecil Taylor Quartet, *At Newport*; Verve
Soprano Sax (quartet); Prestige
1959 • *Reflections* (quartet); Prestige/New Jazz
1961 • *The Straight Horn of Steve Lacy* (quartet); Candid
1962 • *Evidence* (quartet, with Don Cherry); Prestige/New Jazz
1964 • Thelonious Monk, *Big Band and Quartet in Concert*; Columbia
Gil Evans, *The Individualism of Gil Evans*; Verve
1966 • *Disposability* (trio); Vik (RCA Italia)
1967 • *The Forest and The Zoo* (quartet); ESP
1969 • *Roba* (sextet); Saravah
Moon (sextet); BYG
1971 • *Wordless* (quintet); Futura
Lapis (solo); Saravah
1972 • *Estilhaços* (quintet); Sassetti–Guilda da Musica
The Gap (quintet); America (France)
Mal Waldron with the Steve Lacy Quintet; America (France)
1974 • *Solo*; Emanem
School Days (quartet with co-leader Roswell Rudd); Emanem
Scraps (sextet); Saravah
1975 • *The Crust* (quintet); Emanem
Stalks (trio); Columbia (Japan)
Dreams (septet) (text: Gysin); Saravah
1976 • *Saxophone Special* (sextet); Emanem
Stabs (solo); FMP
Trickles (quartet); Black Saint

1977 • *The Wire* (sextet); Denon Jazz (Japan)
Company, *4* (duo with Derek Bailey); Incus
Straws (solo); Cramps
Threads (solo, trio with Alvin Curran, Frederic Rzewski); Horo
The Owl (sextet) (texts: Gysin, Apollinaire, Picabia, Dalí, Ohsawa, Éluard); Saravah

1978 • Musica Elettronica Viva, *United Patchwork*; Horo

1979 • Gil Evans, *Parabola*; Horo
Stamps (quintet); Hat Hut
Eronel (solo); Horo
Troubles (quintet) (texts: Lacy, from the *Manyoshu*); Black Saint

1980 • *The Way* (quintet) (texts: Gysin, Lao Tzu); Hat Hut

1981 • *Tips* (trio) (texts: Braque); Hat Hut
Songs (sextet) (texts: Gysin); Hat Hut

1982 • *Ballets* (solo, sextet); Hat Hut

1983 • *Prospectus* (septet) (texts: Cendrars, Dubois, Gainsborough); Hat Hut

1985 • *Futurities* (nonet) (texts: Creeley); Hat Hut

1986 • *The Condor* (sextet) (texts: Kaufman, Akhmatova, Beltrametti, Balestrini); Soul Note
Masahiko Togashi, *Bura Bura*; Pan Music (Japan)
Hocus-Pocus (solo); Les Disques du Crépuscule

1987 • *The Gleam* (sextet) (texts: Gysin, Waldman, Po Chu-Yi, Kaufman); Silkheart
Momentum (sextet) (texts: Niccolai, Melville, Gysin); RCA Novus

1988 • *The Window* (trio); Soul Note
Paris Blues (duo with co-leader Gil Evans); Owl

1989 • *The Door* (solo to septet); RCA Novus

1990 • *Anthem* (nonet) (texts: Mandelstam, Frazee); RCA Novus
Rushes (trio) (texts: Tsvetayeva, Mandelstam, Akhmatova); New Sound Planet

1991 • *Dutch Masters* (co-leaders: Misha Mengelberg, George Lewis, Ernst Reyseger, Han Bennink); Soul Note
Flim-Flam (duo with co-leader Steve Potts); Hat Hut
Hot House (duo with co-leader Mal Waldron); RCA Novus
Itinerary (big band) (texts: Fuller, Beer); Hat Hut

1992 • *Remains* (solo); Hat Hut
Live at Sweet Basil (sextet) (texts: Cendrars, Kaufman); RCA Novus
Spirit of Mingus (duo with co-leader Eric Watson); Free Lance

1993 • *Vespers* (octet) (texts: Dimitrova); Soul Note
Clangs (double sextet) (texts: Apollinaire, Chaissac, Merz, Schwitters, Kandinsky); Hat Hut

1995 • *Revenue* (quartet); Soul Note
Packet (trio) (texts: Beck, Malina); New Albion

1996 • *Bye-Ya* (trio) (texts: Potts, Raworth); Free Lance
Blues for Aida (solo); Egg Farm (Japan)
Eternal Duo 95 (duo with co-leader Masahiko Togashi); Take One (Japan)

1998 • *Sands* (solo) (text: Ginsberg); Tzadik

1999 • *The Cry* (septet) (texts: Nasrin); Soul Note
The Joan Miró Foundation Concert (duo with co-leader Irene Aebi) (texts: Melville, Schwitters, Soupault, Picabia, Niccolai, Creeley); Edicions Nova Era
Monk's Dream (quartet with co-leader Roswell Rudd) (texts: Ryokan); Verve Universal

2000 • *Outcome* (duo with co-leader Derek Bailey); Potlatch

2001 • Musica Elettronica Viva, *Spacecraft / United Patchwork Theory*; Alga Marghen

2002 • *The Holy La* (trio) (texts: Creeley, Gainsborough); Free Lance
10 of Dukes + 6 Originals (solo); Senators
Mal Waldron, *One More Time*; Sketch

2003 • *The Beat Suite* (quintet) (texts: Kerouac, Ginsberg, Burroughs, Kaufman, Welch, Corso, Creeley, Spicer, Waldman/Schelling, Rexroth); Universal/Sunnyside

2004 • Alvin Curran, *Maritime Rites*; New World

2005 • *One More Time* (duo with co-leader Joëlle Léandre); Leo

Recordings by Others of Lacy's Music

1984 • Rova Saxophone Quartet, *Rova Plays Lacy: Favorite Street*; Black Saint

1998 • Art Song Trio, *Puppies* (texts: Frazee); Ergodic

2000 • Mats Gustafsson, *Windows: The Music of Steve Lacy*; Blue Chopsticks

2004 • Etienne Brunet, *Tips*; Saravah
Michail Bezverhny, *Homage to Steve Lacy*; Afkikker

Performances by Others of Lacy's Music

France and beyond, 1990s to the present • The bass baritone Nicholas Isherwood, who sang in the double sextet on *Clangs*, has been performing a number of Lacy's songs in the repertoire of his vocal group VoxNova, as well as in other contexts (alongside pieces by Ellington, Ives, and Satie). In 2005 he presented this work in Belgium, Mexico City, and Paris.

Paris, May 2001 • For three nights the fourteen-member vocal ensemble the Voice Messengers devoted half its program to Lacy songs, which it maintains in its repertoire.

Argentina, 2001–2002 • In La Plata and in Buenos Aires, the soprano saxophonist Pablo Ledesma, in trio and quartet, devoted entire concerts to Lacy's compositions.

United States, 2004–2005 • Irene Aebi, with singers and musicians from the New England Conservatory of Music, has mounted a new concert version of *Futurities*, begun after Lacy's passing and first performed with Creeley in the audience not long before he too passed away.

New York, 2005 • Dewline, a quartet dedicated to Lacy's music (consisting of Dave Ballou, trumpet; John Lindberg, bass; Kristin Norderval, vocals; Kevin Norton, vibraphone, percussion), performed several concerts including *Tips*, *Saxovision*, and other works.

New York, October 2005 • *Steve Lacy: Songs and Music*, a tribute at Merkin Hall, featured performances of his music by Irene Aebi, Roswell Rudd, Joe Lovano, Dave Liebman, Don Byron, Jean-Jacques Avenel, John Betsch, Bobby Few, Gary Lucas, Richard Teitelbaum, David Wessel, Thomas Buckner, Judi Silvano, Daniel Tepfer, Jeremy Udden, Sunny Kim, and Sean Wood.

Strasbourg, France, November 2005 • *Hommage à Steve Lacy* featured a sextet of Lacy collaborators (Glenn Ferris, trombone; Steve Potts, tenor and soprano saxophones; Irene Aebi, vocals; Bobby Few, piano; Jean-Jacques Avenel, bass; John Betsch, drums), the dancer Shiro Daimon, and Aebi singing *Thirteen Regards* with Daniel Tepfer, piano.

Credits

"The Land of Monk" (1963); courtesy of Down Beat magazine; www.downbeat.com

"On Play and Process, and Musical Instincts" (1976), originally titled "Steve Lacy," an interview by Raymond Gervais and Yves Bouliane, is reproduced by permission of *Parachute: Revue d'art contemporain*, and the authors.

"Songs: Steve Lacy and Brion Gysin" (1981) first appeared in book form in Jason Weiss, *Writing at Risk: Interviews in Paris with Uncommon Writers* (Iowa City: University of Iowa Press, 1991).

"On Practicing, and Exploring the Instrument" (1988), originally titled "Steve Lacy," interview by Kirk Silsbee. © Cadence Magazine 2004. Published by CADNOR Ltd. www.cadencebuilding.com.

"It's Got to Be Alive" (1991), originally titled "Steve Lacy," interview by Ben Ratliff. © Cadence Magazine 1992. Published by CADNOR Ltd. www.cadencebuilding.com.

"In the Old Days" (1997), originally titled "Interview with Steve Lacy," New York City, 9 November 1997, conducted by Lee Friedlander and Maria Friedlander, first published in Lee Friedlander, *American Musicians*, published by D.A.P./Distributed Art Publishers, Inc., New York, 2001, appears here courtesy Lee Friedlander.

"Mind's Heart," poem by Robert Creeley, originally in the book *For Love*, published in *Collected Poems of Robert Creeley, 1945–1975* (Berkeley: University of California Press, 1982). Copyright © 1982 The Regents of the University of California.

"3 Haiku," from *Dewdrops on a Lotus Leaf: Zen Poems of Ryokan*, translated by John Stevens, © 1993. Reprinted by arrangement with Shambhala Publications, Inc., Boston. www.shambhala.com.

The following websites, featuring photographers in this book and others, offer a valuable glimpse of jazz in Europe as well as in the United States:

www.jazzpages.com/Rinderspacher
www.persophotos.com (for Henry Glendover); henryglendover@yahoo.fr
http://www.magnumarchive.com/c/htm/TreePf_MAG.aspx?Stat=Photographers_Portfolio&E=29YL53UWE35 (Guy Le Querrec)
www.mephistophoto.com

http://horace.photos.free.fr
www.imagekitchen.fi (Maarit Kytöharju)
http://www.jazzvisionsphotos.com (Michael Wilderman)

Websites devoted to Steve Lacy's music:
www.stevelacymusic.com
www.stevelacymusic.org

Comprehensive online discography of Steve Lacy, by Patrice Roussel and William Kenz:
http://home.arcor.de/nyds-exp-discogs/index0.htm

Index

Jason Weiss

is the author of *The Lights of Home: A Century of Latin American Writers in Paris* and the forthcoming novel *Faces by the Wayside*. He also edited *Back in No Time: The Brion Gysin Reader*.

Library of Congress
Cataloging-in-Publication Data
Steve Lacy : conversations / edited by Jason Weiss.
p. cm.
Includes bibliographical references and index.
ISBN-13: 978-0-8223-3826-0 (cloth : alk. paper)
ISBN-10: 0-8223-3826-2 (cloth : alk. paper)
ISBN-13: 978-0-8223-3815-4 (pbk. : alk. paper)
ISBN-10: 0-8223-3815-7 (pbk. : alk. paper)
1. Lacy, Steve. 2. Saxophonists—United States—
Interviews. 3. Jazz musicians—United States—
Interviews. I. Weiss, Jason
ML419.L22S84 2006
788.7′2165092—dc22
2006004591